Josef Meyer, August Eggers, Charles Post Culver

The World's Money

Theory of the coin, coinage, and monetary system of the world

Josef Meyer, August Eggers, Charles Post Culver

The World's Money
Theory of the coin, coinage, and monetary system of the world

ISBN/EAN: 9783744796262

Printed in Europe, USA, Canada, Australia, Japan

Cover: Foto ©Suzi / pixelio.de

More available books at **www.hansebooks.com**

THE WORLD'S MONEY.

THEORY

OF THE

COIN, COINAGE,

AND

MONETARY SYSTEM OF THE WORLD.

BY

J. MEYER.

TRANSLATED FROM THE GERMAN
By MRS. C. P. CULVER.

DECEMBER 13, 1878.—Recommitted to the Committee on Coinage, Weights, and
Measures, and ordered to be printed.

WASHINGTON:
GOVERNMENT PRINTING OFFICE.
1878.

TRANSLATOR'S PREFACE.

Hon. ALEXANDER H. STEPHENS,
Chairman Committee on Coinage, Weights, and Measures,
House of Representatives:

SIR: In submitting this translation to the consideration of your honorable committee, I would state that my aim throughout has been to secure as clear and correct a rendering of the text as possible, only deviating from the literal so far as the laws governing the English language make such deviation imperative. That I have succeeded in this is, in substance, the critical judgment pronounced upon the work by the scholar and linguist Rev. W. P. Harrison, D. D., Chaplain House of Representatives.

The etymon of the word MONEY, as kindly furnished me by Prof. J. M. Leonard, Ph. D., of the chair of Greek and comparative philology in the University of Missouri, is a most appropriate introduction to these pages, as it shows at once the high antiquity of the term as well as the dignity of its origin; and while it hints at its importance in national economy, it clearly implies the duty of governments to place its control, no less than the perfecting of its nature, in the hands of their purest and most philosophical statesmen:

Money among the Romans was originally stamped coin, from *cuneus*, a wedge or die for stamping metal, and so called from the government or public stamp imprinted on it, which inscription, often representing a person, *e. g.* Juno, in whose temple it was first coined, served to remind the person holding the coin, not only of the object imprinted thereon, but of the government that issued the coin, and of the value of the coin.

The term MONEY is from *moneta*, which signifies *reminder*, or the *reminding one*, from the Latin *monere*, to *remind*. Tracing the etymology of the word back to the Sanscrit, we find the term *man*, which signifies *to think*, that is, to *remind one's self*.

Respectfully submitted.

Mrs. C. P. CULVER.

WASHINGTON, D. C., *October*, 1878.

AUTHOR'S PREFACE

Money is one of the most important agents in the development of the industrial pursuits, and to its proper management belongs the weightiest, and at the same time the most difficult questions in political economy. The study of this subject has impressed the undersigned with such a lively interest that, for the sake of a true and intelligent understanding of the same, he feels urged to publish his views.

The design of the following pages is to prominently discuss, from a theoretical standpoint, the question of money, and especially that of coinage, and, in consideration of its importance at this time, to assist in the survey and examination of this complicated subject.

May this effort meet with a kind reception.

J. MEYER.

MONEY:

A STUDY IN NATIONAL ECONOMY.

I.

The wants of the people in their primitive domestic establishments are limited, each individual as a general thing producing what he needs for himself. Therefore, comparatively speaking, there is seldom any exchange of products; but where the necessity occurs, the settlement of the business is often interwoven with difficulties. When a person requires a certain article, he first asks the owner of the same whether the goods he offers in exchange can be utilized by him. Then, perhaps, another difficulty arises: the object offered appears less in amount than corresponds with the value of the thing desired. The division is then often attended with inconveniences, and if it is not possible to accomplish a division, then the business of exchange for the dealers (in which one is obliged to give more and receive less) is often followed by hurtful disadvantages. So long, indeed, as the industries are in a primitive condition, these difficulties are comparatively few, but they increase and become more oppressive as culture, and with it the division of labor, advances.

Now, in the course of time it happens that some commodity is discovered which, in the thrifty domestic management of a people, occupies a prominent place, with special reference to their economical, geographical, and social condition, because it meets or satisfies wants which, in the progress of events, have become almost universal. These wants arise from necessity, as, for example, care for the sustenance of life, or from a sense of the beautiful, which induces man to seek to improve his surroundings. For such a commodity persons are ready to exchange their own productions, even if they have not at the time of exchange any wants which this principal commodity, to which we have briefly alluded, is able to satisfy. The business of exchange will be to the individual a matter of reflection that, though no immediate wants exist which this principal commodity can satisfy, yet he may calculate with certainty, or at least with great probability, upon their appearance at an early day. Consequently, in the business of exchange this principal commodity soon takes a wide range, which continually increases as business increases. Among the heads of families there may be many to whom this principal commodity, neither in the present nor yet in the near future, is needful, because they either possess a sufficient amount of the same or else have no desire therefor, which thing may occur without detriment to its universality, because of the absence of all necessity. Yet these persons will be induced to accept this principal commodity in trade, because, with reference to certain increasing necessities, the great advantages which it possesses over other exchange mediums, they can with certainty, or at least with great probability, calculate on the reception of the same from the hands of a third person.

Again, these last may have no wants which this chief commodity of which they have become possessed through trade can satisfy, and consequently it passes into the hands of a fourth or fifth person, and by these it is first consumed.

Therefore, the use of this principal commodity is ever spreading in wider circles; its inherent value is kept in the background, while its exchange value continually increases. Its employment in trade becomes more frequent, until at last it is universally used as an exchange medium—it is MONEY, and the fixed amount of money which is returned for a product is the price.

The history of trade informs us that the commodity which in the industrial pursuits of a people plays the most important part, becomes the universal exchange medium. We have, for example, the old Russians, and the greater part of the American Indians, people whose chief employment is the chase, using for this purpose the hides of wild animals. The Nomads, and also the ancient Romans, employed cattle as money. In agricultural districts, in early times, grain was money; while in Iceland and Newfoundland, dried fish served the purpose. In the trade between the Mandingoes and Europeans, we find iron used as money, which, on account of its great usefulness in the manufacture of war and agricultural implements, is valued above all other commodities.

The natural industries being exchangable for the money industries, the difficulties formerly encountered in the acquisition of any certain object become once for all settled. He who wishes to acquire a certain product need only seek out the possessor of the same, and pay over the demanded or proximate amount of money agreed upon; the possessor of the desired object will, on his part, be ready to supply the same, because the money which he receives in return will enable him to easily satisfy other necessities.

At an earlier period it was not sufficient for him, who desired a certain object, to know that the owner thereof wished or was willing to part with it; the latter must be in want of the article offered in exchange. That this state of affairs was often accompanied with many inconveniences, and that frequently nothing was realized from the exchange, but, instead, material damage was sustained, is truly self-evident. The brisk interchange of commodities, and the closely-united advantageous results therefrom, first became possible through the stability of money.

Therefore it is for the interests of trade, so far as the same depends upon a prompt balancing of the amounts of exchangable goods, and so far as this has not already been done, that a commodity universal as an exchange medium be fixed upon; but the adjustment of this complicated question must, according to its nature, be attended to at a later period.

When once a certain commodity, as a universal exchange medium, is established, then the various objects, in reference to their trade value, are held in consideration above money, they seek money, not, however, as formerly, in the relation of exchange one for the other; the universal exchange medium is the central point about which the trade world clusters. Therefore through this means does it first become possible to form a clear conception of the various values of commodities. Products of the various kinds in trade, when placed against each other in different quantities, can only be compared when they are of the same kind and of the same value; so money becomes the scale of value, the measure of worth. Therefore those products each one of which is exchanged for the same amount of money, have the same value, while those of which each piece brings a greater or smaller amount of money, have a greater or smaller value.

Before the introduction of money, for example, an eimer of wine was exchanged for a certain amount of leather, and 1 cwt. iron for a fixed amount of linen; in such cases, one can have no clear conception of the value of either wine or iron, because the articles placed in exchange for them, leather and linen, were of unlike size. It is first necessary to establish the relation between each of these last articles, leather and linen, in order to clearly understand their relative values against wine and iron, whereby the question arises, whether it is at the same time and place, or whether before or after, or in the vicinity of the place of exchange, in reference to leather or linen, that the relation should be established. This inconvenience is removed as soon as leather or linen appears as money, because these things are exchanged for wine and iron, and from the amount of money given, each one of these two products yields in return the value of the others. That a convenient mode of comparison of the various values of one product with another for the benefit of living industries, is of more than ordinary importance, needs no further proof.

If money is the universal measure of value, then the question further arises, *how* is the amount of the quantity of the exchangeable products, namely, money on the one hand, and the special goods on the other, to be decided? This can only be done in the same way by which the various amounts of the opposite exchangeable goods themselves were decided, before money was used; for the fact that a certain product is used as a universal exchange medium does not, on that account, alter the nature of a fixed ratio.

According to Adam Smith's* published theory, *labor* establishes the ratio for the measurement of the amount of exchangeable products; but in the same kind of work there may be an ability displayed by the skilled workman that makes it difficult to estimate its value; for by great skill, great industry, &c., more and better work is accomplished than where these attributes appear only in a small degree. Therefore, when on this point an average estimate is made, namely, the amount of labor which by ordinary physical strength, industry, skill, &c., can be accomplished, then arises the broader consideration that there is much work of a nature which cannot be compared with any other. Adam Smith has only furnished as example the common hand labor (viz, that of the ditchers); but the puzzling difficulty is not removed through these familiar specifications, for this common hand labor must again be compared with that of which the most is perhaps complicated. It can only, therefore, be possible that of the various kinds of labor, that, particularly, the performance of which requires a specified time, is to be understood as an example for the measurement of the amounts of exchange products.

For example, 1 cwt. iron is offered in exchange for linen, therefore the requisite time for the production of the iron must be established, and as much linen given in return as can be produced in that given time. But here again the difficulty interferes, no consideration has been taken of the intelligence and the skill as the influential agents exercising their power in the completion of the work. Two commodities can be produced in the same time each by labor, the one very simple, the other so complicated as to require rare skill. The consideration here which has most weight is this, that in a simple domestic condition, more than in the progressive division of labor, very many, or the most of the various productive employments are unknown to trade. From what has been said we are satisfied that a universal scale for the measurement of the amounts of the exchangeable goods is neither objectively understood nor employed, and that the decision is more frequently the result of the subjective

---

* Nature and Causes of the Wealth of Nations, Book 1, Ca. 5.

judgment, though it does not always rest upon clear premises. There is a simple law of trade, which, for example, between two products, A and B, requires that double the amount of the latter will serve as pay for the former. But here care must be taken that no mistake is made; there are certain outward circumstances which are closely interwoven with the estimates of the exchange values, the greater or smaller importance of the necessities which are to be satisfied by the exchange, the quantity in which these products exist, the degree of ease by which they can be procured, &c.; these influence the relative value of the two products, but do not establish it.

After this preliminary, the question presents itself, what is money? As has already been shown in the statement as to the origin of money, the use of the chief commodity in bulk grows less and less frequent, as the same on all sides is used as an exchange medium, and therefore it can never become a universal exchange medium until it ceases to be used in bulk, at least that is so in a majority of cases. It has also further been shown that money is the scale by which the value of products is measured. By an examination into the nature of the peculiar value of the superfluous products, the question is properly reached, whether money takes its place in the rank of superfluous products, or whether it withdraws from the same and appears as something else, whether it retains its actuality, or, divested of matter, it is to be looked upon as something ideal, as a representative of value? As a starting point in the solving of the above questions, our attention is directed toward the correct comprehension of the nature of exchange.

He who is ready to exchange his products for the chief commodity may have a necessity for the latter, either immediate or remote, or it may be that these wants are only anticipated by others, yet it is invariably the value of the latter commodity which influences him.

This value can, however, only belong to the material in a certain degree; it is for the possession of the thing itself that the exchange is made. Therefore, when money is once established, the nature of exchange will not be in the slightest degree affected, because, as before, products of the various kinds will still be exchanged for a product of the same value. The exchange is, as formerly, a something given for an equivalent—certain goods in certain amounts are exchanged. Consequently, only the substance and the form of money are of decided importance; if it is the same, it has not, by a change of substance, the power as formerly to accomplish the exchange of products of every kind in bulk. But the fact that money is the universal measure of value, gives to it the stamp of peculiarity. It is one of the superfluous products of various kinds not to be forced out of use. Money is, as has already been shown, only relative, namely, as when one product of simple form is placed in trade against goods of various kinds, by which, according to its amount, the various exchanges can be measured. But money is, as has been stated, no absolute standard of value of the various products.

For example, a shoe-last presents nothing but a size of certain capacity, or space, which the material occupies, and therefore it is a natural measure; but money possesses no such characteristic, because there is no inherent relation between money and the various goods placed against it in trade. A certain amount of money, for example, cannot exactly represent an eimer of wine, except as the eimer of wine establishes this fixed amount of money as the measure, the accuracy of the measure is on both sides the same. Therefore, in this respect, money must not be looked upon as something separated from and standing above the rest of this world's goods. Consequently, money is a product, as all other products, an exchange medium, which is universal, but because of the universality of its application it by no means steps out of the rank of products. It is, as the others, subject to the universal laws of economy.

Money should be clearly comprehended as a sign—a representative of value. According to this idea, a piece of money which any one possesses should have the signification that its owner exchanged for it a certain amount of goods, and is, therefore, prepared to receive for the same a certain amount of other goods which he may desire from a third person. Money is the bill of exchange which the receiver of a product returns to the owner for the same, and through which third persons are commissioned to give to the bearer of the same a stipulated amount of goods.

It is evident that the nature of exchange, as explained, appears entirely contradictory; that he who does not in turn directly give a certain product, that is, the like performance of some material, but only, as in the case cited above, indirectly, namely, by reference to an obtainable good, does certainly only in form satisfy a want. Naturally the object of trade is, through exchange, to come into possession of immediate value. Think you, then, that men are ready to exchange material products for mere signs, or symbols, or ideas? The consideration which follows the attainment of exchanged products, whether a use will be found or not, is of no consequence. The fact that any product, which can be made into money, is very seldom or never used for other purposes, has led to the idea which gives money an entirely formal character. But why should a product, therefore, suddenly, because it is permanently and exclusively used in exchange, appear only as the representative of value?

According to the idea that money is the sign of value, the external characteristics of the pieces of money are of decided importance, namely, the form, color, &c. If these are of like perfection to original money, then it does not stand in opposition to the fixed quantity of true money. If we declare money to be merely the representative of value, and yet assert that the sign accurately exists in a fixed quantity of the fixed material, the conclusion is favorable, for the reality of the sign is evidently the outward appearance—the form, not the material.

II.

If money is a bill of exchange, it is of the utmost importance, especially if it has been long in circulation, that by him who issued it, as in the foregoing case, by the producers of the money, that it finally be redeemed. In what consists redemption? It is possible only for it to consist in this, that the giver of the bill of exchange returns to the presenter of the bill the same material precisely of which the money is composed, perhaps with this difference, that the assignment may have another form or another signature than that contained in the material serving as payment. In the material identity of the bill of exchange with the paying medium, certainly exists a clear proof that money is not to be considered as a mere sign of value. The redemption of money in modern times is an established thing, but this redemption refers only to ideal money, viz, to credit paper, which circulates as money. By further economical developments other materials than the above mentioned, may be made to serve as money, may enter into use as substitutes, and these surrogates, these signs, need no redemption, because they are verily money.

Finally, the view of the case is this, that money is a bill of exchange for attainable value, or by a more correct expression, one thing for another. Because the bill of exchange needs for its efficiency material support, therefore in trade life it does not appear as an independent thing, whilst money, established as the first exchange medium in the industrial developments, rests somewhat upon itself. It certainly appears as a strange precedent in logical inference, that that which from its nature does not stand for itself, but only rests in its development upon a substantial agent, established as a point of outlet, yet takes this agent upon its own self-supporting basis. .

If money is property, like all other property, then the question arises, is it also merchandise; that is, a product which is established in trade to be made exchangeable as a remuneration, whether reference to its supply and demand occurs, and whether, like all other products, it is subject to the laws of trade? When we examine the goods displayed for sale, we certainly do not see money exhibited like the various other products. The ground of this difference lies in the fact that either the material composing the money presents no visible peculiarity, or that its quality is not taken into consideration, whilst, in reference to the various other products, their characteristics are important, and therefore their exhibition is necessary. However, this last is not always the rule. The examination of samples placed on exhibition makes it entirely unnecessary to expose the bulk of the exchangeable goods, therefore many bargains are concluded, and much merchandise bought and sold without immediate inspection.

There exists yet another peculiarity. In trade the sum of money is denoted for which the unit of measure of the various products is to be exchanged; not that, however, inversely, a certain sum of money, as a unit, is laid down for which the various goods in various quantities stand in opposition. The reason of this difference is simply this: that money, being a universal measure of value, and merchandise the things to be measured, it is natural to lay the scale upon that which is to be examined, but not inversely.

The leading points of difference are, however, mere forms of nature. According to the essence of the thing, money may be offered and demanded as other products, for money is, in consequence of its nature, fixed, as exchangeable in trade for everything. It is merchandise preeminently. That which inquires after products offers also products, and that which makes an offer for goods makes also a demand for goods. It is not a one-sided offer, nor a one-sided demand. The difference is simply this: money is a product to be exchanged, and other products are for the purposes of consumption; and also that exchange products find the application of their governing laws in money. When money is abundant, and from that circumstance it is freely offered, then the holders of the same in their endeavors to possess themselves of the overplus of products, will outbid each other; this will call out more money and the price of products will rise. On the contrary, when money is scarce, and for that reason the offer of it is circumscribed, the money-owners will withhold their bids, then the request for it on the part of the owners of superfluous goods will be urgent, less will be offered for products, and the prices will fall.

There are many products which not even remotely are fitted to take their place as money. For, in order that trade be carried on with ease and convenience, the universal exchange medium must possess certain attributes.

The product which serves as money should not contain within itself the elements of corruption, but those of preservation. The person who takes money in exchange for other products may not have an immediate use for the same, or if he have, the market may be in such condition as that he cannot purchase to advantage, consequently his money lies idle, and if from that circumstance it becomes worthless, or loses in value, he suffers a corresponding loss.

The product which serves as money should be of easy transportation. If the place of exchange is at a distance, then the necessary pay medium must either be carried along or dispatched after the close of the bargain. If, therefore, this universal exchange medium is very heavy, the difficulties and cost of transportation will hinder the extension and briskness of trade.

That which serve as money must be easily divisible. This thought was alluded to in the beginning of this treatise as a misfortune before the introduction of money, because it often occurred that various products were offered in exchange of such amounts as did not suit the purposes of the traders, because the goods which served as money, could not be divided without more or less loss. And here let it be specially noticed that the material of which money is made must be of that kind that the compensation for the productions brought to be exchanged be prompt, so as to agreeably meet the wants and designs of both traders, for the avoidance of every disadvantage which might follow. This point will be further descanted upon when we come to speak of coin.

That money may serve its purpose properly it must not be subject to fluctuations in value. If the value of money oscillates in any degree, there can be no reliable calculations in commerce. The industrial interests will be frustrated, or in a measure hindered, and greater or less material loss will follow. The production of that commodity, which is to serve as money, must have, in reference to quantity and cost, a greater proportionate degree of stability than is possessed by other products. Even so, also, the demand for this product must have fixed limits, and that the material under consideration may be applied both to money purposes as also to its original use purposes, the demand in both directions must be proportionately constant. In the early periods of industrial life, the people were in the habit of using various products as money, which did not possess the attributes above mentioned, as, for example, hides, cattle, and grain. The meager development of trade prevented the disadvantages resulting from the want of a proper money service from being disagreeably felt. So soon, however, as trade became brisk and extended, then only such material was given and received which best served the purpose of a universal exchange medium. To such materials the name of precious metal is assigned. Gold and silver resist the influences of the atmosphere, moisture, and most of the acids, and therefore remain a long time unconsumed. Their durability, in connection with their beautiful color, their great malleability, and their great specific gravity, which is in a measure increased by being wrought upon, all of which, added to their relative scarcity, make both these metals peculiarly, objects of high esteem. They hold a large value in small bulk, and for this reason they are easily transported to great distances. The precious metals, in whatever form they may be wrought, are capable of being divided into small and beautiful pieces, and again through fusing can, without much cost, and without loss, be united in a mass or recoined in large pieces.

Another attribute, which will be understood later, and which is of great importance in money affairs, is this, that gold and silver wherever discovered, have the same value. The gold of California is equal to that of Australia; and the silver of Peru like that of Hungary; the value is entirely the same. The precious metals, also, in proportion to other products, continually enjoy a greater constancy or steadiness in value, that is, the fluctuations are not frequent one after the other, but occur slowly after long periods, and the arithmetical variations do not widely differ.

This desirable peculiarity was understood at an early period, for while on the one hand, in the progress of time, the amount which nature, in conjunction with human activity, furnishes, and the cost of acquiring are little changed, on the other hand, the demand remains the same.

The demand for jewelry and other articles of luxury, for which gold and silver are pre-eminently fitted, is, on account of the small number of wealthy people, proportionately small; therefore, the change in value is not affected as it is in other products, which, by their nature and their cost, are fitted to satisfy universal necessities, and which are accessible to all. The demand for money, as such, is constant, as is also the production, experiencing only exceptional expansions in amount and value, so that a demand for a universal pay medium is continually increasing. To this end, in the course of time, banks came into existence, of which we will speak in another place. Now, as the precious metals answer best the purposes of trade, the merchants have by tacit agreement, not, perhaps, in consequence of any outward influence, accepted universally the precious metals as an exchange medium, that is, established the same as money.

Now that gold and silver have become money, it is desirable that in every purchase and sale that only should be used as equivalent in return for goods in which the purity of the piece of money, that is, in which the exact quantity of precious metal is certain. The precious metals do not come forth pure from the metallurgic process which they undergo after they are taken from the earth; for example, after the smelting process and subsequent purging, or through amalgamation with blick silver, there generally remains from 2 to 5 per cent. of foreign admixture, such as lead, copper, antimony, &c. This was more the case in early times, when metallurgy was but little understood; but in modern times the admixture is very small, the fine silver of commerce generally containing but a little over one-fifth per cent. of base metal;* and, consequently, it is important that the precious metals, which on account of their costliness and purity are subject to loss through abrasion, should be further alloyed by the guardians of commerce, or the merchants.

As the purity is ascertained through assay, so the quantity of the precious metal bargained for is weighed, and by this means generally a greater amount is brought into market than the respective business demands; consequently it is necessary to divide the gold or silver. It is evident that the first named of these operations, especially in the small daily trade, which is constantly changing, and therefore demands a quick and easy settlement of the business, is in a great degree burdensome and time-robbing. The endeavor to overcome these inconveniences led to the coining of money; that is, to the introduction of that form of money which should make the first of these operations unnecessary. Originally, and also now, gold and silver were used as pay mediums in bars; that is, in sticks or plates of various dimensions. On the contrary, every separate piece of coin which belongs to the same kind has the same form and the same dimensions, and it is now universally a round, flat form, because this best meets the needs of trade. The purity of the gold and silver bullion, as a rule, is not known, or is not visible, until it has been assayed and stamped at the mint. In the United States of North America the gold and silver bullion is required to be nine-tenths fine, finished and stamped, which stamp testifies to the weight as well

* Karmarsch "Mechanische Technologie," Bd. I., SS. 64 u. 65.

as to the purity of the bullion.* So also in Austria there exists an order that all bullion of home manufacture, and all of foreign importation not already possessing the mark of assay, shall pass through the assay office to be tested and stamped. (Royal edict of May 26, 1866, §§ 7–13.)

The degree of purity is generally represented either by the thousandth part of the weight or by the number of carats contained in a given quantity of the precious metal.

The bullion must also, if the weight is not expressly given, be carefully reweighed, because the signature does not absolutely express the purity of each piece; and even if it did, the dimensions of each piece, and consequently the amount of precious metal therein contained, are different. The purity of the metal is generally expressed by grains and imprinted upon the bullion in the mint; therefore the number of pieces which from the entire amount of the accepted weight of pure metal can be finished, such as mark, zollpfund, &c., is absolutely determined. The weighing of the coin, therefore, for the purpose of establishing its purity is not necessary (except in certain particulars, of which we will speak by and by), because the purity of each particular piece is fixed absolutely; each piece of the same kind has the same dimensions, and, consequently, the same amount of precious metal. While the bullion may vary, one piece from the other, in weight and purity, the coin of the same kind in both relations are alike. On the other hand, there are coins upon which the degree of purity is not imprinted; therefore, so far as concerns the mark, there is no difference between bullion and coin.

III.

The most important difference between bullion and coin is this, that the latter are members one of another, and that the numerical ratio of each member, as well as the denomination, is established; that is, there exists a system of coinage. This system has a basis, a unit, which has on the one side such members as exhibit aliquot parts of the unit, and on the other side a category, which, in a manifold manner, represents the same. The system of coinage has a formal character. It is a plan for counting, and therefore it may happen that one or the other member is not represented by real money. For example, the unit may not be coined, but only one of the next higher or lower members, in which case the coin is merely used in calculation. Yet, notwithstanding the nature of this one member is according to an ideal coin system, its real expression is found in the different metal quantities. The determining upon what coin to stamp the amount of its purity and its alloy, how great the remedium of weight and value in grains to be fixed, what amount to pay for coinage, as well as the establishing of the relation of value between gold and silver, do not belong to the system of coinage, but instead to the coin laws.

It has been already stated that commerce demands an accommodating exchange medium, and that the precious metals above all other things, on account of their divisibility, are especially fitted to perform that office. Therefore, in the progress of Political Economy, coin has won a place, so that a perfect coin system, as one of the most powerful agents for promoting the life and comfort of trade, occupies an important position. When the subdivisions, in sufficient amounts, and in corresponding numerical value, are easily obtained, then the adjustment of prices will speedily follow, and the necessities, the energy, and the interests of the merchants, and especially of the retail dealers, will be met. When

---

* Zeitschrift für die Staatswissenschaft, Jahrgang 1862, S. 20.

a judicious division is made in the higher money category, then the small pieces may be exchanged for larger sums, which is of great advantage when payment is to be made in distant places, for if the money species is too largely represented by small units, then payment becomes burdensome and slow, and the conveyance ceremonious and expensive.

The position which a coin takes in a system is made manifest through the specification of its denomination, and also by the number of its money units. In reference to that, on the one side is the system of coinage, on the other the metal value, and the dimensions of each kind of coin, through the publication of the usual legal directions, is universally known. Therefore the signature upon a coin expressing the kind of coin may appear superfluous, although a correct judgment as to what place a coin takes in a system is not by a mere glance easy to give by a large number of persons. The security and the facilities of trade admit these signatures as being practical, if they do not appear immediately necessary.

The next question which arises is, what does the stamp signify? The usual opinion is that the stamp testifies to the purity, and in every case also to the weight of the coin. It should be remembered that although governments, as a rule, especially in modern times, have their money coined of a lawful purity, yet that the coined precious metal circulates through a long period, until, by abrasion, it loses part of its weight. Even so, too, by the lapse of time, the coin loses a considerable amount of its purity, and, further, false coin is brought into use, and therefore governments, especially in early times, have given out coin which contained less precious metal than the law demanded.

The stamp, then, is no universal and authentic guarantee for the existence of a quality which, although intrinsic, does not continually and in all cases exist. The stamp can at furthest but denote that a given quantity of the precious metal *should* exist in the coin. But the express attribute, to have a certain name, and to stand in a certain arithmetical relation to other coin, that is, to be a member of a system, remains forever and in all cases independent of the material of the coin. Consequently, as a general thing, the stamp only denotes the money units which the coin, according to the present fixed system of coinage, represents, or, better expressed, it points out the place which the coin takes in the system. But the stamp does not designate the various proportions which the unit coin bears to the lower or higher coins in the category. For example, the coin which a kreuzer represents has only the inscription " kreuzer," but it is not made apparent whether it is the one-hundredth or the one-sixtieth part of a gulden, or whether the double standard legally exists or not. The stamp gives only the name of the gold coin, and in no way designates how many silver unit coins it represents.

These proportions are to be taken with exactness according to the legal directions concerning coinage, and which, through the requisite explanations, are to be brought to the universal knowledge. The money unit is also by the stamp only shown indirectly; a direct specification is only used in coin of the same material, which in several pieces forms the unit, or in such which in one piece expresses several small units, as, for example, when the unit is a silver gulden and there exists a double silver gulden, or a twenty-kreuzer piece. It is not the design of the stamp to express the fineness of the coin. On the contrary, there are coin upon which the degree of fineness is not impressed, as, for example, the so-called small coin, which are formed out of base metal, whose degree of fineness cannot be expressed. It does not follow, however, that coin has no higher value than uncoined metal, because the latter must be assayed and weighed before and after every purchase and sale. The consideration that the impression on the coin is not arbitrary, but done according to established legal directions, that, consequently, only certain kinds of coin are issued upon the basis of a coin system, of which every single piece contains a fixed and lawful degree of fineness, the confidence of the citizen that the government, as the highest authority, is called upon to watch over the enforcement of the laws, to see that the laws be properly respected, as well as that the coin, through length of time, does not lose its value, are the causes which bring coined money into active circulation, without the operations necessary in the use of bullion, and that, too, whether the degree of fineness is impressed on it or not. It is the coin laws which immediately decide how great the amount of precious metal shall be contained in coin.

Although an inspection of coin as to its degree of fineness does not take place at every purchase and sale, yet the merchants, especially lately, exercise a strict control over coinage; the sad losses of former times have in this particular awakened an active watchfulness. Coin is carefully examined not only for the purpose of detecting counterfeits, but also to ascertain whether the legal impression has been properly placed upon it by the government. After a certain coin has been in circulation a long time, an examination is made in reference to its remedium or passable weight, to determine whether it still retains its original degree of fineness; and if a depreciation is discovered, its value is reduced in proportion. It is true that in interior and remote districts, in daily trade, and especially where only small amounts circulate among retail dealers (of whom we will speak by and by), money passes current, although it may have lost a part of its original value, so long as it is not counterfeit; further than this no attention is paid to it, because the retail merchants, of their own accord, will not take the trouble to ascertain the exact value of the coin. But, in those parts of the country where wholesale business is carried on (and in this kind of business it is important that the coin in circulation shall maintain the characteristics of its full value), there is notice taken of the smallest departure from the legal value of the precious metals, and therefore bankers, wholesale merchants, manufacturers, and the like, make frequent examinations of the coin. In international commerce, where money is strictly used as an equivalent, gold and silver coin are only received after close inspection, and, like bullion, weighed and assayed. In modern times, governments exercise a care in supporting the regulations for coinage. (See, among others, art. 12 and 13, Abs. 2, of the Coin Treaties of the German Government for January 24, 1857).

Finally, it is worthy of notice that the stamp serves a technical purpose, namely, to protect the outside of the coin, that no important damage can be made by cutting, scraping, filing, &c., without being at once detected.

In early times not only the rulers, but also clerical and secular corporations, and often, indeed, private individuals, coined money. But it is evident that, in consequence of the practice of this privilege on the part of so many, the want of union caused confusion, and as the stamp is one of the most important agents in inducing a free circulation, it is only by the utmost care, when in the employ of private interests, that a trust in its genuineness can take any deep root. In fact, there would be brought into circulation much coin whose value is less than its legal measure demands. The continually increasing demands of trade call for a fixed law in coinage, as one of its most serviceable mediums, and that the right to coin money exclusively be gradually assumed by the state sovereignty, as the highest authority in the country, and which is called upon to protect and promote the universal interests, and in which therefore, the greatest reliance can be placed. History establishes the fact that it is not a matter of mere National economy, but of fiscal interest to the citizens, that the state assume this right. The exclusive right to coin money makes the coin laws sovereign. The practice of this sovereign right is now exercised in various ways.

IV.

Money is coined either for the benefit of the government, or for that of private parties who bring metal to the mint. Moreover, in both cases, coining either opens a source of revenue to the public treasury, or it does not. If the government secures an income from coinage, then it is of that kind which either (as, *a*, only covers the cost of production) yields a small mintage, in an exact sense brassage (or, *b*, mintage in a broader sense, called in coin laws seigniorage); that is, apart from the compensation for the cost of production, a clear gain is secured to the public treasury. If the operations of the mint secure no revenue to the government, then the cost of coinage must be defrayed by the public treasury, but indirectly by taxation.

The cost of coining varies in different countries, and, as a rule, it is less for gold than for silver; and, for small coin, the established cost in proportion to the value far exceeds that of the large. For example: In Prussia the cost of gold coinage is $\frac{1}{6}$ per cent.; for the thaler piece, $1\frac{1}{4}$ per cent.; for the 5 groschen silver piece ($\frac{1}{18}$ part of a thaler), $2\frac{1}{4}$ per cent.* In France the cost of coinage has lately been established by law for 1 kilogram of gold, 6 francs 70 centimes; for 1 kilogram of silver, 1 franc 50 centimes; making a little over $\frac{1}{5}$ per cent. for gold and $\frac{3}{4}$ per cent for silver.† In Russia the cost of gold is 0–85, and that of silver 2–95 per cent.‡

As regards the establishment of seigniorage, the different countries have at different times enacted various laws, which are yet extant. In England, under the reign of Charles II, 1666 (but which has in part undergone frequent changes since), a very heavy seigniorage was imposed; but in 1817, when silver coin was again introduced, and which to the amount of 40 shillings was declared legal tender, 66 shillings were coined from 1 pound Troy, instead of 62 shillings as before, and 4 shillings were retained as seigniorage, which amounted to $6\frac{1}{4}$ per cent.§

In France, according to Necker, they pay for the coining of gold no more than 1.162, and for silver 1.295 as seigniorage, and 14.6 per thousand for silver, and 2.8 per thousand for gold, as brassage. In Russia, as also in the United States of North America, the cost of coinage is borne by the public treasury. In the Netherlands there is not only a mintage but a coin royalty imposed.‖

The fact that the business of coinage is a source of revenue to the government, might lead to the opinion that the seigniorage is generally a tribute, and it is from that circumstance that the idea has been expressed that the seigniorage is an entrance fee for the introduction of gold and silver bullion into money circulation, which for that reason the

---

* Karmarsch, Mechanische Technologie, Bd. I, S. 541.
† Zeitschrift für die Staatswissenschaften, Jahrg. 1862, S. 32.
‡ McCulloch, Money and Banks, p. 28.
§ McCulloch, Money and Banks, pp. 28 and 29.
‖ Oppenheim, "Die Natur des Geldes," S. 430–431.

producers of the precious metals must pay, because as a general thing they cannot dispose of their entire product to the consumers, therefore it is necessary to bring the overplus into money circulation.*

The producers of gold and silver, and those who superinted the sources of money, or the owners of bullion, as a general thing, exchange their gold and silver for coin; this is evidently done for the reason that coin is of that form as best accomplishes the functions of money, for which reason it always obtains its value in trade. But if coin is once made a universal exchange medium, then the gold and silver bullion, which is offered by the producers of the precious metals, will not be accepted at all.

In international trade, money, according to its nature, (namely, as a material product,) is received as other products. For this reason, coin is always accepted according to the exact amount of precious metal which it contains, and to that end it is weighed and assayed. But foreign commerce differs widely from internal trade. In the former, ready money is but seldom used, and when it is accepted in purchase and sale it appears only in large amounts. Further, the conclusion of the business and the time of payment are generally widely separated; therefore the money is for the most part exported, and the adjustment does not occur immediately. In internal trade a large amount of business is transacted through coin, the conclusion of the bargain is immediately succeeded by payment, and the adjustment by the full amount in cash very frequently takes place.

Again, in international commerce an examination into the weight and purity of coin, corresponding to the nature of the money, is made, because highly judicious and even absolutely necessary; but in home trade, when it is unhindered in its course, there exists the regulation of cash payments, which makes the before-mentioned operation altogether superfluous. Therefore coin is better adapted to internal trade than gold and silver bullion, because it is a more convenient exchange medium. The special conclusions reached are these: that the entire system of coinage is regulated by law; that each piece of coin is made, not according to the pleasure of any individual, but contains its legal measure of purity. This fact helps greatly to strengthen the confidence which the citizen of a country has in his own government, a circumstance which naturally can find no place in international trade. For the advantages which coinage gives to trade, the citizens of a State are disposed to return to their government a compensation, when the same is demanded, and consent to receive the alloyed coin, as though it contained the full amount of pure metal.

As, with reference to the fixed value of a thing, a fabric has a greater worth than the raw material of which it is composed, so also is coin of more value for internal trade than the gold and silver in a raw state; and as the manufacturer adds the cost of manufacturing to the cost of the raw material, so also is the government justified in reckoning with the cost of the material the additional cost of its production, in order to invest the coin in circulation with a higher value than the actual amount of fineness indicates.

However, because the establishment of a seigniorage, on the part of the government, imparts a higher value to the coin, it by no means follows that the coin was not previously accepted as a more perfect exchange medium than the raw material, and that the additional value placed upon it by the government is not in consequence of the character or nature of the article, but instead a pure arbitrary act of taxation.

---

* Oppenheim, "Die Natur des Geldes," S. 436–439.

So long as coin consisted only of certain pieces of precious metal, with a simple impression, it was easy to manufacture the same; but with the further development and perfecting of the coinage, especially since the concentration of the work in the hands of fewer persons, or, as has been done lately, placing it entirely under the control of the government, the business is no longer a simple or easy one. If the work of coining is performed exclusively by the government, and to the cost of the raw material is added the cost of refining, it is exactly as if a certain article, of which a known amount is capable of satisfying a human necessity, and which up to a certain time was produced in large amounts, is now produced in limited quantities. The exchange value of this article is increased, notwithstanding its real value was known long ago. This illustration will explain the increased value of coin, as its actual value over that of the raw material has always been acknowledged.

It is affirmed* that as the demand for coin has not increased, therefore its value has not increased; but it must be evident to every one that between the greater perfecting of an article, and the demand for that improved article, there exists no *causal nexus*. This perfected article often satisfies special wants, peculiar to certain districts, and necessarily brings with the improvement an increase of consumers, and it often happens that the product in question is more durable than formerly, so that it is finally evident that while the cost of a product is increased by its improvement, the demand for it may be rather diminished, or at farthest not increased. Therefore there can be no conclusion arrived at concerning the advance in the value of coin from the fact that the demand for it has not increased. It is evident, therefore, that the above-quoted assertion is incorrect, so far as it relates to internal trade, because it is a fact that products are exchanged on better terms for coin than they can be for uncoined metal.

Although the government, like other enterprises, calculates the producing cost in the manufacture of the coin, and for that reason reduces the amount of precious metal in the coin below the normal value demanded by the coin laws, yet for all this the presumption is assumed both by the government and the owners of bullion, in their exchanges for coin, that the market value in offer and demand has not changed— the same amount of goods is delivered by the owners of other products as before the imposition of the seigniorage, and again, these latter pay out this coin to third persons for the same quantity of merchandise. There is, apparently, no change in the prices, but in reality there is a change effected. According to the nature of money, that which contains a depreciated amount of precious metal should receive in return a correspondingly small amount of merchandise. That this is not the case, can only be accounted for from the fact that coin has universally a higher known value than the raw metal. It is the opinion, also, that the seigniorage does not affect trade so far as the consumers are concerned, because they neither give more merchandise for the coin, nor by the transferring of the coin receive a greater quantity of goods in return, and, that therefore, the seigniorage only taxes the producers of the precious metals.† However, it is certain with reference to the real relation of the seigniorage, this opinion is in no case confirmed. It would be easy, according to the nature of the seigniorage, to establish it as a tax, in order to explain to the receivers of the coin that the real change in the price of products is caused by the removing of the seigniorage. But the impropriety of establishing the seigniorage as a tax

* Oppenheim, "Die Natur des Geldes," S. 439.
† Oppenheim im obeitirten Werke, S. 436.

is plain. The removing of a tribute can only ensue when it is allowed by the condition of the market. The desire to have the tribute abated may be ever present to the tax-payer, but the carrying out of the desire may depend upon circumstances beyond his power to control.

From the preceding argument it must not be inferred that after the introduction of the seigniorage, the offer upon the part of the merchants who desire coin in exchange for their merchandise, is unconditionally increased, or, contrariwise, the demand upon the part of those who are ready to exchange coin for other products is lessened; that for the depreciated coin as much merchandise is furnished as before the establishment of the seigniorage—that is, properly speaking, more is furnished, or, in other words, the tax is virtually removed. That such an understanding is, from the nature of the case, contradictory, needs no proof to establish.

In order that a larger quantity of merchandise may be exchanged for a smaller amount of depreciated coin—that is, an amount of produce greater than the cost of the coin, or, what is the same, greater than the seigniorage—it is necessary that the gold or silver coin should only be manufactured from such gold or silver bullion of the same value which in the sum total of its seigniorage contains more precious metal than the coin. The basis of the difference, as has already been plainly shown, lies in the increased value of coin. It is true that the idea has been advanced, that the cause of the difference in value is directly the reverse, viz., the depreciation of bullion, and that the worker in gold and silver, as well as the consumer of bullion, in order to prevent the sellers of bullion from being benefited by the saving of the coin-tax, threaten to melt down coin, and that, therefore, the owners of bullion, to whom no alternative remains, justly force the bullion up to the full value of the seigniorage, that is, oblige the buyer to pay more for his bullion.* But if, on account of the easy fusibility of the precious metal contained in the coin, those who wish to purchase bullion put themselves into an independent attitude toward the bullion merchants, and by that means work an easy change in the market-value of this product, the question arises, why are the owners of bullion unwilling to return as much more bullion for coin as the difference of the seigniorage amounts to, but must first be forced to it by the holders of the coin, and that too when gold and silver bullion ranks as merchandise, and according to the earlier tenets of this theory the receiver of the coin voluntarily returns the same amount of produce as before the introduction of the seigniorage?

Finally, there is one point which claims attention decidedly opposed to the conception of the seigniorage as a tax. If, for example, the government issues coin not only for private parties, but also on its own account, or if it does this exclusively for itself, and limits the coin to a legal, fixed fineness, then a seigniorage is established from which the government enjoys an income. And yet neither in this case is a direct tax imposed, because the coin circulates freely without enforcement, and not merely as a systematized medium of payment by which the tax is collected through deduction; yet there is a tribute lifted (indirectly), because no act will be undertaken by private parties upon which it is possible for the government to fasten a tax. Notwithstanding the amount of seigniorage is fixed in the coin laws, it is not, therefore, invested with the character of a tribute, for a tribute can only be fully enforced in one of the two mentioned ways; for this reason the fixing follows, that the character of the coin be in accordance with correct rules and that every piece be legally and properly executed.

_____

* Oppenheim im obcitirten Werke, SS. 438 u. 439.

It is only in this that a tribute can be detected, when the owner of produce who receives coin from the government is obliged to give more produce than corresponds with the depreciated value of the precious metal, and then the tribute appears to be transferred. But the transferring of a tribute is not considered regular, because after the introduction of the seigniorage, by which the market ratio is not changed, the owner of produce is obliged to give a larger amount of goods than formerly. Now if the nature of a phenomenon is to be made clear, then the explanation must be of a kind as will suffice for all forms in which this phenomenon is known. Whether the issuing of coin by the government, either for itself or for private parties, be only a method for the collecting of seigniorage, the spirit and the effect are the same. This is, however, a comprehensive explanation, that coin is a fabric, and the seigniorage collected a reimbursement for the cost incurred by the working of the precious metal.

When a seigniorage is levied, the purity of the coin is diminished to an amount equal to the exact legal value of the seigniorage; therefore it is on account of the greater value of coin for internal trade that the seigniorage is considered an advantage, and the coin, though minus a certain quantity of pure metal, is, nevertheless, unchanged in its market value, the same amount of produce is exchanged for it as formerly; this is especially the case with gold and silver bullion, of which as much more is given for coin as the full amount of seigniorage. This is the case so far as internal trade is concerned, as, for example, the principal and interest on public and private debts, contracted previous to the establishment of the seigniorage, can be discharged by the coin upon which a seigniorage has been paid, upon the same terms as by that coined previous to the establishment of a seigniorage.

But the question is, can coin subject to seigniorage be used to advantage in foreign countries? For example, in country A, as in country B, a like coin standard exists, namely, 20 silver coin pieces—of which the denominations differ—are made from one fine Cologne mark; consequently every piece of coin contains $\frac{1}{4}$ lothe fine silver.* In country A there is no seigniorage, while in country B 2 per cent. or $\frac{1}{50}$ lothe pure silver is retained as seigniorage. Now if A has a debt of 100 coin pieces to pay to B, it must, in order to fully meet that debt, send to B $81\frac{95}{100}$ lothe bullion silver, or $102\frac{3}{8}$ coin pieces. Because in the latter $\frac{78}{100}$ lothe fine silver is equal in coin form to every $\frac{80}{100}$ lothe pure silver which the coin of country A really contains; therefore the creditor in B in trade with the foreign country can demand the full metal value, namely, 80 lothe pure silver. But, on the contrary, if B has a debt of 100 coin pieces to pay to A, the debt can be fully discharged by sending 80 lothe bullion silver, that is, if bullion and coin are of like weight, while at home he would discharge the debt of like amount with 100 coin pieces, or 78 lothe fine silver.

It is plain, therefore, that the country in which no seigniorage exists finds it more expensive to pay a foreign debt than does one in which a seigniorage is established. According to the coin laws of international trade, the expressed value of the precious metal can only be rendered, when in two countries engaged in commerce there exists a seigniorage, and that, too, whether the amount of the seigniorage is the same or not. For the creditor receives payment according to the money laws of his country, and he is, therefore, obliged to carry to the mint of his country as much precious metal as shall by recoining furnish money of a full legal fineness. Countries A and B have the same mode of coining es-

---

* One lothe equals one-half ounce.

tablished by law, viz, 20 pieces out of 1 fine Cologne mark. B claims of A 100 gulden containing 80 lothe fine silver. Now if the seigniorage is the same in both, viz, 2 per cent., then B demands $81\frac{95}{100}$ lothe bullion, or $105\frac{5}{8}$ coin pieces. If the seigniorage is 4 per cent., $107\frac{4}{8}$, and if it is 1 per cent., $103\frac{3}{10}$ pieces of coin must be paid.

It is self-evident that the variations in the condition of the gold and silver market change the relation between bullion and coin. When the supply of gold and silver declines, and the demand increases, then the difference between coin and bullion is small; it may even happen that the value of the two will be equalized, and even that of bullion may rise above coin. If the supply increases and the demand declines, then the difference between coin and bullion becomes greater, and this happens because the value of bullion is really lowered.

In treating of the operations of the seigniorage it was shown, that notwithstanding the diminishing of the amount of pure metal in the coin, there occurs no variation in its value as an exchange medium, and this leads to the question, whether this is unconditional; that is, without reference to the degree of adulteration introduced, or whether its operations are limited to a *certain* degree? For the answering of this question two considerations are necessary. Coin is an industrial product, therefore its cost must be reckoned as that of any production of a private enterprise. This, however, must always be considered: the principal invested, the loss by the transfer of that principal, as well as the continual additions to the standing capital, and the cost of carrying on the enterprise. It is certainly just that when a state creates a benefit, or undertakes the performance of a service which is of vast importance to the industrial life of its citizens, as, for example, the coining of money, or the superintendence of the transportation of produce by railways, the financial point of view should have no prominence. If a government labors to advance the interests of its people, it must not, like a private individual, after full compensation for all outlay, aim at an overplus for itself, and reckon the cost in proportion; but it suffices when, after accomplishing its work, it receives remuneration for its capital.

In the foregoing case, however, the question is not, how shall the cost of coinage be reckoned, but whether the merchants will permit the calculation of heavier charges. This question must be answered in the affirmative, because coin is a fabric, which, like any other product, is better suited to meet the wants of trade than the raw material. Coin is not comprehended as something exclusive, and therefore the calculation of the cost of coinage by the government, from the standpoint of a private enterprise, will be willingly acquiesced in by the citizens. This view of the case is, however, subject to restrictions; money is, according to its nature, an equivalent for the various products; it is a merchandise through which is effected the exchange of products for a certain amount of precious metal. Therefore, if coin is a more convenient circulating product than the raw gold and silver, and notwithstanding it contains a less amount of precious metal, it possesses the same power as an exchange medium, then the character of money is not changed by the mere change of form, it cannot be lowered to a mere sign of value. The government should certainly be permitted to calculate the expense of coinage, the interest on the capital, as well as the cost of establishing and carrying on the enterprise according to the custom of the country; yet this privilege should not go so far as that a revenue should accrue therefrom, after the manner of a private enterprise.

The judgment upon the part of the merchants may certainly not always be confined to proper limits, but an exact knowledge of the productive condition of coin is necessary, and by constantly examining the worth of the same a dividing line can be drawn, so that on the one side the cost is covered, and on the other there is no opportunity for excessive gain. The rule by which coin, in trade, is established according to its full value, makes it possible for the government to secure a gain, if it exceeds its utmost limits, but that seldom occurs; it is only important that the power is not conceded to the government to make, out of choice, a large gain by coinage. Moreover, of late a knowledge of the nature of coin is more general, and governments themselves take pains to give a greater dissemination to this product in their districts, and the estimate of the cost and gain, with reference to the various branches of industry, is fixed, as well as that of other things not immediately connected therewith, for example, with reference to taxation, the estimate of which is always at least approximately correct.

If a government establishes a seigniorage which the mercantile community considers too high, then the coin will not circulate as freely as if it contained the full legal amount of precious metal; the coin is depreciated in proportion as the seigniorage is too high. It is just as if the government actually coined money of less metalic value than is demanded by law. It is evident that the coin must be received at its nominal value in home trade, because it represents, according to law, the pay medium through which, by a fixed sum of money, the performance of an obligation is discharged. Therefore the damage which the merchants suffer through the depreciation of coin cannot be repaired simply by a formal change in calculation, that is, the value of coin of the different countries, or the old and new systems calculated according to the par value of coin, but only by raising the price of their merchandise.

The same effect will follow if in the course of time the cost of coinage is reduced, and the government still retains the original seigniorage, because it has no longer any ground to continue to deduct from the coin a part of its metal-value.

In both instances, when the seigniorage is too high, or when the coin contains less than its legal value, the price of merchandise in the sum total rises. This advance in price can only take place when the efforts of the merchants to obtain compensation for the depreciated coin are upheld by the concurring circumstances of supply and demand. Sometimes it is received at its full value, as for example, under the obligations and payments for service rendered toward the government or private parties for interest upon public or private bonds of indebtedness, with the payment of the debt-principal, and generally all amounts of money stipulated for under former contracts, and which specially depend upon former public or private agreement. For those who are entitled to a stipulated amount there can be no compensation for a deficiency in the metal-value by the mere naming of the depreciated coin after that of true value, unless through concurrent circumstances, after the lapse of time the coin is declared a legal tender, and the rendering of a bare nominal amount annuls all past obligations. The dealers must pay more in the sum total for their merchandise, while the income therefrom is lessened, the claimant loses a part of his claim, and the government itself, notwithstanding it derives a gain from the depreciated coin, yet it loses in tax and other sources of revenue, unless as a remedy it resorts to an oppressive impost duty.

The imposition of seigniorage has the same effect as if the value of coin was increased by an increase of its precious metal. When the fact is published that gold and silver have advanced, then the seigniorage becomes a preventive against the disappearance of the coin, under the presumption that the value of gold and silver is less than the full amount of the seigniorage. As coin in home trade has a higher value than the like weight of bullion, the merchants have no inducement for the sake of a possible gain to melt down the coin and sell the metal at its market value. But the seigniorage can only prevent this so long as the value of bullion, that is, the value of each piece of raw metal containing the coin quantity does not reach the amount of the seigniorage, or at least does not overreach it. In the first case, the coin would leave the country, because of the constant opportunities to buy bullion, or to be remelted, and in the second place, a certain and greater gain would accrue by remelting and selling the metal. For example, if 16 silver gulden are coined from 1 fine Cologne mark, and the seigniorage is 5 per cent., so that 1 silver gulden contains $\frac{18}{20}$ lothe $= 57$ kreuzers, and only so much additional value in silver is admitted as that 1 lothe of silver $= 1$ florin $3\frac{3}{10}$ kreuzers, making $\frac{18}{20}$ lothe $= 1$ florin (60 kreuzers), or even more, then the coin cannot be retained in home trade.

When the government establishes no seigniorage, in the hope that by the supply and demand of bullion being equal, they will remain the same in value, it generally happens that so soon as the value of bullion rises above coin, a greater or less outflowing of the coin takes place. And this occurs for the reason that the coin and bullion contain an equal amount of precious metal, and, as there is no difference in value, the coin is preferred for the sake of convenience. Where a seigniorage is established there is, of course, a difference in value between coin and bullion in favor of the first. There is, therefore, an existing motive for payment in bullion instead of coin to foreign countries. While in international trade the coin form, at least as a rule, is equivalent to bullion, therefore, in a country where no seigniorage exists, coin becomes a lively and easy circulating medium in internal trade, and the cost of coinage, at least in part, is uselessly spent.

But there is another consideration to be thought of in connection with the above opinion. It no longer appears that the coin of a country is retained so long as the price of an equal weight of bullion with coin does not reach the full amount of the seigniorage, because in a short time there follows the emission of a large sum of coin by the government or by private parties, causing a depreciation of money, and an advance in the price of all kinds of merchandise, or at least of a large majority of them. Now, the enhancement of the price of foreign merchandise, brought about by the large sum of money thus called out, will be followed, under like conditions, by a rise in price of the precious metals. If this rise is so important as to reach the difference of the seigniorage, or to go beyond it, then the owner of the coin will either melt it down and sell the metal, or send it abroad. In no case will it be used in payment at home, because the addition which must be made in consequence of the depreciation of the coin would be as great a disadvantage as would the coin be which is not subject to a seigniorage, when the precious metal from which it is coined advances in value.

The purposes of the seigniorage are exemplified in other directions. Notwithstanding the completeness in the arrangement for the manufacture of coin, there is a difference in the weight and purity of the various pieces. Sometimes these are greater and sometimes less than the exact legal amount. The cause of this variation is this: the ingots, that is, the plain bars of cast metal, through imperfections in the roller, are not flattened to a uniform thickness, therefore the plates cut therefrom are of unequal weight and unequal fineness.* Consequently, for the avoidance of a too great irregularity in the plus and minus of the variation, there is a limit established in the coin laws (Toleranz, Remedium).

Coin sustains a loss of its precious metal by abrasion, and for that reason new coin is constantly forced into circulation, which is naturally of more value than the old. This is more observable where the government neglects to seize the coin which has been too long in use and to recoin it. Through the citation of these two examples it is evident that there is coin in circulation whose value is unequal, but which by law is made of equal power for buying and selling. When the government of a country fails to establish a seigniorage, then the coin which accidentally has a higher degree of fineness than the worn coin in circulation, is melted down and the raw metal sold either at home or abroad, so that the higher value which the heavy coin pieces possess cannot be used in internal trade in place of the depreciated coin. On the contrary, where there is a seigniorage established, the money-owner has no inducement to melt down the coin for the sake of selling the metal, becsuse he finds in the seigniorage a compensation for the gain which he would receive by changing the coin into raw metal. It is presumable, then, that in consequence of the universal increase of value given to metal by coinage, notwithstanding the losses resulting therefrom, there will be a corresponding increase of value in the precious metal.

For example, 16 gulden† (á 60 kreuzers) are coined from 1 fine Cologne mark; therefore 1 gulden contains 1 lothe fine silver; the waste by coinage is $\frac{1}{20}$ lothe; therefore the gulden piece really contains but 57 kreuzers. Now, under the presumption that there is no seigniorage, and when 1 lothe of fine silver is worth in the market 1 florin $2\frac{2}{15}$ kreuzers, then the newly-coined gulden pieces will be melted down, because they are in value to the amount of 3 kreuzers greater than the larger part of the old pieces in circulation, and the gain is therefore 3 kreuzers to every lothe. But, if there is a seigniorage of 5 per cent., so that the gulden piece contains but $\frac{18}{20}$ lothe fine silver, and $\frac{1}{20}$ lothe is lost in coinage, then the gulden piece actually contains but $\frac{18}{20}$ lothe fine silver, or 54 kreuzers; so, then, if 1 lothe fine silver is worth in the market 1 florin 3 kreuzers, the newly-coined gulden piece is only worth $59\frac{11}{20}$ kreuzers, and the remelting of the coin does not occur.

From the foregoing examples we further learn that the seigniorage can only prevent the disappearance of the coin from trade, so long as the difference of the loss exceeds the difference between the coin of the largest metal value and that of the smallest, or, at least, reaches it; for if it is smaller than this difference, then the higher value which the coin possesses in consequence of the greater amount of precious metal contained therein, has in its coin-form no available worth, it can only be utilized by selling the excess of gold and silver in the coin. It is natural, and cannot be prevented by the seigniorage, when coin of different degrees of fineness are in circulation together, that the energetic money speculators, for the sake of the resulting gain, should gather up the coin of the higher metal value; and when this occurs, then that of a lower metal value will circulate as before, and indeed be advanced in worth. As in the previously-mentioned case, when the average amount of the gain by the selling of the old coin is $\frac{1}{20}$ lothe, then the new coin gains $3\frac{3}{20}$ kreuzers, which altogether is more than is gained by remelting.

---

* Karmarsch, "Mechanische Technologie," Bd. ss. 546 u. 547.
† 1 mark = 16 lothe = 8 ounces.

V.

If foreign productions can be obtained at a lower rate than goods of the same kind at home, then the seigniorage is not able to retain the coin in the country.

Has the extent of the seigniorage in any country, in a proportionate degree between coin and bullion, an influence upon the precious metals in the market? If in a country there is no seigniorage, or but a very small one, then the sellers of precious metals (the producers, the metal traders, as well as all trades people who receive bullion from foreign countries for the purpose of putting it upon the market), hold, in proportion to other countries, a greater amount of coined metal. It makes no difference to the home traders in precious metals, if they choose to convert their large amount of precious metal into coin at home, whether the seigniorage is great or small, because they hold in any case, by its unchanging market value, the same amount of merchandise. But the foreign dealer in precious metals, who, perhaps, competes in a country in which a high seigniorage exists, has no advantage; because if he really obtains the coin of his rival's country, which has a greater metal value than that of his own, the overplus must serve to the payment of the seigniorage which he is compelled to discharge for the legal recoining, and so the foreign owner of the precious metal must, when in a country where a small seigniorage exists, bear the expense of a second payment.

In this case the inland traders in precious metals have no special basis upon which to offer their products, and the foreign traders no inducement to prefer seeking out a country in which a low seigniorage exists. The foreign metal sellers gain no advantage in endeavoring to make their payments abroad in bullion which they have taken as compensation in trade, and which it was their purpose thus to employ, when they are dealing with a country in which there is no seigniorage, or at least a very small one; for this latter only ranks as bullion in their own country, to which, besides, if the seigniorage is small, an addition is made, in order to give the coin standard a correspondingly full value. Coin subject to a high seigniorage would circulate in their country on an equality with coin of full value, and have the power to push the latter entirely out of circulation. If, for example, the 16-gulden standard is established (16 guldens from 1 fine Cologne mark), in county A a seigniorage of 10 per cent. exists, and in country B one of 20 per cent. In the former the gulden contains $\frac{9}{10}$ lothe of fine silver, in the latter $\frac{8}{10}$; then the owners of precious metals in B, if they sell to A and take its coin, whether it is to be remelted or not, receive really but a bullion of $\frac{9}{10}$ lothe. Now if B has a payment to make to a third country in which the same coin standard exists, the deficiency of $\frac{1}{10}$ lothe of pure silver must first be supplied. Now, if instead, the holder of bullion disposes of his property at home, he receives for every lothe of fine silver in bullion form $\frac{9}{10}$ lothe in coin form. This coin, however, is able to supply to its owner in trade 1 lothe bullion fine silver. The precious-metal owners of that country in which a high seigniorage exists find themselves in no worse condition than do those whose government has established no seigniorage, or at least a very small one, and *vice versa*, the latter are in no better condition than the former. So far as bullion furthers foreign payments, there is no reason why, on the part of the sellers of the precious metals, a large supply of precious metal should be offered to that country in which no seigniorage or a very small one is established.

A real gain to the foreign dealers in precious metals is only possible when they are paid for in the coin of their own country, and which is remitted to them either directly or in the manner of a bill of exchange, because in this way only do they realize more than by selling them at home. For example, in countries A and B a 16-gulden standard exists. In A there is no seigniorage, while in B there is one of 10 per cent.; therefore, in A a gulden contains 1 lothe, while in B it has only $\frac{9}{10}$ lothe. Now the dealers in precious metals in B when they sell to A receive for every lothe of bullion 1 lothe of coined silver, which equals in their money 1 florin 6 kreuzers, so that they really receive more than if obliged to sell at home, where they would only receive 1 gulden of $\frac{9}{10}$ lothe of fine silver. With reference to a country in which there is no seigniorage or a very low one, when engaged in trade with other countries, the exchange payments can always be stipulated for, and in every country where the seigniorage is very small or nothing, the supply of bullion, as a rule, is great, while the demand is small and the price low. In the case where there is no seigniorage imposed, the difference between coin and bullion is in favor of the former; but where there is a small seigniorage, the difference between coin and bullion is greater, and this is always in proportion to the extent of the seigniorage; that is, more bullion is required in payment for the same amount of coin.

But is the possession of the coin of full value any advantage to dealers in precious metals in a country where there is a high seigniorage? A question which, under the consideration that the recoining in the mint attains the object quicker and safer than by selling, is identical with another, which is, whether if coining is done for the benefit of private persons, and there is no seigniorage imposed, the precious metals will flow more strongly toward the mint, and whether they will not also be imported from foreign countries? The owners of gold and silver in that country which has a high seigniorage, when they carry their products to a country where there is no seigniorage, or, at least, a very small one, and make their purchases with the coin of that country (of full metal value), under the supposition that the ratio of prices for merchandise is the same, do not gain anything, because of the difference in the seigniorage, for they receive the same amount of merchandise in their own country as abroad, according to the respective coin.

And further, the coin of a foreign country, as a rule, has no circulation away from home, so that it would not benefit the owners of gold and silver to have their products coined in a foreign country into money of a full metal value, and bring it home. And then, again, the foreign owners of bullion who have purchased merchandise in a country where there is no seigniorage, or a very small one, derive no advantage from paying with the coin of this country, because they can, with the necessary bullion of a like coin-standard, operate as well at home with as small an amount of precious metal as the coin in question contains. It can only benefit the owners of precious metal to purchase the coin of full metal value as merchandise. As a metal pay-medium for international trade, as far as they supply such a medium, the bullion and the coin of those countries where accurate payments are enforced, compete with each other. When the manner of payment is not stipulated, then the difference must be determined between the price of bullion and the foreign coin referred to, for the purchase of the one or the other of the two pay-mediums.

In comparing the two kinds of coin, it will be found that the foreign coin, on account of its greater metal value, will be held as the par coin, and that several home coins answer to one foreign coin; consequently the foreign coin is of more value than bullion, making the trade with this coin, at least as a rule, advantageous. But if the price of bullion is higher than the coin under consideration, then not only the traveler, to whom on account of his residence in a foreign country the latter is indispensable, but also the trades-people, and especially the debtor to the foreign country, will seek for that same coin, and under these circumstances it may possibly happen that the foreign owners of precious metal, and even those of our own country, will have the metal coined into money of full value and find the selling of the same very profitable.

This will especially be the case when the coin of full value is receivable in other countries, and when the country with the depreciated coin is in full lively commercial relations with the former. In this case the precious metals tend more strongly toward that country in which there is no seigniorage, or at least a very small one. For example, in each of the two countries, A and B, 16 gulden are coined from 1 fine Cologne mark, so that 1 gulden contains 1 lothe of fine silver. Now if the seigniorage in A is 5 per centum, and in B 10 per centum, then the gulden in A really contains but $\frac{19}{20}$ lothe, and in B $\frac{18}{20}$ lothe fine silver; so that B is obliged to equalize the difference of $\frac{1}{20}$ lothe through fractional coin (as no other way is possible). Now, for example, under the supposition that 3 kreuzers of small silver coin represent $\frac{8}{200}$ lothe, there are yet wanting $\frac{2}{200}$ lothe $= \frac{2}{3}$ kreuzers, then it requires 1 florin $3\frac{2}{3}$ kreuzers in B to equal 1 gulden in A. If then the market price of 1 lothe of bullion, that is, that amount which B for the value of 1 florin must pay to A, is in B equal to 1 florin $3\frac{2}{3}$ kreuzers, then the gulden coin of A is cheaper than bullion, there is competition in the demand for the coin of A, and the piece of 1 florin $3\frac{2}{3}$ kreuzers is easy to obtain. But if the foreign coin of full value obtains in any country an equal circulation with the depreciated domestic coin, then the precious metals of the foreign country will more rapidly seek the mint, because the foreign coin in a country with a high seigniorage is no longer mere merchandise, but possesses a purchasing power, and, on account of the greater amount of precious metal which it holds, it has a greater power than the domestic coin. But that the foreign coin may circulate as the domestic coin, there must be a calculation of the respective values of the same, that the plus of the metal value be taken into account upon the abolishment of the high seigniorage. According to the above example, when $\frac{18}{20}$ lothe fine silver in B=1 florin (60 kreuzers), $\frac{19}{20}$ lothe, that is, 1 florin,=1 florin $3\frac{2}{3}$ kreuzers in A.

When a certain seigniorage is established in any country, then the sellers of bullion receive a smaller relative quantity of coined metal as equivalent. For those wishing to purchase bullion, but whose residence is in a country in which no seigniorage, or a very small one, exists, it will be advantageous to make their purchases in a country where a high seigniorage obtains, and that too, whether they wish the bullion for use, or for the purposes of payment, or to send it to the mint of their own country for coining, and whether they make their payments by remittances of metal, or by exchanges drawn on the bullion merchants, because in any case they receive their demanded amount of raw metal for a smaller amount of coined metal than is necessary to make the same purchase at home. For example, the merchant of A receives in B but $\frac{9}{10}$ lothe of coined silver, or, according to their money, 54 kreuzers for 1 lothe bullion. There is a stronger competition in a country with a high seigniorage to make precious metal valid in bullion form according to the demand. The difference between bullion and coin decreases as the amount of seigniorage diminishes; that is, there will be more coin returned for the same amount of precious bullion.

When a seigniorage is introduced, and in consequence thereof a depreciated coin enters into trade, then the price of the precious metals in the country is changed, and with that also the original manner of coining, because from now on there are more pieces coined from the same weight of metal. If 16 guldens from one fine Cologne mark is the legal reckoning, and there is established a seigniorage of 10 per cent., then the gulden contains but $\frac{9}{10}$ lothe, the ratio of bullion to coin is as $1 : \frac{9}{10}$, and therefore $17\frac{6}{10}$ guldens are coined from one mark. But this change is only outward, for it is so arranged that the perfection of the work compensates for the loss of the small quantity of precious metal from the original value. But the coin is not changed in appearance, its agency as a measure of value is the same, and for that reason there is no change effected in the money system.

According to a former statement, which will be further noticed, as soon as a seigniorage is established, there is an actual change in the market price of precious metal. With a low seigniorage the value of bullion falls, and with a high seigniorage it rises; in the former instance there will be more and in the latter fewer coin stamped. But the real change is effected only through the introduction of the seigniorage, and remains in conjunction with the same; it is not on account of a change in the production of the precious metals, or in the necessity for them, nor that their value is not understood, because the coining follows a certain mode, after as before, agreeably with the coin laws, so that the seigniorage, if not legally, is yet really changed ; in the first place raised, in the second place, lowered.

Should so high a seiniorage be established as to secure a monopolizing gain, then, on account of a rise in prices, there is danger that false coin, that is, imitation coin of gold and silver, will be introduced, because the important gain accruing therefrom will be considered a compensation for the great risk involved. In this case it is not necessary that base metal be used in the production of the false coin; gold and silver may be used, and indeed in their employment there is larger exchange secured with less risk. The method of manufacturing, by which base metal is galvanized, or thin plates of precious metal made to receive the impression of genuine coin, and then soldered to plates of copper or lead, makes the production of false coin comparatively easy. If the coining of real gold and silver is carried to a great extent, the accumulation of money resulting therefrom enhances the price of bullion, and depreciates the value of coin, and thus the incentive to the production of false coin is removed.

Moreover, the difficulties attending the false coining of gold and silver, in order to secure a successful imitation of the genuine coin, especially by private management, confines the work to narrow limits, and then the public and private vigilance exercised in the department of coinage, makes it almost impossible that any considerable interruption should occur in the money circulation.

We have as yet only spoken of the natural form of collecting the seigniorage, namely, that the deficiency of the pure metal in the coin exactly equals the amount of the seigniorage. But the collecting of the seigniorage may be accomplished in this way : the coin contains the precise amount of pure metal established by law, the amount of alloy is also explicitly stated, and private parties who bring precious metal to the mint may pay for its coining either a certain amount of coin or a certain amount of raw metal. There may be in the coin laws a seigniorage which is not fixed, and the collection of such a seigniorage has the effect of causing a higher value intentionally to be put upon coin than it actually possesses. This happens when a reduced amount of precious metal is made to enter into coin which formerly contained a larger quantity, or when by a change to another denomination of an advanced coin system the new unit coin, or basis, assumes in opposition to the old a higher ratio numerically without increasing the value of the precious metals in the market. In reference to the two modes above mentioned for collecting the seigniorage, when the value of the coin is outwardly stamped upon it, exactly according to the coin standard, its value will be less than is required, according to the market value of the precious metal. Let, however, either mode be adopted for the collection of the seigniorage, the ratio of coin to bullion as to the various other wares, as well as the attending operations and appearances of the seigniorage, are ever the same.

Finally, as concerns alloy, that is, the addition of inferior precious or base metals, copper with silver, silver or copper alone, or both together with gold, it is to the principal coin in reference to its compounds—and perhaps, too, to its subdivisions—merely a ligature, a preservative against the too speedy waste of the precious metal; in no way can the addition in connection with the precious metal be considered as an independent material—a chief thing; the functions of money can only be performed through the precious metals. In the manufacturing of money the cost of the alloy must be taken into consideration, but it only affects the value of coin when a seigniorage is established. When on account of the wearing away of the coin it is necessary to stop its circulation and recoin it, the cost of separating, in case that is technically necessary, is not reckoned apart as a special expense, as where a seigniorage exists to be borne by the public treasury, but it is counted in with the entire cost of coining, because the process of recoining is necessary to the maintenance of the respective repairs of the circulating medium; therefore, the cost, as in every department of business, is, for the earnest prosecution of labor, necessarily reckoned with the expense of the whole cost of production.

It is indispensable that the chief coin, that is, the coin which forms the basis or unit of the real coin system, be graduated in order that the necessities of trade, the requisites of retail dealers, for goods for which the unit coin is more than equivalent, be easily met. The actual coinage either embraces all these gradations of the ideal system, or only one of them, while the others, for example, the small ones, exist only as an idea in calculation. The actual coining of several units of the same category united into a high unit should be done to further the interests of trade, so that real intermediate members may be found among the several grades of the abstract coin system; as, for example, the 10-kreuzer piece of the Austrian coin system. The aliquot parts of the chief coin should strictly be taken only from the same metal as these last and coined in the same degree of purity, as corresponds to the respective parts of the chief coin; they should also share the seigniorage with the chief coin. Only by following these principles can either, all, or certain subdivisions, which on account of their small size are very inconvenient in business, become a pay medium. Where gold is the basis of the coin system, one or more of the next lowest in the category may be coined out of gold, only useful in trade, but the coinage must be of that kind, relative to the large class, that only silver, either in a preponderating or subordinate ratio to alloy, to the exclusion of a base metal, enters into circulation. The same is the case with the silver standard. One or two of the higher subdivisions are of silver, but the lower ones have relatively either a small silver value, or are entirely of base metal. The difference is this, that where a high standard, that is, where gold is the chief coin, a larger amount of silver is made to serve for the purchase of small amounts of merchandise, and to balance small sums in trade, that is, to divide the chief coin.

It is not the purpose at present to consider all small coin, but only those subdivisions of the chief coin which serve as easy, practical, successful circulating pay mediums, and which can only be manufactured out of the precious metals, in the same way as the larger coins. For the genius of speech unites the expression *divided coin* to the idea of a small value. By this relative idea is expressed the corresponding practical representation of the coin, and it is the best starting point for the critical examination of the extent of its value. All small coins are of insignificant value, but we refer particularly to those fractional parts of the unit coin which, if formed of precious metal, would be of such small dimensions that their handling would be inconvenient. Of the base metals for the representation of small coin, copper is generally employed; but of late other metals have come into use. Thus, for example, since 1850, the small silver coin of Switzerland is made from a mixture of silver and argentan, that is, copper, zinc, and nickel; and the latest small copper coin of Switzerland, France, Sweden, and Denmark contain a small addition of· tin and zinc.*

As only gold and silver are valid as universal pay mediums, the amount of precious metal which the small coin, as aliquot parts of chief coin, contain, are not to be considered in a corresponding manner as a money function in the requirements of trade; this is at once apparent on account of the proportionately large amount of base metal, or yet from the small quantity of precious metal represented, so that the small coin appear as representatives, as signs of the parts of coin, and contemplated as forming the other members of the money system whose preponderating elements are gold and silver. On this basis, then, the small coin, in contradistinction to the other coin of the country (the chief coin, however various, and though one or more may be only subdivisions), need not contain a fraction of the precious metal of the chief coin. On account of the value of gold, the higher subdivisions are made of silver, and the lower coin in the scale, not only on account of the value of gold but also of silver, are formed entirely of base metal, or, if silver is used, it is but a small per cent. of the chief coin, which is dropped in the calculation of the small coin.

In a critical discussion of the character of small coin it is necessary to understand clearly the value of the alloy of the lower divisions, where it exists in large amounts, not as in the chief coin, only used as a means of preserving the precious metals, but as the principal material from which the coin is formed, because the precious metals alone are not in a condition to perform the functions of money.

This view of the character of small coin in no way contradicts the former explanations of the nature of money, because the coining of the precious metals in small amounts is impracticable, and the small coin, therefore, is but a seeming basis, which is the mere sign of the substance of a certain kind of money.

The idea that the small coin is only a sign or symbol of the parts of coin, introduces another important consideration. It was stated, in speaking of the seigniorage, that the coining of the small coin, in the ratio of its value, was more expensive than any other coin of a country, and it was further remarked that, with reference to the large coin, the calculation of the cost of coinage appeared admissible from the stand-

---

* Karmarsch, Mechanische Technologie, Bd. I, S. 540.

point of a private enterprise, but beyond this it should not be allowed to go, because that would reduce coined money to a mere sign of value. But it is different with small coin, because this is only a symbol of value, a representative of a part of a coin; therefore the cost of coinage without regard to the former is greater, and the estimate is also higher than that made of the other coin. It is possible in the manufacturing of small coin to secure a monopolizing gain, and, notwithstanding the price of the raw metal and the greater cost of manufacturing, to secure a profit.

However correct this view of the case may be, the government from another consideration, namely, from the danger of counterfeits, takes the precaution, by giving to the small coin a mere nominal value, to confine it within narrow limits. The imperfect counterfeits of the small coin are of that kind that the metal value (especially that of the small silver coin), is either less, or it entirely differs from that of the legal coinage. If the government, in fixing the value of the small coin, permits, from the nature of the coin, too great a latitude, then false coinage will gain an advantage, because, without mentioning the fact that the counterfeiting of the smaller kind, especially the small copper coin, is attended with little cost and trouble, and therefore is more frequent, and that in consequence of the great gain, which is an important premium for the risk, there is offered a strong inducement to false coinage, and the employment of the complicated contrivances makes the easy production of a coin possible, which, in material and form, would not differ from the genuine. Therefore, to prevent a too great accumulation of small coin, and the subsequent attending evils, the government, in conformity to that purpose, will retain, after calculating the value of the metal and the cost of coinage, but a small overplus as profit.

In conclusion, we would remark that if the government in the issuing of a coin, as small coin, would treat it in a manner different from its character, that is, with reference to the value it has in the coin system, and form the greater part of it from precious metal, the effect would be the same as when gold and silver coin is covered by seigniorage, which is understood by the people as an excess of the cost of coinage, that is, should be estimated in trade only according to its real value in precious metal.

The characteristics of the small coin are further exemplified in this, that the material of which the whole, or at least the greater part, consists, is only employed for that purpose, because the precious metals alone cannot, in the small traffic, perform the functions of money in an equally practical manner. Consequently, on account of the nature of the precious metals, the representation of the parts of gold and silver coin by small coin is of itself a necessity, and is not the result of other adventitious circumstances. When the government, as is frequently the case, employs paper as money instead of gold and silver, it is, as a rule, for the reason that a more extensive pay medium is necessary than that already in use, and the precious metals in sufficient amounts are either not at hand or their production is united with too much expense. As a rule, by the employment of other materials, an increase of money is brought about, while, on the contrary, the small coin necessarily assists to supply the aliquot parts of the chief coin in small traffic.

Paper is generally used as the representative of the money unit in large amounts, but this difference is not intrinsic, for the government can, by an enlargement of the money system, employ to a certain amount a representation of small coin, as for example in Austria, where for the past fifty years there has been in circulation the money representative of the 10-kreuzer piece. In the latter case the essential difference is this, that the small subdivisions of the chief coin are made entirely of the same material as these latter, and consequently these subdivisions are not signs of the parts of the chief coin under consideration, but are themselves the parts. With reference to this circumstance, it is possible, then, that the apparent value of these small aliquot parts exceeds the intrinsic value, but as for that, where other material than precious metal is employed for money purposes, every member of the money system may possess an apparent value greater than its intrinsic value.

In the economical development, the precious metals, if not immediately, yet proportionately early, assumed the functions of money ; and because of the availability of their corresponding attributes, they quietly retain over everything else the position of a universal trade medium ; and for this reason is the idea identified with an exact money standard, making the accord of an intrinsic and apparent value a necessity. All other materials, therefore, which serve the purposes of money, lack the universal importance of gold and silver; they only belong to that country in which they are fixed to perform the service of money; they are strictly considered as only substitutes of gold and silver, and for that reason it is possible for their apparent worth to exceed their intrinsic value.

VI.

The money-surrogates (the substitutes for money), which circulate as coin made of precious metal, are of a twofold character. They are either, 1st, of that kind as rest upon gold and silver as their basis, and whose circulation to the full nominal value as regards the possibility of their redemption, depends upon the precious metals. Accordingly, this kind of money-surrogate is credit-money, because the emission of the same results from the assumed name of credit, and its reception in trade is voluntary, that confidence in its redemption be not forced. Or, 2d, the money-surrogates have no dependence upon the precious metals ; they have no need of redemption; they are simply independent money. When a bank receives authority to issue notes, then these notes are credit-money, because their issue is based upon the promise that they take the place of the precious metals, and their circulation is possible only because their redemption to their full value is secured by the precious metals. Credit-money then exists, when the government issues paper certificates, with or without interest, with the explanation that its redemption shall follow after a certain time, and its acceptance is always obligatory, because the government possesses the power ; but, in this case, the characteristic sign of the credit-money depends upon its redeemableness. On the contrary, paper certificates which are issued by the government as irredeemable, is independent money, (state paper money), the acceptance of which, in extensive trade, may be voluntary, although this is not generally the case.

For example, when on account of a too large issue the notes of a bank are declared irredeemable by the state authority, and yet possess an exchange power, then the character of the notes as credit-money is changed, and it becomes independent money. It is only by the emission, or, at least, by the intervention of the *government* that a legal-tender money can exist.

Because the small coin is only a subsidiary means for the representation of the corresponding gold and silver divisions of coin, then, according to their nature, the obligation attending the acceptance of the so-called base coin, should be restricted to that amount which cannot be equalized by the smallest coin made from pure metal. Over and above this amount there should be free choice granted, whether the small coin be received or not, and it is in this manner that a criterion is furnished, whether the pure credit-money will be accepted or not. In the German-Austrian Coin Treaty of January 24, 1857 (in § 14, latter part), it was properly determined that small coin, as legal tender, need only be received in such amounts as cannot be rendered in the small base coin (namely, ¼ florin, according to the 45 and 52½ florin standard, ⅙ thaler, according to the thaler standard). However, this limit is not positively fixed by all the legislatures, and the obligation is expressed to receive such an amount of small coin as can be equalized by coin of full value. So in England, for example, the silver money which there has always the character of small coin, is declared legal tender to the amount of 40 shillings (£2 = 20 florins Austrian standard), notwithstanding this amount can be equalized by gold coin. The legal declaration that the acceptance of small coin above a certain amount cannot be enforced, is to be understood as a rule of measure, taken with reference to the nature of small coin, but not for the purpose of preventing a too great issue of the same. This declaration only regards the conduct of the trades-people in their respective employments, and is not strong enough to bring a pressure to bear upon the government to exercise the power of circumscribing the issuing of money.

It is understood in all states that small coin is only manufactured for the benefit of the government, and not for private parties, because it is presumed that the government possesses the honorable intent and the right judgment, and under this declaration is in a condition to regulate the circulation of the small coin.

Because the small coin is only a make-shift for the corresponding parts of standard coin, it seems only consistent with the peculiar nature of coin, that there be given to the holder of small coin the power of exchanging it for the corresponding larger coin, and also the power certainly extended for the exchanging of the base coin for a corresponding amount of small coin.

The small coin, certainly bears in its nature the character of credit money. Only where a government issues a legal-tender, its destiny, whether it belongs to one or the other above-mentioned categories, depends entirely upon the estimate of the latter. In fact, small coin is differently esteemed in different countries; while in one it is independent money, and is therefore not redeemable, in another its exchange for precious metal is possible. Thus, for example, in the German-Austrian Coin Treaty of January 24, 1857 (§ 15, Abs. c.), it was determined that small coin to the full amount of its legal circulation could at any time be exchanged in the treasury for the base coin of the country. Where the privilege to redeem the small coin is allowed, there is properly from a practical point of view this conclusion admissible, that the redemption serves as a preventive against the overflowing of the circulation with small coin. Indeed, it is the acknowledgment of the redeemableness of the notes which a bank or state issues, which serves as the best guarantee against a too large issue of small coin, together with the evil consequences resulting therefrom, of which we will speak by and by, and, if there is opportunity, also of a corresponding means by which the standing evil may be removed. If a government knows that when small coin is presented at its treasury, it is obliged to redeem the same with genuine money, it will limit its issue to a smaller amount than when it does not feel the constraint of such an obligation. When there is an excess of small coin in circulation, where its redemption is legal, it soon seeks the public treasury and is exchanged for genuine money. The rapid inflowing of small coin into the treasury is a token that there has been too large an issue, and therefore as a safe check to a still greater increase of small coin, the prohibition of a further issue of the same must be enforced.

It has been already stated that the privilege of exchanging the smaller base coin for a corresponding amount of small coin, should be granted. At this point, the consideration of greatest weight is, as it is with the redemption of the money-surrogates, that the greater the measure of the sum total allowed in the exchange, the greater proportionate amount of small coin remains in circulation, because the amount of small coin is distributed among many trades-people beyond the limits of redemption. In the legislatures of the several states there are declarations to be met with not in harmony with the theoretical pretensions upon which the above-mentioned opinion concerning the character of small coin, is based. For example, in the German-Austrian Coin Treaty of January 24, 1857, (in § 15, c.), latter part, it is declared that the exchange of the base coin of the country for the small silver coin is not obligatory in amounts under 20 thalers, covering 40 gulden, and of small copper coin not under 5 thalers covering 10 florins.

Apart from the changes in the value of the material, there enters into the so-called hard money—that is, the gold, and especially the silver coin, of which we have before spoken—a depreciation if it is coined of a less fineness than the coin laws demand, or if (what is only a difference in form, but at the same time the only practical manner of securing a gain in coin without changing the system) the gold, and especially the silver coin of each member of the system, contains the nominal value of the next higher member, as, for example, in the Austrian coin system (45-gulden standard), the quarter-gulden contains relatively the value of 1 gulden; the gulden piece, the worth of a 2-gulden piece.

In order to make the gain more certain, the government is careful to make the adulteration as little noticeable outwardly as possible, and to supply the absence of the pure metal with base metal, that the dimensions of the coin may approach as near as possible to that established by law. In such a case there is a depreciation of the gold or silver money, for this reason, because the amount of precious metal, like any other product, is taken in trade as the measure of reciprocity. Such change, whether earlier or later discovered, cannot be equalized in trade; for to receive as much merchandise as formerly, a larger amount of precious metal must be returned—that is, the price of merchandise rises in the same ratio.

It is entirely different with the small coin. As this is only a representation of the parts of gold and silver coin referred to, therefore it makes no difference in trade whether it contains a greater or a less amount of metal, or, what is the same, whether it holds the nominal value of the next higher in the category or not. The fact that a certain amount of metal is fixed upon in the coin laws for every kind of small coin, determines nothing more than that the coin laws relating to small coin have only the signification that the government declares by the coining of the same, as strictly by its deeds in other respects, not to proceed arbitrarily, but to observe a regular course, and that the manner and way of its proceeding is universally known. A government not in pursuit of gain will retain, in the issuing of the small coin, the normal legal amount; but a government that sees only its financial interests (as was referred to in connection with precious-metal money), in order not to attract the attention of the merchants to the mentioned variations, will lessen the metal value of the small coin, by making its dimensions less than the law demands. But if the public discover this variation, the trade will endeavor to prevent the further alteration of the small coin, and the consequent rise in the value of merchandise. This occurs as soon as the outward appearance of the small coin ceases to correspond to its normal measure, for by this sign (and the small coin is but a sign of value), is its exterior value known.

The depreciation of small coin can never be real, but only apparent. This is always the case when the amount of any product on hand is too great for the existing wants of a community. The same causes produce a depreciation in gold, and particularly in silver money, if a too large issue of coin takes place either for state or private purposes, because either foreign commerce has brought in much precious metal, or because an especially rich profit of gold and silver has been secured in the country under consideration. The depreciation of small coin, then, is caused by a too free issue by the government, where the redemption is established by law, the consequence of neglect, just as is the case with paper surrogates issued by the state, or by banks, authorized to issue note-paper. The greatest difference, however, is this, that the increase of the paper-money surrogates, from the supply of the material, has no fixed limit, while the increase of metal money, especially gold and silver money, as a rule, more than that of copper or any other metal money, is really curtailed in its amount to the supply of the material. The increase of small coin is only so far arbitrary as the government is free to declare how much of the material under consideration shall be issued in small coin, and how much in standard coin, but it is only in silver (and, as a rule, under the silver standard), in which this change can be effected at pleasure. As regards independent materials, gold can only be used for standard money and copper for base coin.

To the disproportionate increase of small coin, as has before been stated, is traced, in a great measure, the imperfect imitations, which are always large in proportion to the profits drawn from this kind of coin.

The excessive increase of small coin results either through premeditated intent of gain to the public treasury, or unintentionally from an erroneous judgment of the necessities of trade for this species of coin. The result is either that a part of the standard money formerly issued is now compensated for by small coin, whereby either the amount of money, which was coined at the same period, remains unaltered, or the extraordinary increase of small coin is followed by an increase of money; or else the undue increase of small coin is not at the sacrifice of the standard money, which is issued in the same amount after as before, naturally causing an increase of money to follow. If the usual issue of small coin, and a part of the standard coin, is compensated for by this species of coin—and in this manner a glutting of trade with small coin is effected without an especial increase of money—then as soon as the absence of standard money is felt there follows an issuing of the latter, either alone for government purposes or for the advantage of private parties. But aside from the fact that only standard money is used to equalize the claims of foreign countries, when that cannot be done by an exchange of merchandise, yet also at home this kind of money is needed; for example, money consignments, which are necessary in home trade, are more easily made through gold and silver coin than through small coin; so, too, the exchange payments upon which foreign trade is established can be equalized by precious metal in a manner impossible through small coin, as there is no law by which the reception as payment of a fixed amount of small coin is made obligatory. Immediately where a lack of standard money is perceptible, the properly-executed order, which obliges no one to receive in payment the small coin above a certain amount, will be strictly adhered to, in spite of the inconvenience, and, perhaps, directly in opposition to it, thus producing a sensible impression upon trade.

The great scarcity of precious metals, when compared to the old supply, causes a difference between the small coin and the standard silver and gold coin, and the value of the latter is enhanced. The standard coin becomes merchandise, whose premium, according to the ratio of supply and demand, rises or falls. So soon as this occurs, the standard coin, between which and the small coin there exists in trade no legal difference as to value, will be withdrawn from circulation, and also the supply through new coinage will disappear, the standard coin being an object in great demand for speculation. They who carry on a wholesale business, as they receive from the small craft and trades-people nearly all small coin in payment, find themselves obliged to procure a supply of standard coin by purchase, and on account of the great expense thus incurred and which they have no disposition to bear themselves, they endeavor, as far as the market value will allow, to impose the extra expense upon their customers, the retail dealers; and these latter, in turn, endeavor as far as possible to burden the consumer with the advanced price of their merchandise. Although in a measure the supposition is that an increase of money is not the result of a too great emission of small coin, yet in consequence of the difference between small coin and standard coin, there always occurs a greater or less advance in prices.

If the large emission of small coin causes an increase of money, as it usually does, whether it be at the sacrifice of the standard coin or not, the result is, an increase in the price of merchandise, in opposition to standard money as well as small coin. The standard money is no longer employed merely in the purchase of such merchandise which, until now, was imported, but for other reasons it is crowded out of the country. It is effected in this way: the small coin now performs a large part of the money circulation formerly accomplished through standard coin, and it is possible to form a surplus, which will serve to enlarge foreign trade. Again, in consequence of the circumstance that through the extraordinary amount of money the prices at home are considerably advanced, while abroad they are stationary, making importation profitable, the standard money is used in the purchase of such goods as, until now, were not imported.

If through this circumstance a large part of the standard money is forced out of the country, then at last specie becomes scarce, and the price of merchandise again falls. But here it is well to reflect that the probability is very great that after the emission of small coin, and after the outflowing of a large part of the standard money, the amount of money at home in opposition to the supply of merchandise is yet too great. It is also further to be meditated upon, that the gain from small coin only too easily induces a new issue, whereby the proportion between money and produce is continually interrupted. This latter event is common. But whether the one or the other takes place, the certain consequence of an undue issue of small coin in every case, causes a scarcity in standard money; for the stock of metal from which the pay medium for foreign trade was formerly taken, is, since the large issue of small coin, considerably reduced, perhaps nearly exhausted, and the usual supply through coining for the benefit of the state or for private parties, together with the amount on hand, is not sufficient to satisfy the demand of foreign trade for bullion. In the mean time these demands increase, for the presumption is that the existing amount of money always considerably exceeds the amount of home products; so the prevailing high prices always make the importation of those goods profitable which were formerly produced at home; and of the remnant of the standard coin, a part finds ample employment as business capital in foreign trade. Specie now becomes subject to speculation, as was formerly stated, which causes a scarcity, with all the accompanying evils induced by a rise in the price of gold, and especially of silver coin, occasioning, as before, a too great issue of money. The fall in the price of merchandise, which took place immediately upon the removal of a large part of the precious metal, is either checked at once (which is the case if in the mean time new issues follow), or it is so important that former prices are again reached.

Through a too large issue of small coin, made regardless of the advance in the price of merchandise, and the inconveniences to tradespeople, and the industries, occasioned by speculation, trade (entirely in contrast with the issue of paper money) becomes overstocked with a burdensome pay medium; in consequence of this, the small coin, especially in wholesale trade, circulates not in single pieces but in rolls or packages, giving large opportunity for the employment of counterfeits.

The depreciation of the small coin alluded to above is universal and enduring, extending throughout the country and continuing for a long time. But if it does not arise from an inherent cause, it may be confined and local, extending only through a certain district, or in a certain place. The small coin, as formerly, is by small industries and retail dealers collected together in large amounts, at certain points, and after the lapse of time the greater part is bought up in small quantities. In this case the demand by the small industries and retail dealers for produce is the same as formerly, only the kind of pay medium is changed, the price of merchandise remains the same. If a larger number of retail dealers than formerly are drawn together to a certain locality for the purpose of making purchases, there is then a greater inflowing of small coin; the demand for produce is consequently increased, and prices advance. But in this case, those traders who conduct business on a larger scale, and who come in contact with retail dealers, in like manner receive more small coin than formerly. So long as the circulation of money was limited the large dealers, because they needed but little small coin, on account of their manner of doing business, dealt mostly in a circular manner, which, though very active, required but small advances, receiving, of course, the excess in specie. The wholesale dealers, because the large coin is more important to them than the small coin, concede a small premium for the former, and, contrariwise, the same dealers do often, when they have small disbursements to make and greatly desire the possession of small coin, either obtain the same by selling a greater amount of merchandise for it than for large coin, or by exchanging large coin for it, allowing therefor a percentage. But so soon as a partial overplus of small coin occurs, the aforesaid dealers, who were formerly so interested in small coin, no longer retain it; its possession is burdensome and unprofitable, and they are constantly receiving it in payment.

Small coin does not enter the circle of the real wholesale trade, because it is inconvenient, and its accumulation in masses is neither universal nor continuous; consequently, there is in these circles sufficient standard money to exclude the small coin above a certain amount, which can be used without detriment to the dealers. By a previous local overflow of trade with small coin, the latter is in a great measure drawn into the circle of the trade districts. The producers of these districts cannot refuse its acceptance without considerable interruption to their business, as has previously been stated; but it has no longer the former quick outflow from these circles; consequently it remains unused for a long time, until the cause of the overflow is removed. The traders, for the sake of the gain growing out of this state of things, return to the retailers, who pay in small coin a less amount of merchandise; that is, they raise the price. The retailers then naturally endeavor to impose the extra price upon their customers, but whether this succeeds depends upon the condition of the market.

From this representation it is evident that, according to the manner of glutting the trade with small coin, and the resulting depreciation of the same, the domestic circumstances vary, while the results to the small dealers are the same.

As with small coin, so also with paper currency; the like consequences result from a too large issue. If a credit paper is in circulation, it is held at its nominal value only when it is redeemable upon the stipulated terms of its issue. If it is redeemable only to a part of its nominal value, then the credit paper only circulates to this amount, and very likely the mistrust and fear of a yet greater pay restriction causes a yet greater fall in value. As soon as the redemption is but partial, or the entire irredeemableness of the paper is declared by the government, then the ratio of the already emitted notes based upon the supposed store of metal over the value of credit-paper money is determined. If only so much paper money is issued that the necessary store of metal exists at home, by which it can be redeemed, then the irredeemable notes pass at their nominal value; their partial redemption secures their circulation upon the credit of the course of exchange prescribed. If, on account of the large issue of notes, the former amount of specie at home becomes less, and therefore scarce, the market ratio of value between notes and standard money now used as merchandise, and the future value of credit-paper money, is determined, and under such circumstances it may happen, if the sum of the notes to be redeemed is greater than the necessary store of metal, that the circulation of such notes, on account of the contraction of their circulating value, will cease.

The same results follow whether the government issue redeemable or irredeemable money surrogates; the same, too, is the case with small coin, which was originally to be redeemed, but whose redemption was afterward annulled by the government. Just as has before been plainly proven, the depreciation of small coin, as well as that of money surrogates, occurs altogether through their inferior value compared with specie. The cause of this does not arise from the fact that there is too much specie, but in a general economical relation, namely, this, that with reference to the necessities of trade for a pay medium, as a substitute for money (to which, properly speaking, small coin belongs), there is too little specie.

It is, perhaps, wrong to seek for the cause of the depreciation of small coin in this, that as soon as it begins to circulate in large quantities, its small intrinsic value is not equal to what it was before, but sinks in proportion to its abundance. For, as has been previously stated, there is no account taken of the intrinsic value of small coin; that is, its metal contents and their price. From its nature it is but a sign quickly changed; at least, that is the conclusion drawn from the extraordinary increase of this agent. It should be carefully noted that the necessary large excess of small coin determines immediately, and not gradually, the value of the trifling inherent worth of small coin in contrast with the standard coin.

Finally, the amount of coin does not affect its intrinsic value. A large coinage upon the part of the government, or of private persons, may bring into trade a considerable amount of money, but this does not lower the price of metal; on the contrary, it often raises it, or, as will be noticed later, inversely, very often an increase of coin results from the sinking of the metal value.

VII.

In the course of this argument we have seen how gradually coin became incorporated with the industrial life, and discussed the special phenomena in the department of the nature of coin; the seigniorage and small coins have also been carefully considered. Now the question to be discussed is, whether an exchange operation exists between bullion and coin, and, if so, to what extent.

First, then, the precious metal in bullion form, on account of the large increase in the demand or the decrease of the supply, rises to an important increase in value, and where a seigniorage exists the difference is still greater. The easy fusibility of these metals, makes them valuable above all others. The material can be wrought into form with little cost and difficulty, and without loss of weight, while with other products upon which, likewise, much labor is spent, the completion is either not effected, or it is accompanied with considerable cost and difficulty, or is perhaps only finished with detriment to the material. And, further, it is to be noticed, that, through coining by the government, either for itself or for private parties who bring metal to the mint, either directly from the mines, or through trade have obtained it from abroad, there has gradually accumulated, in the course of time, a large store of precious metal which circulates at home, and remains subject at any time to the disposal of the public interests; while, on the one hand, many owners of coin, in perceiving the greater value of bullion, are prompted, for the sake of gain, to melt down their coin; and, on the other hand, those who need bullion as a foreign pay medium, or for the necessities of the arts, instead of purchasing the bullion, the price of which has risen, prefer melting the coin and using the raw metal in one or the other way. The competition in the demand for bullion decreases, while the supply increases; consequently the price gradually falls nearly or entirely to its original level. Therefore it is *coin* which regulates the worth of bullion, and it is *coin* which effects the necessary change in the fineness of bullion to the attainment of its original value. This rule applies to metal bullion in general; but as regards copper, the increase in the price of bullion on account of the already high nominal value of copper coin is not so easy to regulate.

On the other hand, if the value of bullion sinks below its usual level, the owner of bullion takes pains to obtain for it the most favorable price; a part he sells abroad, if by so doing he secures a greater gain, but preferably it is carried to the mint, as its coining is the simplest and easiest way to obtain the highest value. Metal bullion, like every other product, possesses the faculty of attaining the greatest possible value, and when this is depreciated, to rise to its first level; but bullion cannot attain to this by itself; there is an outward agent necessary to accomplish a reduction in the value of bullion, and thereby restore it to its former market ratio. This agent is coin; that is, in the case in question, coin in itself, not, as in the former case, the individual circulating coin piece. This argument is based upon the presumption that the government does not coin exclusively for itself, but that the privilege is granted to private persons to have their bullion coined, and indeed the latter make use of this privilege. If the government coined only for itself, there would only be larger purchases of bullion made by it, and the former value partly or wholly restored.

The above explanation refers solely to gold and silver bullion; as to copper bullion, whether larger coinage and heavier purchases should be made by the government, does not come within the province of this argument. The emission of small coin lies exclusively in the hands of the government.

VIII.

We will now consider the various changes in coin. When a large amount of coin (be it gold and silver, that is, properly speaking standard coin, or only small coin), is suddenly drawn into circulation, then, in consequence of the depreciation resulting therefrom, a more or less important and general advance in the price of produce, and a large outflow of precious metal (as well perhaps in bullion form as in coin form), toward foreign countries, are apparent, and the wholesale dealers import their goods chiefly from abroad where the price is cheaper. Thus by the purchase of cheap goods, the gains, which to many were lessened through the depreciation of money, are again restored. Yet others, and particularly the retail dealers, who buy only at home, and therefore in spite of the competition of the cheaper foreign merchandise, always pay a higher price than before, are not placed in the same advantageous position. This state of things continues until the coin is remelted and the metal put upon the market. For, in consequence of the rise in prices caused by the abundance of money, there is, as a rule, a great demand for bullion, both for consumption and for paying purposes, and its price is such, that by its sale, it is possible to restore the loss sustained by coin on account of its depreciation when used in trade for the purchase of merchandise. Thus, through the gradual reduction of the surplus coin, it is restored nearly or quite to its original value. The bullion, in consequence of its greater value, is the agent which causes a change in the stability of coin, and coin in return determines the material which seeks for it a profitable investment; that is, the value of coin is regulated by bullion.

If the stock of coin in a country is suddenly diminished, producing thereby an unexpected panic, and a universal fall in prices, then as a rule the price of bullion also falls. The difference now between the high price of coin, and the low price of bullion, to the detriment of the latter, induces the holders of the raw metal to send their produce to the mint. In this manner, through the increase in the stock of coin, its value is brought nearly or quite to the original standard, and consequently in this case it is manifest that bullion is the power, which, on the one hand, disturbs coin, and again, with equal weight, re-establishes it. Under these circumstances, as before stated, private parties have full liberty accorded them to have coining done. If the government coins merely for its own purposes, it can influence the value of coin only by an issue greater than ordinary. The above conditions do not apply to copper coin independent of the large issue by the government, the emission of copper coin being solely under the control of the government.

IX.

From this exposition it is evident that the value of bullion is quickly regulated through coin, but that, again, the value of coin is as quickly regulated through bullion, and that in this the kind of metal causes no difference. The effort has been made* to establish a difference between copper and the two precious metals, gold and silver, and it is maintained that the value of coin through bullion is only established by copper, in opposition to the precious metals, even in those cases in which either an important increase or lessening of the coin follows, the coin regulates the value of bullion; that in the first case especially bullion falls in value through the remelting of coin, yet in the latter case through recoining, the bullion again rises to the value of coin.

To establish this assertion, it is argued that the greater part of gold and silver is used for money purposes, and, consequently, in the course of time there is a coin magazine established which is far greater than the existing store of bullion, and that the place is seized upon by copper in a parallel ratio; that it is therefore natural that the functions of the worth regulator should be assumed by the greater instead of the smaller amount. And, further, it is asserted that if bullion represents the regulator of value, then, as before stated, the bullion itself would undergo a change; namely, that by depreciating the coin, and the consequent rise in prices, the bullion falls in value, and, on the contrary, by the introduction of a rise in value in coin, with the accompanying decrease of prices, an increase in the price of bullion takes place.

But should the gold and silver which circulate as coin in the course of time exceed the amount of that which appears in bullion form, and the place, on the contrary, be seized upon by copper, this one thing is certain, that, at one time on the side of coin, and at another time on the side of bullion, a change will take place which will disturb the equilibrium between coin and bullion. If those standards which have suffered disturbance are placed back again to their former value, then there must be a variation in prices as a natural result. But this neither can nor will be accomplished by the disturbed portion; an outward agent is necessary to effect such change in the market as shall restore the former equilibrium. The assertion, therefore, that this regulator belongs only to the larger amount which governs, independent of the money functions, is, with reference to the above explanation, inadmissible.

It is certainly correct that if bullion regulates the value of coin, then, in the event of the fall or rise of the latter, a change of value occurs in the former. But this circumstance is of no further importance; the determinate point is this, that the bullion first of all produces that change in the coin measure, through which the former steadiness in value of the same is again produced. It is an inherent necessity that the regulator itself undergo a change of value, because coin and bullion are in active exchange; every variation in one portion naturally effects a variation in the other. This would be evident if, in these cases, coin was taken as the regulator; for if, through large issues, the value of coin falls, then, by curtailing the amount through remelting, the value rises, thus causing an increase in the amount of bullion, which, in turn, reduces its value. On the contrary, if the value of coin rises by decreasing its amount, then, by recoining the bullion, the amount of coin is increased, but its value lowered, while the amount of bullion is decreased, and thereby its value is raised.

The rise and fall of the value of coin is known to induce a rise or fall in merchandise; none can deny its agency. But it is a denial of the same to take but a partial view of the falling or rising of bullion, without reference to the value of coin, and it is not far from an adjustment of the question—that is, a reconducting to the former value, or yet the

* Oppenheim, Die Natur des Geldes, SS. 127–136.

nearest possible approach to the same—when the highest or lowest value of the coin to which the bullion either raises or depresses it, is taken as the point of observation.

But, finally, it is not understood why there should be a difference made in respect to the regulation of value between precious and base metal. For example, copper is employed in the various domestic and individual uses in much larger amounts than that used for coin, so at farthest the result may be a demand for that metal as lively and great as for the precious metals; but as soon as a change in value is introduced, the adjustment will be accomplished in the same way as it usually is between coin and bullion.

It was mentioned in the beginning of this essay, that the proportionately great stability in value in precious metals, besides other advantages, was the foundation upon which they were established as money functions; the same idea has been held up continually; and now, therefore, this attribute cannot be slighted. It was also mentioned that in the easy fusibility of the precious metals, which effects their circulation, there exists a regulator against a too great advance in price in the above-mentioned metals, collected through ages in the coin treasuries. Whether coin be issued for the advantage of the citizen, or exclusively for that of the government, it offers in return a remedium against a too great fall in value in the precious metal, and it is universally admitted that where coining is done for the advantage of the government, it cannot be considered as a regulator as certainly, nor to such an extent, as where the privilege is granted to private persons to have their precious metal coined.

The reason of the greater proportional stability in value of the precious metals, is not merely that they are subject to smaller fluctuations than other metals, for instance, copper, but it is to be sought for further; the supply and demand is uniform in a far greater degree than that enjoyed by all other merchandise together. The production and exchange of goods which require a specie pay medium, as well as the consumption of gold and silver in the arts, do not in the whole and entire amount produce such a sudden change, that in the same time these agents are not able to maintain an equilibrium in the usual profits on precious metals. But then again these agents are not generally so backward in their development, that by this means any deficiencies may arise in the demand for precious metals. The demand for gold and silver has, up to the present, been entirely met by the supply, and this fact is of weight in favor of the idea that if but two kinds of metal were used for coin purposes, the deficiencies in the one kind might easily be compensated for by a richer gain in the other, and so contrariwise, the large amount of the one kind of metal might be equalized through the scant supply of the other.

What has just been said of the great staple value of the precious metals is established by the late reports. From January, 1849, to 1860, the average yearly product of silver in round numbers amounted to 2,100,000 pounds. The exports of this metal from Europe to East Asia from 1851, to 1860, was a yearly average of 2,053,000 pounds. The export of silver from Europe, has exceeded the import from America, and the average silver product of this part of the world amounts to 1,800,000 pounds.

Apart from this, on account of the increase of population, and of prosperity, there is an increased demand for specie for home use; then on account of the extensive use of silver in the arts, the demand for this metal is increased to an extraordinary amount. Notwithstanding these increasing claims, however, the supply has not remained so far behind the demand, that, according to analogy, under the circumstances, one is disposed to accept the usual merchantable price. The reason for this peculiar phenomenon is, that during the time from 1849, to 1860, the gold profit increased over the same space of time previously in round numbers, 400,000 pounds yearly; for while, in 1800, it was 48,000 pounds, in 1846, it was 90,000 pounds. It is possible that this large increase in gold drew the silver from circulation, and threw it on the market. In consequence of this the highest reported relative value of the two precious metals changed in favor of silver 3¼ per cent., properly speaking on an average of 2.7 per cent., by which it is seen that the proportion in general between the supply and the demand of the precious metals, is not sensibly disturbed.*

X.

When industrial progress has reached that development that coin is the model for the universal exchange medium, and the nature of coin is regulated in its most important parts, then the coinage will be so managed that from the authorized unit weight of the precious metal (mark, zollpfund, &c.) will be coined as many pieces of the coin unit (for example, gulden) as are given in the market for this fundamental weight; or, in other words, the coin price and the market price of the respective precious metals will reimburse each other. We would here remark that there no longer exists between coin and bullion, as was originally the case, an artificial difference; that is, one established by order of the legislature. For coin in its origin is nothing else than a certain amount of precious metal that appears in a certain form, with a certain exterior, with simple signature, and with a proper name (whether the amount of weight is impressed thereon or not), but upon which there is no seigniorage.

If, for example, there is a certain piece of silver containing ¼ lothe, with a certain form and signature, called a gulden, and 20 of these pieces are exchanged in the market for one fine Cologne mark=16 lothe, then the resulting coin standard is the 20-gulden standard. If, subsequently, the government establishes a seigniorage, then naturally every single piece of coin contains the same amount of metal, minus the cost of manufacturing, and therefore by recoining the mark there is an overplus which may be coined into pieces of smaller value. By the seigniorage, as before stated, the established market value between coin and bullion is so far changed, that for a certain quantity of bullion a less amount of coined metal is given, although this does not necessitate a change in the coin standard; the plus of the bullion is employed only to the perfecting of the raw metal, and the real, originally-established price ratio of coin and bullion toward each other is presumed to have experienced no change.

There should also, as before stated, be as much gold or silver coin issued from the received unit weight of precious metal as shall establish the price of the same upon the market. As soon as the universal exchange medium has taken the form of coin, the various amounts of coined metal become, on account of the natural evolution and imperative influence necessary to the forming of the various kinds of money, a different thing from the raw metal. They are, especially if a very small amount of labor has been expended upon them, industrial products, in contradistinction to the raw precious metals as natural products. If, after the coin has been forced into circulation, it becomes desirable to introduce a new coin, then the necessary material and worth is exchanged for the

* Zeitschrift für die Staatswissenschaft, Jahrgang 1868, SS. 8–17.

existing original coin; the new coin, like every other industrial product, only represents a money value, namely, that amount of precious metal, which must be returned for the recovery of the necessary raw material, and where a seigniorage is established, also for the production of the necessary work, (that is, the cost price of the coin money). Now, because coin and bullion are different things from each other, an exchange may not at first be possible; there may be a divergence, so that more or less precious metal may be returned for the coin than the latter contains. Variations in the cost of manufacturing are not to be considered here, because the metal contents of the coin can be raised or lowered to the standing, unchanging, legal quantity, and the total value always answers to the actual value. It is different when the precious metal under consideration undergoes a change in value; according to this presumption the legal amount of precious metal which the coin contains is not changed.

Money, and coin as a kind of money, is like every other product, and *purchase* is only an exchange of the various single products for gold and silver; therefore, the variations in the cost of the production of coin money, as well as the variations in the cost of the several special products, must find their expression in the price. Money, relatively coin, is not, therefore, to be comprehended in the sense that in every kind there must be present a legally acknowledged amount of precious metal in each particular coin piece, but it is to be comprehended in the sense of merchandise, in which the nominal value of the coin agrees with the real value of the same. It is the artistically wrought coin, although containing the same material in the same amount as that supplied with a certain name, yet with but a simple inscription, an exchange medium from precious metal, enduring and universal, not identical in kind with the latter, which by a change of value of its constituent parts, particularly delivered from the raw metal, which is possible to become an unvarying satisfactory standard.

If precious metal rises in value, coin is represented by a smaller amount of precious metal than it possesses; and if precious metal falls in value, then coin is represented by a larger amount of precious metal than it possesses. In accepting coin as a settled money value, representing industrial productions, it is a false perception which leads one to insist upon the inviolable, original amount of precious metal in the coin, without reference, in the meanwhile, to the variations which in the course of time have taken place in the market value of gold and silver through recoining.

Concerning the uncoined and the coined precious metals, the price of the former is subject to sudden and constant fluctuations. Now, trade needs a solid basis for its computations and transactions; therefore, for every country it is judicious, yes, necessary, that its coin in one or the other precious metals signify a fixed value, so that this coin corresponding to the legal quantity of precious metal under consideration, without reference to the fluctuations in prices, which in the mean time may enter, possess the power to discharge the introduced money obligations, whether the same proceed from loans or from supplies of merchandise. In this way, coin from these metals establish the legal pay medium. But if the value upon which the foregoing fluctuations turn is itself changed, and if this change according to the nature of the circumstances is permanent, and of financial importance, then the necessity is urgent for calculating a new ratio of value between coin and bullion, and also for the recoining of a legal pay medium.

If the market price of gold or silver rises, and the equilibrium between coin and bullion is sensibly disturbed, then because payments of a fixed amount, the interest and principal of loans as the case may be, only recognizes in the coin the present paying power of the amount of metal therein contained, therefore, the venders, not considering the advanced value of metal to their advantage, carefully seek to maintain the old prices. On the other hand, the purchasers, because they receive from the venders a correspondingly larger amount of merchandise, seek to lower the price. In examining the above detailed statement, the postulate is at least theoretically and securely based. But it is a question whether it is safe and easy in all cases for the purchasers to secure to the full, for the advanced value of metal, a corresponding lowering of prices for any length of time, and, further, whether such will take place in all branches of business.

The holders of coin who desire to purchase can attain their object, viz, the higher value of the coin, much more certainly and easily by remelting it, and placing the precious metal material upon the market, as the place where every product most certainly attains its true value. In any case, therefore, in which a decline in prices is difficult to secure, the holders of coin prefer melting it and selling the precious metal; and when this is easy to accomplish it tends to abate prices, or if (of which we will speak by and by), the business interests do not permit an easy remelting of the coin, the venders, to secure a higher rate for coined metal, are induced to lower their prices; but if it is possible, according to the standard market value, to attain a corresponding fall of prices, or if that is actually attained, the holders of coin still have a great advantage in remelting their coin and selling the metal, because in this way a greater gain is secured than when a decline in prices is effected. If, for example, 1 gulden (equal to 60 kreuzers), in consequence of a rise in the value of silver is made to equal 1 florin 6 kreuzers, then 100 florins equal 110 florins, and, therefore, in purchasing, this latter sum secures a corresponding amount of merchandise. In selling, however, because there is no change presumed in the market value of merchandise, this amount only aims to effect the value of 100 gulden pieces; but if the above 100 guldens are melted, there will result from the sale of the precious metal 110 guldens, which initiates a greater cost of production, and besides under like circumstances yields a larger gain. The holders of the coin metal which is rising in value, especially trades-people, who in their industrial pursuits have to deal with large sums, melt the coin under consideration (although that causes speculation in money, the coin being bought up for the sake of the premium), and place the remelted precious metal upon the market as merchandise along with that of the gold and silver producers and traders.

The increase in the price of the precious metals has its foundation either in a decrease in the supply, or what is principally the case, the increased demand for the same. This increased demand, which either exists at home or is induced by foreign influence, is further affected by an increased employment of the precious metals for domestic purposes, for the special designs of consumption, or by a large coinage by the government for its own advantage, but more particularly by a greater requisition for bullion as a pay medium, for the large amounts of merchandise, which cannot be equalized by home productions. Let us suppose that at a given period of time the same amount of money as previously, is requisite for the exchange of the products of a country, then it is self-evident that for the supply of merchandise, which the country itself produces, or which it imports, there is a corresponding supply of pay medium, that also in the above case, for the excess of foreign products, the remelted coin metal, thrown upon the market, so far as the same is sold, must relatively be more than equivalent.

Now, this excess depends either upon the greater liveliness of the money circulation, so far as thereby a greater traffic in merchandise is effected, or in the saving of capital which arises therefrom, that now the same amount of produce can be furnished with a smaller outlay, or finally in the credit system in all its various forms, especially, however, in the issue of notes. The increase of an equivalent for the redemption of produce results either through economy—that is, the sum of money which is collected and not yet paid over for produce—once more enters into trade, no matter whether this capital originates at home or comes from abroad; or else the increase is effected in this way, that sums of bullion are sent from abroad in payment for furnished home products, or as interest, or back payments on loans of home capital. If a foreign country desires gold or silver, and there has been brought therefrom a corresponding amount of other products, the purchased amount can be equalized by exchanging bullion therefor, or by returning a compensation in metal currency, either bullion or coin. Now, the deficiency which exists in the coin depository through the remelting and sale of coined metal, is again reimbursed, provided the purchase of the requisite pay medium in either of the two last-cited ways is made of the same metal; however, this last circumstance does not always happen, and although, by a long continuance of the melting in the three first-cited ways, there results an improvement in the necessary pay medium, which was purchased as coin and remelted, yet one or the other of the metals belonging to the coin depository is successively more and more decreased.

In this way the advantage is lost which was hoped for from one or the other of the materials used as currency, and the same inconveniences occur, though perhaps in a less degree, which generally follow a contraction of the metal currency, and of which, in connection with the seigniorage, we have already spoken. On account of the amount of coin remelted, there is naturally much of this production withdrawn, for it is not merely the amount of interest, but also the principal, which is remelted and sold. But for this reason the latter must not be injured, for the increase of the currency, especially the use of credit, so long as the decrease of the money store follows, reimburses every deficiency which exists through the melting of coin for the productive trade, and so far is the production not injured by speculation. The amount of coin, also, which is bought up at a premium, or which is used in exchange, becomes immediately remunerative, and being at once put upon the market usually finds a ready sale. However, should speculation rapidly absorb the greater part, it is possible for the production to be so far interrupted that the means necessary for the prosecution of active business, as formerly, will fail, and with the loss of that hope, the whole amount of coin will be withdrawn from trade.

Moreover, if the existing want of a reserve capital is fully determined by the merchants, money speculation is at least checked, for this is only undertaken in order, through the rising value of precious metal, to increase stocks or revenues, but above all the former income, and, of course, the former productions remain undisturbed. In such an event, the precious metal, which has risen in value, disappears more slowly from trade, but a complete check to its disappearance does not occur so long as only a partial means of remuneration for the carrying on of production is employed, and, as has already been mentioned, an immediate equivalent is returned for large amounts of coin.

It has been until now presumed that the original and proper ratio of coinage is affected by the rising price of one or the other of the precious metals. But the above-cited phenomenon appears when, in the first measurement of the coin, a too heavy coin standard is adopted; that is, too few pieces of the unit coin is made from the fundamental weight, and in this way the amount of precious metal in each coin piece represents a smaller value than it holds in the market. If the increased value of precious metal is permanent and important, then the inconvenience spoken of can only be remedied through the introduction of a corresponding light coin standard.

If gold or silver decreases in value, the rule produces an opposite result. The venders, because they now hold a depreciated value in coin, and possess no other means of restraining this retrenchment, seek to supply the loss through a greater metal value, through more coin; that is, by raising the price of merchandise. The fact that coin must still be received at its old high value, allows the merchants no indemnification, because the original coin value is only represented through a greater amount of precious metal; for that reason the latter must be given at its natural, and not merely its nominal value. The purchasers, on the contrary, in seeking to guard their interests, endeavor, as formerly, to equalize the price of merchandise with the present amount of precious metal contained in the coin. Most productions rise in value, and it depends upon the strength of the two competitors, whether, by length of time, the complete equalization of the difference between the depreciated and the original value of coin is established. The opinion may be entertained that the depreciation in value of the precious metals has no influence in shaping the prices, because the coin continues to be recognized, after as before, at its full legal nominal value. Standard coin, by the way, under like conditions, being subject to the same rules as small coin. But the mere acknowledgment of the full value of coin does not restore it to its full value; it must really be what it outwardly appears to be, as far as the substance is concerned. For, according to the opinion just cited, either no standard coin should be issued, although the depreciation of the metal value in most cases is far from being sufficiently important to prevent the issue of coin in amounts large enough for practical purposes, or else the standard coin should only be a sign of value, an imitation; a view which, with reference to the former decision, is declared to be inadmissible.

If gold and silver in coin form have always a greater value than in a crude state, then those in whose possession it is held, either through production, or foreign trade, or money transactions, will carry it to the mint in preference to selling it, and then if in the mean time an advance in prices takes place in various articles, the holders of the precious metals acquire, at least partially, more means by which to meet the advance in prices. If the fall of gold and silver is caused by a lessening of the demand, because there is for either one or the other less necessity for articles of luxury, or as a foreign pay medium, then there is no essential change introduced into the money circulation. But if this depreciation is caused through an increased supply, then, especially if that is brought about by a rich yield from the mines, in a short time there will be a large amount of coin forced into circulation. For in this case not only the producers of the precious metals under consideration, and those who receive from abroad in payments either bullion or coin, send the depreciated metal to the mint, but also the government, as a rule, for its own advantage, will undertake larger coinage, because on account of the large supply, the purchase in large quantities is cheaper than if the sinking of the price was caused by a lessening of the demand.

But if trade is overstocked with money, then the price of most articles rises, which makes the satisfying of the indispensable wants very difficult, and it falls the heaviest upon those who draw a fixed income. When in consequence of a rich gain in metals, the supply is increased, then the advance in prices takes place from two causes, which consequently produces a double amount of influence. Where coining is practiced by the government on its own account alone, and it holds the management of the circulation entirely under its own control, then if in the emission of coin it in any way becomes subject to shrinkage in value, it can prevent the advance in prices by curtailing the coinage, much more effectually than where private parties are unrestrained in their privilege of coining.

It is possible, in first establishing the coin rule, to adopt a too light coin standard, that is, to compute the amount of precious metal in each piece at too great a value, and thus have too many pieces of unit coins made from the adopted weight. The same condition of things exists as was before mentioned, when speaking of the establishment of the seigniorage, namely, that the coin laws contain no rule for seigniorage, but that, however, by the establishment of one, there really takes place an advance in the value of coin, to which the real value upon the market of the precious metal under consideration, does not correspond.

In the results referred to, do the active operations of trade enter? Is the seigniorage, because its establishment is not expressly stated in the coin laws, but only quietly acquiesced in, not generally recognized in trade, but is the seigniorage coin only contentedly considered, and estimated according to its standard; or is the higher value of the coin recognized, at least to that limit which was laid down in the previous discussion upon the allowable height of the seigniorage?

For an answer to these questions we are, in the domains of economy, restricted generally to the proportionately valid proposition, that as soon as one thing satisfies a want more completely than another, the higher value of the former is for that reason recognized, and this recognition is expressed by the exchange of the thing in question for other products. Now, certainly the trades-people know how to value the advantages which the coined precious metal, as it relates to the money functions, possesses over the raw product, and for the cost of the work which accurately fashioned the raw metal to the proper measure for the purposes of trade, will allow the same compensation which is granted according to the customary calculations to the productive enterprises; that is, up to that point where the higher value of the coin is recognized, where the imposition of the seigniorage is not expressly limited in the coin laws.

If, in the money system, a coin standard is adopted of a weight so light, that the government draws a monopolizing gain from every piece, then the same ratio exists, and the same results follow, as if a seigniorage was established which far exceeds the cost; or, as if the coin, in its legal normal value, was secretly diminished. Now, if the depreciation in the price of metal is confirmed by long-continued causes, and the imparity is considerable, then, in behalf of the re-establishment of the normal trade ratio, the existing necessity demands that the government change the present mode of coinage, and adopt a heavy, instead of a light coin standard.

XI.

We have hitherto considered in each of the precious metals the ratio between coin and bullion of the same metal species, but the reciprocal relation between the two precious metals has not been fully discussed. Gold and silver as a pay medium, mutually circulate together in trade, while each possesses certain specialties. Gold is a costly material on account of its external attributes; a small quantity is of great value, and for that reason it is particularly adapted to the payment of large sums, especially when they are to be forwarded to distant places. The coinage cost of gold also is not so great as silver; and because of the smaller value possessed by the latter for the payment of large amounts and for transportation, it is certainly an inferior metal, yet it is much harder, and therefore in circulation loses less through abrasion. But, if the coinage cost of silver is greater than that of gold, on the other hand the necessity for a recoinage does not so soon occur. Then, again, for the payment of small amounts of money, represented in part or whole by precious metal, the silver coin, strictly on account of its low value, is particularly adapted.

The amount of gold which is exchangeable for a certain silver coin, and contrariwise, the amount of silver which is exchangeable for a certain gold coin, varies according to the ratio between the supply and demand, as is the case with every other kind of merchandise. These variations are either universal, extending through the entire international trade, or they are only partial, and confined to certain countries; and further, they are permanent or transient, according to circumstances, which operate continually through a long period of time; or they are called forth by causes of a secondary nature.

In early times the value of gold, compared to silver, was very great. The comparative ratio in Europe in the first century after the discovery of America, was, according to Humboldt, between as 1 : 10.7 and as 1 : 12.;[*] in the last century it was between as 1 : 14 and as 1 : 16. In Germany, according to Nebenius,[†] until 1665, the real ratio between gold and silver was as high as 1 : 15, notwithstanding a much lower ratio was established by the coin laws. In Prussia the ratio stood in 1508, as 1 : 9.2; in 1536, as 1 : 14.4; in 1556, as 1 : 12.5, which latter remained until 1615.

During the seventeenth century gold advanced in most of the European countries. In Germany, in 1665, the ratio in the three districts, Bavaria, Swabia, and Franconia was fixed at 1 : 14½. The tin standard in 1667, was 1 : 13½.[‡] The Leipzig standard, in 1690, was 1 : 15$\frac{7}{12}$. In Scotland the ratio was 1 : 12; in France 1 : 13½, and in Spain 1 : 14.§

In the eighteenth century the average ratio between gold and silver appears to have been as 1 : 15. In the convention of 1753, the ratio adopted was as 1 : 14$\frac{22}{72}$, and in 1750, the old Prussian standard was 1 : 13½.

In France, 1720, the comparative ratio of value was limited to 1 : 15; the royal edict, however, in 1726, lowered it to 1 : 14$\frac{9}{16}$. In 1785, the ratio was fixed at 1 : 15$\frac{2}{5}$, and according to the coin laws of 1803, the valid ratio was 1 : 15½.||

In the nineteenth century the limited medium ratio from January, 1807–1812, did not rise above 1 : 16, nor sink below 1 : 15.91.¶ According to Dumas de Colmen, from 1818–1838 gold did not advance more than 2$\frac{3}{10}$ per cent. According to Soetber, the average ratio between

---

* Humboldt, Neu-Spanien, Buch iv, S. 216.

† Nebenius, Oeffentl. Credit, S. 735, Anm.

‡ Tin, half pence and farthings—token coins—were issued largely in England under William and Mary, in 1690, and by Charles II, in 1680.—(Dr. W. P. Harrison, D.D., chaplain House of Representatives.)

§ Anderson's Handelsgeschichte, Bd. iv, S. 335, und Humbolt: Neu-Spanien, Buch iv, S. 217.

|| Dutot in d. Collection Gullaumin, p. 904, n. Hufeland über Geld, S. 294.

¶ Chevalier, De la monnaie, p. 167.

gold and silver upon the London price basis during the period from 1831–1850, was 1 : 15.78. From 1851–1860, it was 1 : 15.35. Gold had fallen $2\frac{7}{10}$ per cent., or else silver had advanced that much.*

The ratio between gold and silver can be regulated in the coin law edicts in a double manner. By law, the ratio of gold and silver to each other is either direct or indirect, viz, established through the expressed signature of the coin standard, which no longer depends upon the market fluctuations, or else the coin of the one or of the other metal is declared merchandise, and consequently the regulation of the value of the same depends entirely upon the change of ratio between the supply and demand. In the one case, silver is the foundation of the coin system, and all the members of the same (with the exception of those classed as small coin), are represented by silver coin of preponderating silver contents, the gold coin representing only a multiple coin unit. In the other case the coin system is represented by gold, and either all or most of the higher subdivisions of the system are expressed only by silver, and the coin of this kind is called small coin. In the latter case it is not easy to coin such silver pieces at their contemporary full nominal value as represent the gold unit coin or its compound, because these coin pieces, on account of their small silver value, must be made too large in circumference for practical use. And, further, the silver coin which represent the subdivisions are small coin, and in coining they properly receive a smaller metal value than their nominal value represents, so that silver is generally considered as a material which represents gold, and, therefore, the danger is imminent that great difficulty will be experienced in circulating the larger coin pieces in home trade at their full nominal value, and the small coin, with a corresponding depreciation of their metal contents, will suffer much more.

There would be an exception if these larger coin pieces had no legal exchange at home, and were only made for foreign trade, or if the larger subdivisions between the unit and the small coin were issued at their full value. The legally established relative value between the two precious metals, either agrees with the existing market ratio, or it does not. The basis of this disagreement is found either in an error referable to an average estimate, or in the design of the government, or this difference enters in consequence of a later variation in the relative worth. In this way gold may be rated too high, and silver too low; or contrariwise, silver too high, and gold too low.

If gold is estimated above silver, at a too high rate, there will be an effort made to employ the former in trade as much as possible. If, for example, the market ratio between gold and silver is 1 : 14, that is, for a fixed weight of gold, a 14-fold weight of silver is demanded, as equivalent, while the legal weight is 1 : 15, then the 1-fold gold represents the 15-fold silver coin, and for that reason, a larger amount of merchandise can be purchased, and a larger debt discharged with the gold coin, than can possibly be effected with the silver coin, according to the existing market ratio. With the exception of those who are selling silver and hold it at its true ratio to coined gold, all who receive their payments in gold coin, are damaged. It is hardest upon the public and private creditor, especially all those who draw a fixed income, because they are legally bound to accept the nominal value as the real full sum.

It is different in free trade. The merchant raises the price of his goods as much as the gold is above par, and this rise in prices is universal in the sense that it extends not only to gold, but also to silver, because as a rule he does not know beforehand whether the payment will be tend-

* Zeitschrift für die Staatswissenschaften, Jahrg. 1862, S. 17.

ered him in gold or silver, and because the privilege is not legally granted to make a difference between the two metals. The price of as much merchandise as formerly cost 15 florins, is raised to 16 florins; this rise in prices, so far as it is permanent and easy to realize, is, according to the market ratio, only nominal as regards gold coin, but as regards silver coin it is real. The presumption here is, that the ratio of gold and silver coin toward each other is not too great, and that gold coin is more frequently met with in trade than silver coin. If the amount of circulating gold coin is less than silver, then the real depreciated value of gold coin, at least as a general thing, is not further regarded. The legally established high value of gold, however, always incites the government to an increased issue of this metal, and when such a calamity occurs, the gold held by private parties is, notwithstanding the rise in prices, pressed rapidly into the mint, while in trade the exchange of gold coin for merchandise is small compared with silver. The silver money, which is presumably measured according to the standing market ratio between silver coin and silver bullion, and whose material is valued too low in comparison with gold coin, and which is lightly estimated both at home and abroad, is remelted and the metal sold for gold coin, by which means, on its own account, by a small additional payment in case of a rise in prices, an advantage is sought. A tariff too low induces an increased importation of merchandise, and on account of the better ratio of value abroad the importation is profitable, and the surplus is equalized by the depreciated metal.

When gold, in comparison with silver, is estimated too low, then in the purchase of merchandise, as well as in the payment of debts, which is generally a stipulated amount, smaller effects will be produced compared with what, indeed, according to the existing relation of value, should be produced. For example, the market ratio between gold and silver is 1:14, but the legal ratio is 1:13, the simple gold coin is only equal to 13-fold silver value represented in coin form. Now, the purchasers, if they make their payments in gold coin, receive a smaller quantity of merchandise than really belongs to them, according to the actually represented relative value of the two precious metals. And if gold coin circulates in trade as freely as silver coin, the buyer, upon the basis before explained, will seek to lower the price of merchandise, that is, seek to obtain a larger amount of merchandise for the same amount of coin. If the decrease in prices really occurs, then, by the legal relative value of 1:13, the amount of merchandise will be increased one-thirteenth for every gulden, and that, too, without difference whether the payments be made in gold or silver; the depreciation in prices is nominal with gold, but with silver it is real.

If the purchaser, as it actually is the case in many branches of business, is not able, without difficulty, to insure the continuance of the depreciated prices, he finds it then to his advantage to melt the gold coin and exchange the raw metal for silver coin. The remelting of the gold coin promises more gain, and is, although perhaps a slower, yet a surer way of obtaining it; and because of the universal abatement in prices, the ransomed silver money is by the sale exchangeable for a larger amount of goods than gold. Gold coin seeks an outlet abroad, because it is there estimated at its true value, and the importation of merchandise is profitable. If gold is estimated too low, then it seldom, as was shown in the case of silver, finds its way to the mint, for a precious metal of low value is only coined for private purposes, when the favorable conditions of trade allow the importation of larger amounts of foreign goods which demand payment, and to which purpose the coined metal of depreciated estimate is adapted; or for trade operations entered into before the metal fell in value, by stipulations that dare not be set aside, and especially for the payment of money in distant places for which gold is a very favorable medium. If the estimate of gold is low, then the coining of gold by the government is naturally less profitable, and for this reason it is issued in small amounts, unless the government by the sacrifice of its financial interests feels itself bound to supply the general necessities of trade with a corresponding pay medium.

In the two instances just mentioned, as these are generally united, the presumption is that the unit coin is represented by silver, and that the unit is expressed in a compound form by the gold coin. For, as has before been stated, it is possible, even where the coin system is based upon gold, that, with the exception of the silver small coin, such silver pieces found in legal circulation do not, by virtue of their coinage, bear the character of small money. Under such circumstances, if gold is rated too high, that is, if the unit coin legally equalizes a larger amount of silver coin than according to the market standard of precious metal it should, then the lowering of prices, and the remelting of silver coin, are the means by which the owners of silver coin can restore the silver to the gold value. If gold is rated too low, so that a smaller amount of coined silver than corresponds to the market ratio is legally at par with the unit coin, the result is the prices rise, and the gold coin is remelted; the first takes place to prevent the depreciation of silver coin, the second to make valid the higher worth of gold over silver. Therefore, in case an incorrect relative value enters, circumstances must determine whether, of that precious metal which does not furnish the unit coin, a greater or less amount is necessary to equalize the unit coin than is demanded by the relative value of the two precious metals upon the market.

It has been stated that the coin of the lower-valued metal is remelted and exchanged for that of a higher value. The attempt to paralyze the real relations of the two precious metals, whose value is not in a corresponding manner legally defined, is expressed in another way. In order to attain more speedily and certainly the object of a better realization of the low-valued metal, the holders of the coin of this metal use it to purchase the higher-valued metal and send it to the mint to be coined. The wrong estimate of the relative value of the two precious metals is the cause of a universal exchange process, which, later, will undergo a rigid investigation.

If much of the coin from the low-valued precious metal becomes depreciated by abrasion, in consequence of long circulation, or by clipping and the like, it is exchanged for coin of the other metal, in proportion to the value of its contents, and finally, sold upon the market.

As soon as the coin of the legally low-estimated metal leaves the mint, it begins to lose its full value in circulation, and its reduction in value is continually augmented through the decrease of its metal value; this increases in degree as the difference is greater between the legal and real relative value, because the greater the number of pieces of the coin of depreciated value, the greater the increase in the gain through the cutting of the same. Coin of a low estimated precious metal, whose actual fineness varies more or less from its legal fineness, can only circulate at home. This fact does not prevent the exchange of the two metals, one for the other, as formerly mentioned. If the reduction is important, the price of merchandise certainly rises, and therefore more coin of the legally depreciated precious metal must be given for the other metal in bullion form; yet the measure of the metal diminution, and the rise of prices consequent thereon, remains under the signature of the legal relative value; therefore, there may constantly be an exchange of metals, though, perhaps, to a limited extent. If, however, the metal depreciation of the coin of low estimate, and the consequent appreciated price of the other metal vary little or none from the legal relative value, then the exchange of the two precious metals, one for the other, being no longer profitable, ceases. The depreciated coin of the low-estimated metal is not remelted, and the raw material sold, because the net proceeds therefrom are smaller than the nominal amount.

If the exchange of the low-estimated coin is active, then, as with every active business, it is effectual only for the payment of a premium to the holder of the depreciated coin. On this account, therefore, the price of the raw metal of low estimate, especially if yet more depreciated, would not need an advance. For they who depreciate coin, not only hold the latter at their full nominal value, but they sell with parsimonious care a part of the same. This speculation, therefore, easily yields to the holders a portion of the gain of the metal under consideration; and, possibly, they also receive from this source an advantage, if they maintain the depreciated coin of the same metal at the purchase price.

From the foregoing investigation any real deviation of the ratio between gold and silver, namely, between gold coin and uncoined silver, or between silver coin and uncoined gold, is clearly disproved; and the presumption is evident, that there is no variation between coin and bullion, either of gold or silver, but that they balance each other. The above conclusions would be evident, if, originally, the legal and market ratio between gold and silver agreed with each other; but lately there is seen a difference in the mutual exchange of gold and silver in the market, by which it is presumed that gold and silver circulate together in nearly the same amount.

If the legal and commercial ratio between gold and silver is 1 : 13, and yet silver so much advanced that, for example, besides the amount of bullion silver which 1 gulden contains, an addition of $\frac{1}{13}$ of coined silver, that is $1\frac{1}{13}$ gulden must be given in the market, then the value of gold falls, and it requires but $12\frac{1}{13}$ guldens as equivalent for a single gold coin. Silver from now on is rated too low, and gold too high; therefore silver is melted, or gold is bought up with silver coin. Now, as concerns the price of merchandise, there is given for silver, on account of its rise in value, a correspondingly greater amount of produce; so that really the prices fall. For all that, merchants endeavor to retain the old prices, and, if possible, to have their payments in gold, the value of which has not risen.

If silver falls in value, so that, for example, the ratio between 1 gulden and the silver coin is 1 : $1\frac{1}{13}$, then there must be given for a single gold coin a greater amount of silver coin, and consequently the real market ratio between gold and silver is 1 : $14\frac{1}{13}$. Silver continues to be rated legally too high, and gold too low, and of course gold is melted or silver bought up with gold coin. Now the merchants endeavor to raise the prices of their goods by desiring the payments to be made in silver, the value of which has fallen.

If gold rises, for example, $\frac{1}{13}$, then for the metal quantity contained in a single gold coin an addition of $\frac{1}{13}$ in gold coin is given, the ratio of gold to silver is 1 : 14, so that on account of the advanced value of gold more silver coin is required as equivalent. In this case gold coin is rated too low, and silver coin too high, and in consequence of this difference, silver coin is either remelted, or it is bought up with gold coin.

On account of the actual advance in gold coin, purchasers seek to lower the prices, and the merchants strive to retain the old prices at the same rates according to the standard silver value.

If gold falls in value, for example, $\frac{1}{15}$, then $\frac{12}{13}$ uncoined gold is equal to 1 of coined gold, the actual ratio between gold and silver being as 1 : 12. In this case, then, contrariwise, gold coin is rated too high, and silver coin too low; consequently, silver coin is remelted or exchanged for gold, and merchandise, on account of the high nominal value of gold coin, rises in price.

From the four illustrations presented, the conclusions are, that the introduction of the one or the other economical result is determined by a material change; that is, that change determines, which takes place either in the supply or demand referring to one kind of metal; in no case is it a change of form; that is, that which happens with results strictly defined, entirely apart from the relation of the two precious metals to each other, because the other metal has undergone a change in the market ratio. Now the material change is restricted by the change in prices, or much more by the efforts to change the price of merchandise to the corresponding change in the precious metal under consideration, because the actual price depends upon the concentration in the market, and often accords in no way with the intended price. An advancement in the unit of prices can only occur through the depreciation of gold or silver, and in no way through the increased value of these precious metals; for in case one metal falls in value, this depreciation is not effected through any agency which changes the ratio between coin and bullion of the same metal. Only in case of an advance in gold or silver do the merchants endeavor to maintain the old relative value of the former prices. This endeavor to retain the old prices, is not, however, as it appears, with reference to the advanced value of precious metals for the purpose of establishing an advanced price, but the solicitude arises only to prevent retrenchment, which would be introduced by the lowering of the prices through the coin of the other metal which had not risen in value.

▸ Let a variation in the ratio between coin and bullion occur in either the one or the other species of metal, then in any of the four cases mentioned, the same results follow, no difference whether the system of coinage be based upon gold or upon silver.

It is, therefore, presumed that it is the prerogative of the state to maintain the fullest liberty in reference to coinage, that it is allowable for it to exchange one metal for another, and at its pleasure to coin one or the other. If this were not the case, and if the government issued coin only for its own purposes, then there would occur changes in prices, and abridgments of just claims; but the exchange of metals mentioned would not take place because the metal thus exchanged could not be coined for the benefit of private persons. It is true, that under these circumstances, the metal of low value is remelted and sold for the coin of the other metal; but through this means the amount of coin of low value which disappears is inconsiderable, at least so long as the state undertakes no coinage of the other metal in large amounts; because it is difficult for those who remelt coin of low-valued metal entirely for speculation, to act in concert with the metal producers and metal dealers, who for business purposes sell their bullion of low value for coin of the same metal.

Coin of this kind cannot be legally held back, but even if its material is not advanced in value it brings no gain to the speculators. This depends upon the activity of the government in coining. Because, if a gain can be drawn from a rise in value of a species of metal, then, generally, a larger coinage of the same ensues. Where the government coins exclusively for its own advantage, its efficiency takes the place of private persons, and the same condition of things exists, though perhaps not to that extent, which will be discovered later in investigating the double standard.·

The history of coin supplies abundant proof of the accuracy of these conclusions.*

XII.

In the United States of North America, by act of Congress of 18th January, 1837, it is declared, that from 1 ounce troy of gold of $\frac{9}{10}$ fineness, there shall be coined $1\frac{44}{41}$ eagles of $10 each, and from 1 pound troy silver of $\frac{9}{10}$ fineness $13\frac{159}{496}$ dollars shall be coined, and, to favor gold, the ratio was declared $1:15\frac{0}{100}$, while, in the period between 1830–1840, the ratio between the two precious metals was in reality $1:15\frac{83}{100}$. The result was that, by means of the gold coin, the pure silver coin was remelted or bought up for exportation, and only mutilated or depreciated silver coin remained in circulation. Previous to 1848, this inconvenience, on account of the relatively smaller circulation of gold coin, was less felt. Afterward, in consequence of the large gold gains in California, the relative value of the precious metals at the close of 1850, was $1:15\frac{45}{100}$ and under, and the amount of silver coin of full value continually decreased, and, even of the coarse, mutilated pieces, the heavier ones were sought out and remelted.

Gold paid upon the best silver coin a premium of from 3 to 4 per cent., and only the old Spanish silver coin remained in circulation, whose separate pieces were represented by piasters, but which had lost more than 10 per cent. of their intrinsic value through abrasion.

By a law of France, instituted 28th March, 1803, it was ordained that the unit coin (franc) should contain 5 grams of silver $\frac{9}{10}$ fine, and that gold pieces of 20 francs be coined, and the subdivisions of the latter in the following manner, viz, that from 1 kilogram 155 pieces should be issued. The relative value between the two precious metals was fixed at $1:15\frac{1}{2}$, while the same, up to the close of the year 1850, was higher in open trade, that is, more favorable for gold. The result of this fixed value is that the silver coin remains constantly in circulation, while, to a great extent, this is not the case with gold, for, up to this time, gold coin has found only an exceptional use in France.

However, as, after the year 1850, the ratio of gold to silver had fallen to $1:15\frac{45}{100}$ and under, the silver coin of full value, and even the inferior mutilated silver coin, was either remelted or sold abroad, so that in the course of the year 1857, the government passed an ordinance to hinder the exportation of silver; but, on account of its loose operations, it was quickly nonsuited. For that reason, there was continually more and more gold coin issued, and from information furnished by seventy tax-collectors, and by the branch departments of the Bank of France, collectively, on the investigation of the banking interests by an appointed commission during the year 1857, it is plain to see that at that time already gold was exclusively the circulating medium for all wholesale trade.

Subsequent to 1850, the fall of gold, as compared to silver, made itself very sensibly felt in Switzerland. In May, 1850, a law was passed that only silver coin (5, 2, 1, and $\frac{1}{2}$ franc pieces), but no gold coin, should be issued, and that no one should be obliged to receive other kinds of silver, and the public treasury was forbidden to accept in payment, at ordinary times, any other as legal coin ; but, as early as 1855, the pure silver coin, especially the new 2, 1, and $\frac{1}{2}$ franc pieces, became scarce. In consequence of the large issue of gold in France, and the manifold trade intercourse with Switzerland, the gold coin began to enter the latter country. The banks and several of the private banking-houses of Switzerland, on account of the large trade with Paris, obtained advantageous and accommodating custom, and no longer made their payments in 5-franc silver pieces, but in French gold, and received the same in return, and partly by means of public advertisements, and partly through special arrangements with their customers, they forced the repeal of this law. The public treasury find it necessary to give and to receive gold coin almost entirely at its nominal value ; even the wages of the soldiers and like expenditures are usually paid in gold. It is true that the exchanging of gold pieces for the necessary silver coin is often attended with difficulty, and through the want of small silver coin the ordinary retail trade is somewhat embarrassed.

The same condition of things exists in Belgium. By a law passed 5th June, 1832, as in the French coin laws of 1803, the ratio of gold to silver was established 1:15$\frac{1}{2}$, the coining of 20-franc pieces was permitted, and it was also further ordained that the French decimal coins of gold and silver be received at the public treasury at their nominal value. Subsequently, however, toward the close of the year 1850, the value of gold to silver having fallen 2 per cent., and therefore below the ratio of 1:15$\frac{1}{2}$, gold became demonetized. By a law of December, 1850, the legal exchange, not only the French, but also the other foreign gold coin which had in the mean time been introduced as national gold coin, was called in, and a further issue prohibited. This arrangement produced no great inconvenience, for the amount of the large French silver coin was yet considerable, the real average silver contents of the circulating pieces being nearly up to the coin standard, because but little remelting of the best coin had taken place, and the actual circulation of the French gold coin continued yet, (only under restrictions) for a long time. The increased issue of gold, however, which, subsequent to 1855, took place in France, caused a backward movement in Belgium, which holds a very lively trade with her neighbor. The silver coin of full weight in Belgium was from time to time gradually bought up with gold and sent out of the country. On account of this selection of the heavier pieces, the average quality of the large circulating silver coin became constantly meaner, until finally the silver coin grew very rare, and the attending perplexities became constantly greater. At last the public treasury received only silver money in payment, and the large banks only gold coin.

The variations alluded to in the nature of the coin of these states were effected through the mutual operations of opposite agents. On the one hand, were the rich gold discoveries in California and Australia subsequent to 1848, causing a fall in the value of gold, as well as the issuing of such a large amount of gold coin that it became, in a measure, the most prominent pay medium. On the other hand, an extraordinary desire for Asiatic products increased the price of the same, and caused a demand for silver, thereby increasing the price of the latter in those countries, and this increase in price would have been greater had not a considerable amount of silver been redeemed through gold exchange, thereby increasing the supply of silver. Then, too, a quantity of depreciated coin made its appearance, causing the remelting of that of full contents, and thus increasing the demand.

As has before been alluded to, gold and silver coin can in a manner circulate together, though only the coin of one metal has a fixed value attached to it by the authorities. The establishing of the value of the coin from the other metal is ceded entirely to free trade. This transpires in the system of a single standard, in which naturally the standard coin only is understood.

The other metal is, therefore, demonetized; that is, coin of that metal is issued, but it is divested of the character of a legal pay medium. The single standard, it is true, is understood to be this, that coin of a fixed nominal value is issued from one kind of metal, while the other metal is not used for coin purposes. Where the coin system is based upon gold, silver coin is only used as the natural measure of small coin. Only under the two conditions mentioned above can it be issued in pieces of large value as merchandise, for the fact that the value is not fixed cannot prevent an average exchange, and each piece, according to the analogy of small coin, is lessened in the fineness of its contents to the per cent. of its average value. If, however, silver is the standard currency, then it is not judicious to reject gold absolutely, and not permit it to be coined for the advantage and use of private parties, because this metal affords many commercial advantages, which are acknowledged in practice. Consequently, the single standard is only understood in the sense first mentioned.

Because the demonetized coin always circulates with greater difficulty than the legal, then, on the one hand, many in the possession of the former are not able to use it in payment; and again, on the other hand, many who desire to collect payments cannot receive it with advantage to their business. Now this, as well as the fact that of the demonetized coin there are proportionately fewer pieces issued, will operate to establish for them a separate market. Now, the exchange, because it usually adjusts the money trade, is the natural market and the standard regulator of the value of that coin considered as merchandise, and the coin referred to is conspicuous in establishing the basis of the official estimate of value. But, naturally, this in no wise prevents, beyond this center, for example, by brokers, metal dealers, &c., a free trade being carried on in this coin, in which the price may differ from that of the exchange. In reference to coin whose value is variable, those who produce precious metals, or trade with the same, or obtain possession of the metal in question through foreign dealers and have it coined—in broader terms, bankers and money-changers—these furnish the supply, while those engaged in either domestic or foreign trade, and to whom coin as a pay-medium is necessary, furnish the demand, and by the mutual operations of these agents with each other the exchange of coin arises.

XIII.

Now, concerning the circulation of coin as merchandise, it can occur in various ways. Because this coin is not legal tender, then the acceptance of it is not obligatory, but permissible. In private business, as well as in government affairs, both the contracting parties must be at liberty to choose the kind of coin which they will receive in exchange. But in order not to resign to the discretion of the officials the acceptance or the rejection, in every case, of a particular coin, the administration, the land and revenue magistrates, public corporations, jurists, as well as all large manufactories, and institutions in general, such as banks, railroads, &c., should openly publish beforehand what kind of coin they purpose receiving, and what rejecting. The coin which is not legal tender, is, on account of its depreciated value, less eagerly received, and for that reason has a limited circulation. Now, the government has the power to receive such coin into the Treasury or not. Nevertheless, it is for the interests of commerce that the circulation of coin, pronounced merchandise, so far as it does not exclusively serve the purposes of foreign trade, should not be confined to narrow limits, otherwise the advantage expected from this other species of metal is lost to trade. Now, the extension of the circulation is very beneficial, if the administration insures the acceptance of such coin at the Treasury, and performs its promise. The free circulation of this coin is yet further promoted, if, besides the public Treasury, (the common Treasury of the country), the large monied institutions and the railroads receive it; for it is not compatible with the nature of the coin under consideration to impose a formal obligation for its acceptance upon the treasuries and institutions, especially the latter. If there is full liberty relative to the exchange, then any further obligation for acceptance is unnecessary.

Now, concerning the value of the coin in question, it can either be determined upon in the daily exchange, or by the average exchange, the day before payment, or its adoption can be based upon a periodical rate. In the latter case, namely, a fixed period of time, three or six months is taken, during which the daily average value of the coin under consideration is calculated, for which the coin during the next following equal period of time is taken as payment. Further, if several treasuries exist in different parts of the country, then, if the treasury of the chief city does not make the decision, either the given average exchange collectively for the period agreed upon is taken, or the first-named treasury declares the general average, or else for each of these chief centers of money exchange, a certain territory is indicated to which the known average exchange is restricted in trade. Periodical rates are instituted by the state, or by the public treasuries, by large money institutions, manufactories, &c. By these rates the fluctuations in value become less frequent, and the trade in demonetized coin with these treasuries becomes easier; so, on the other hand, the longer the period taken for the average, the more correct it is, and the compensation to these treasuries for the variations in value more certain. Where no rates are fixed beforehand by public corporations and institutions, and also in private trade, where no particular agreement determines a different arrangement, which is naturally binding, the exchange on pay-day, or at any rate, the payments of preceding days, is examined by the legislature, in order that so far as a refusal to accept the demonetized metal, the obligation to pay that which is lacking after the referred to daily exchange is discharged is annulled, and against this course of exchange no objections can be raised.

If the government takes a seigniorage from the coin of fixed value, then it is not clear why it should not also establish the same upon the issuing of that coin regarded as merchandise. If coined metal, at least at home, under all circumstances, whether it has a constant or variable value, answers the requirements of trade better than uncoined metal, then the claim for compensation in its accomplishment is only reasonable. Coin which has a variable value is, on this account, by no means excluded from home circulation. The other chief basis of the seigniorage, namely, the retention of the coin in case its material value is increased, has no bearing upon the coin in question. The latter is considered merchandise, to make permanent in trade the increased value of its precious metal.

As the price of any industrial product is naturally computed upon the value of the raw material added to the cost of labor in its production, so naturally the exchange of the coin under consideration is settled by the value of the metal added to the seigniorage.

On account of the variations in the market, the exact exchange is suddenly above and then as suddenly below this level, just as the exchange of foreign coin is suddenly above and then suddenly below par coin. In no case do those who tender the coin in question, place it in the same rank with the raw precious metal, without great allowance being made for the expended labor, and being satisfied with the price of the latter. Home trade is made easier and more convenient by coined metal, and the merchant looks rather to that which *can* serve his purpose than to that which really *may* do so.

Those who need a pay medium for foreign trade, purchase either bullion or coin of that country to which they are indebted. If, however, the home debtor desires the coin in question, it is either because the difference between the price of home and foreign products is sufficiently important that, notwithstanding the seigniorage, the purchase of foreign merchandise is more advantageous; or else it is merely because the coin in question is, perhaps, on account of the dimensions of its issue, a very acceptable pay medium. In the latter case the home debtor, in calculating his business expenses, reckons the seigniorage, together with the cost of the foreign merchandise which he sells at home, and for the payment of which he purchased the coin in question.

The coin form does not afford the same advantage in international trade as it does in home trade; for that reason, although the appearance of the several pieces of coin is very agreeable, yet they are not sufficiently esteemed as to be received as equivalent in wholesale dealing, because in international trade the dealer looks only to the amount of precious metal, and examines strictly whether the same is present or not. But if a coin is issued for the sole purpose of foreign trade, as, for example, the Levantine thaler of Austria, the same has no circulation at home; it is just as if there was no seigniorage established. If the government in issuing its legal tender establishes no seigniorage, then naturally there can be none imposed on the coin considered as merchandise. In this case the price of the coin in question is exactly that of the raw metal, whereby the coin form, whether it is for home trade, or, in special cases, for foreign trade, is in greater demand, and operates to effect a difference in price from that of the uncoined metal.

If the administration receive payment in demonetized coin it can either sell it, or, like any private person, use it again in payment. In the latter case, however, the reception of the demonetized coin must be by the other party an act of entire freedom, and, according to the nature of the thing, only such disbursement of the demonetized metal is allowed as presents the government in the light of a private person, as, for example, the purchasing of the various things must be an act of previous contract. On the other hand, all obligations of a public character, for example all salaries, the interest and principal, of State debts, &c., can only be met by legal tender. Therefore, the fact that the administration permits the entrance of demonetized metal into its Treasury, does not confer the right to compel those who enter into free trade with it to accept the demonetized coin. The payments which the government draws should be strictly taken, with the exception of those especially stipulated, as are those between private parties in trade with each other, the exchange of pay-day, or, at any rate, of the previous day, to be restricted. Those, however, who receive demonetized coin from the government in payment, such as government clerks, and those who have at any time taxes to discharge to the public Treasury, and especially where prolonged tax-periods exist, should be allowed to pay back into the public Treasury the demonetized metal at the same price at which they received it; for it cannot be considered unreasonable if the government, by anticipation, determines that if it make payments in demonetized coin, that the same demonetized coin shall be again received in payments. In this manner of exchange there can be nothing improper.

Shall coin, considered as merchandise, be issued by the government for its own advantage?

Because coin which is considered merchandise is not legal tender, then, agreeably to the nature of the thing, it appears that the administration which takes upon itself the issuing of such coin entirely for its own advantage should be equally interested that the coin in question pass current, the same as the legal tender issued by the government exclusively for its own advantage. If the government receives demonetized coin into its treasury, it can either sell it or use it again in payment. The administration must do the same when it issues demonetized coin for its own advantage. But the interests of the public treasury should not be damaged by the sale, and the payments should induce the reflection, that the reception of the coin in question, cannot be enforced, and that, as a general thing, a considerable part of the government outlay cannot be discharged with this coin. The government must certainly do one or the other, because the final acceptance of the demonetized coin is of general interest, and, considering the difficulties which the continual use of the coin under consideration produces, especially by an increased issue, and the open disturbance of private trade, in which the coin category, according to its nature, is so clearly indicated, it is not very judicious to encroach farther than is, in consequence of the sale of coin by the government, unavoidable. But it is not easy for the special coinage to regulate the currency, yet in those cases where the valuation, always corresponding to the occasional market ratio, is shared by the precious metal in the coin the stock of coin naturally adjusts itself to the occasional exigency.

XIV.

Which of the two systems is preferable, the system of the *double* standard, or of the *single* standard?

Where the ratio of value of the two precious metals, one with the other, is legally regulated, this regulation may either be originally erroneous, or, because of the variation in value of one or the other metal, it may become incorrect. In the former instance the market price of the too highly estimated metal approaches the coin price, but in the latter case, if the value of one metal falls, the sinking movement is partly, at least, a check to the advance. The advantage afforded by the difference between the coin price and the market price of the higher estimated metal, increases the demand for the latter; therefore, the price either rises or it does not fall as low as it would if it depended upon the condition of the supply alone. This causes an important circumstance to occur. They who put upon the market the precious metal most highly estimated by the mint, especially they who have received the same in payment from abroad, very often prefer carrying it to the mint rather than to take as equivalent the ordinary coin from metal of depreciated value, by which means the supply of the precious metal of the higher value is proportionately diminished. A too wide separation of the two precious metals is in this way prevented, and by the double standard system there is certainly introduced a proportionately greater stability in the reciprocal ratios of value of the two precious metals. The presumption naturally is, that the demand for the metal of high value, by the government, is not too small to afford a sufficient circulating currency to effect the exchange of the two precious metals, and to allow trade its ordinary, or even a wider circuit ; and, on the other hand, that the supply upon the market is not so great as to allow a large store of precious metal to lie unused. If these suppositions are incorrect, then certainly the system of the double standard cannot prevent a great shrinkage in value of the two metals.

In consequence of the difference in foreign prices compared with home prices, the depreciated precious metal of the mint will, in the way of purchasing merchandise, partially, at least, be sent abroad; but it is not certain that there will be a large foreign demand for the depreciated metal, because of the variation of the market price of the two precious metals from the coin price, thus making another great foreign change possible.

Should the foreign demand cease, then the coin issued from this metal remains at home, and a surplus of money is the result. Now, the price of merchandise rises, and this advance in prices induces a large importation of goods, which, in turn, draws a proportionate amount of specie to foreign countries, preferably that coin which at home is of depreciated value.

The consequences of this surfeit are only checked when home productions and home or foreign trade induces the necessity for an increased exchange medium corresponding to the increase of money. In this event, there will certainly be a foreign demand for specie.

But it is possible that, contemporary with the exchange of the two precious metals, there is a large foreign demand for that metal which is of small legal value, and that the metal-producers, metal-dealers, &c., have concentrated in their hands a considerable part of the latter in exchange for the metal of greater value at home, or for merchandise received from abroad. In this event, it may happen that the metal of low estimate is drawn out of the country without causing a rise in its home value, because the loss is reimbursed by the same coin of another metal, and consequently, the increased demand is counterbalanced by the increased supply of the emancipated coin.

The argument, until now, has been based upon the presumption, that the precious metal of a legally higher value is produced entirely at home, and in this way the supply is furnished to the market. If this were not so, a part of the supply in the home market would come from abroad; so, whether contemporary or not, the extent of the supply must increase, and remuneration be rendered through an exchange by merchandise, that part of the higher estimated metal purchased abroad, being equalized through specie based upon consignments of merchandise. This will cause the metal of low value at home to disappear.

If the system of a single standard is legalized, then, according to the nature of the thing, it cannot happen that one of the two precious metals is rated too high, and the other too low. For coin whose value is not legally fixed, underlies the fluctuations of the market, and this certainly does not cause a proportionately greater stability in the ratio of value of the two precious metals. When there exists no metal of depreciated value, the foreign demand for specie of low estimate ceases.

If the two species of metal, with reference to their value, are of equal weight, then independent of that there can be no fluctuation in the price of those which have a stipulated amount to require and to pay, because one metal alone does not possess that attractive power which can effect an important exchange between the two precious metals ; and, therefore, upon this ground alone, neither an excess of money takes place, nor does the coin of one metal disappear; clearly the latter event cannot occur for this reason, because one species of metal is not reimbursed by the other, and consequently no new employment can be undertaken.

But if in that precious metal whose coin has a fixed value, there occurs an important variation which cannot be disregarded, then certainly a single standard offers no remedy against the inconvenience. If that precious metal which is prohibited by law from serving as legal tender rises in value, then the coin issued therefrom disappears; if it becomes really scarce, the result is, a fall in prices. If the value of the metal spoken of falls, then a rise in the price of merchandise takes place. If the double standard is legalized, there would, in the first case, be no noticeable difference in the economical appearances of the change in value of the one metal, but in the latter case, besides the advance in prices, there would be an outflow of the too highly rated metal. In the majority of cases the double standard has decided disadvantages. From the illustrations given above, and the further consideration, that by the double standard not always, but only under certain suppositions, a ratio of greater stability in the relative value of the two precious metals is aimed at, the conclusion is that the single standard appears to be preferable.

It is certain, that coin of variable value is of small advantage to trade, because in business transactions the secure basis of calculation is wanting, and thereby merchants suffer disadvantages and losses. However, the coin spoken of, whether of gold or silver, is well adapted to commerce on a large scale, for this relatively demands less mere currency; for this reason the number of pieces of this species of coin in circulation is comparatively small. For foreign trade the fluctuating value is of no consequence, because even bullion has no stable value. But the reception or giving out of coin of variable value is a matter of choice with every one, and the possibility of this coin being used in payment for a long time by the government, and, perhaps by other public treasuries, serves to facilitate the use of the coin.

Finally, it should be noted that trade always has coin of a constant value, and that a great difference exists between industrial conditions, by which, on account of the glutting of trade with paper currency, metal money, especially gold and silver coin, holds a premium. It is certain, however, that the disadvantage of the fluctuating value of coin is smaller than the united disadvantages attending a double standard, namely, the disappearing of the coin, rise in prices, and the power to damage all claims of a stipulated amount, or the obligations for the payment of the same.

If a foreign country has a payment to make in bullion to a country where a single standard exists, it can execute the same either with the coin of the latter, or with its own coin, or with bullion.

The two latter pay mediums are used by the country with a single standard to discharge money obligations either at home, or in other countries, or they are sold. In this respect there is no difference between a country with a single, and one with a double standard. But, if the foreign coin, or bullion, is brought to the mint and reissued in home coin, and if the foreign pay medium belongs to that metal the coin of which has no fixed value at home, then the country with a single standard is only receiving coin of a variable value. The system of a single standard certainly permits only a limited use of foreign currency, because the coin is not sold, but used immediately in payments. This can only be effected through exchange, when a mutual sale is brought about. The effect upon individual industries is the same, whether it raises the price of the metal of which we speak, or not. The sale of metal whose value is not fixed would be more frequent where a single standard exists, were it not possible that, under the circumstances mentioned, the free use of the metal referred to is prevented, for it constantly happens that the citizens of a country where a single standard exists, prefer to stipulate for payment in that metal from which coin of an invariable value is issued.

Trade with this country presents no great difficulties for other states, because both metals are easily obtained either in its own, or foreign markets, and it pays its creditors of those countries in which either a double standard exists, or where the single standard is of that kind of metal whose coin has a fixed value, with that money material which is never, or seldom, used as equivalent for received goods. If the system of the single standard was understood in the sense that no coin is issued for private parties from the other metal, then the merchants who receive bullion, or coin from abroad, would naturally be more limited in the use of the received metal.

It has already been stated that the government either sells the coin which it receives in payment, and which has been declared merchandise, or it uses it in the discharge of certain obligations. Now, the two standards, with reference to their advantages and disadvantages, have been balanced and proven; therefore this is the place to discuss the manner and way of the application of coin of variable value.

The objection can be made, and indeed has been raised, that the government, by the continuance of the single standard, may speculate in the sale of coin declared as merchandise, and that through the example of the government, the officials are induced to speculate. But the administration, in the sale of the questionable coin, must in no way suffer itself to fall into the forms of speculation, and in the attainment of its object use no hidden means to serve the purposes of speculation. The administration does not buy up coin at a low rate and sell it again at an advanced price; and it is evident that the assertion formerly expressed, that the government shall not issue coin of inferior value for its own advantage, is very much in place as security against these objections. The government, as a producer, is under obligations to have the interest of all in view, and labor to secure none, or at least a very small gain; but of far more importance is the case just mentioned, where coin considered as merchandise is accepted and sold by the state treasury for universal advantage, because it can use it only in small amounts where the question is not one of a real enterprise. Strictly speaking, it should be sufficient to sell the coin for the purposes for which it was received; but it is quite certain that there is no necessity to realize a large gain. But the apprehension that the opportunity to secure a gain, which by abuse, the government can easily use, is dissipated by the reflection that the amount of coin found at one time in the hands of the government is not large enough to secure any considerable gain to itself, when other means are at command to the attainment of the same end. It is also true, certainly, that each official who is employed in the financial and treasury departments, by virtue of his position, possesses such information regarding the existing condition of the currency as to make it very easy for him to enter into speculation; but the number is always small; and, surely, the disadvantages of a single standard are not worthy to be taken into account against the advantages.

Financial embarrassments are not increased through the sale of coin considered as merchandise; for where large disbursements are impossible because the coin, on account of unfavorable exchange, cannot be sold or used without too great damage to the public treasury, then it is comparatively easy to secure the necessary means by the establishment of a floating debt, which may be again liquidated upon the introduction of more favorable conditions. Moreover, where the disadvantages are inconsiderable, the coin can always be sold, or used in payment, and the loss can be afterward remedied through a higher exchange.

Finally, the danger that, whenever it is possible to secure an advantage, whether from the rise or fall in the value of coin, the government will rate the periodical average exchange lower than agrees with the calculation, is not to be apprehended from a government which practices right and justice. Moreover, the difference in trade by the calculation of the exchange, is far less than the difference between the exchange in the open market and that caused by the periodical fixing of the value of coin by the government. If the former is higher than the latter, then the coin, at least as a rule, is sold or used in payments. If it is less, then it seeks the public treasury with great rapidity, and that, too, though the estimated value of the latter is less than the result should be according to the basis of the calculation. Moreover, if the rates of the coin declared as merchandise are, as a rule, very low, then the government should disapprove or entirely disallow the reception of the coin into the treasury as a means of advancing its circulation.

XV.

The views hitherto advanced have shown that the system of the single standard, according to the idea that coin without a fixed value, and from other than the legally-established metal issued for the citizens, is neither disadvantageous to the trade with foreign countries in which this standard is current, with reference to payments, nor yet to the government relative to the production of the coin declared merchandise, but, indeed, that, for the perfection of the coinage within the country under consideration, and for the accompanying industrial results, it is of decided advantage.

From the coin laws of modern times we learn that the single standard, partly legal and partly real, has prevailed in many countries.

In England, in 1717, the ratio of the two precious metals was fixed at $1.15\frac{233}{284}$; afterward the guinea, which had hitherto equalled 21 shillings 6 pence, was reduced to 21 shillings. But in spite of this reduction the guinea, in comparison with silver, was rated too high. This excess was about 4 pence in favor of the guinea, or about $1\frac{11}{11}$ per cent.; for although the value of silver, compared with gold, rose during the greater part of the former century, and subsequently considerably more, yet the interests of all classes required the use of gold as payment rather than silver. In this way gold became practically the single legal tender. The silver money of full value ceased to circulate at home until by act 56 George III, chap. 68, it was stipulated as legal tender to the amount of 40 shillings; and instead of 62 shillings coined from 1 pound troy, 66 shillings was declared legal, thus retaining 4 shillings as seigniorage. At the same time the authority to issue silver money lay exclusively in the hands of the government.[*]

In the United States of North America, in consequence of a mistake already alluded to, by act of Congress of 21st February, 1853, and a supplementary clause, the coin standard for gold coin was strictly retained unchanged, and, besides the previous issue of eagles and half-eagles, there were $3, $2½, and $1 gold pieces ordered to be coined. The future issue of entire silver dollars was silently abandoned, for although the coin standard was not changed, yet the further issuing of that kind of

* MacCulloch, Geld und Banken, S. 28, 29, 41, u. 42.

coin was fully nonsuited. Regarding the other silver coins, which up to that time had been measured by the same standard as the dollar, an essential reduction was declared in their silver contents, so that they presented a ratio of value as $1 : 14\frac{88}{100}$. According to the previous legal coin standard, there were $41\frac{6688}{10000}$ half dollars coined from 1 pound fine silver, while now 1 pound produces $44\frac{9538}{10000}$ half dollars. At the same time it was ordained that the reception of these new coin above the amount of $5 was not obligatory, and that the issuing of this new silver coin could only take place for government purposes. From these circumstances, and the entire discontinuance of the issue of silver dollars, the double standard since June, 1853, has been in the United States, not only legally but practically set aside, and the gold standard alone made valid.

In France, although the coin law of March 28, 1803, which recognizes the double standard, is still in force, yet, as has before been stated, since 1857, the gold standard actually prevails.

In Switzerland, since 1850, the system of the single standard has existed, only with this difference, that the material of that coin which serves as legal tender has changed in the course of time. By a law of May 7, 1850, the coin system of Switzerland was based entirely upon the silver standard. No gold coin was allowed to be issued; there were only silver kinds (5, 2, 1, and $\frac{1}{2}$ franc pieces), and no one was obliged to accept any other kind of coin. The Confederacy, according to a former examination, had stipulated that they be issued in strict conformity to the established coin system in the law of May 7, 1850. The Confederacy also forbade the public Treasury from receiving any other coin as legal tender, with the exception of large bills of exchange. On the contrary, by a law of January 21, 1860, the gold standard was exclusively established. Through this law the French gold coin, whose ratio of value is $1 : 15\frac{1}{2}$, as is also in France, its nominal legal exchange value, was accepted as currency at the same nominal legal value, and it was further declared that every other foreign gold coin, which should be reissued according to the previous examination and interpretation of the Confederacy, should have the capacity of the corresponding French coin. The 2, 1, and $\frac{1}{2}$ franc pieces were legally held merely as small coin, and of these no one was obliged to accept above the amount of 20 francs.

In Belgium, December, 1850, the legal exchange of all foreign gold coin, (the English sovereign, the Hollander 10-gulden piece, the French gold coin), was abolished; the government was empowered to call in the national gold coin, and by an ordinance of August 11, 1854, there followed the settlement of the latter. By a law of June 4, 1861, it was further declared that French gold coin, which held a ratio of 1 kilogram of fine gold to $15\frac{1}{2}$ kilograms of fine silver, should be received at their nominal value so long as they retain, in legal exchange, the same nominal value in France; and this ordinance was extended to the gold coin of other countries which were issued of full value with the corresponding French pieces. The Belgian Government was also empowered to issue gold coin of 20 and 40 francs, after the standard of the coin laws of 1832; also gold pieces of 10 and 5 francs of the same ratio, with the corresponding French coin. For the last fifteen years Belgium has had the single money standard. The cause of the change of the legal coin material was explained above.*

---

* Zeitschrift für die Staatswissenschaft, Jahrg. 1862.

COINAGE UPON A COMMON UNIT BASIS.

A SUPPLEMENT TO MONEY AS A STUDY IN NATIONAL ECONOMY.

BY

J. MEYER.

TRANSLATED FROM THE GERMAN

BY

MRS. C. P. CULVER.

AUTHOR'S PREFACE.

An aim to reform the conditions and regulations which are deep-rooted in the life of a people, even though the latter exhibit many defects, is sure to meet strong opposition, which is more energetic and persistent when personal interests are involved. This was the fate which attended the late movements to unite the various countries and peoples by a common coin system. Independent of the obstinacy, strengthened by custom and selfish motives, national sympathies and antipathies, no less than vanity, present impediments to the important and beautiful conception of establishing a system of universal coinage. That certain skepticism, which always questions improvements, and adheres to the old as the best, shakes its head suspiciously and looks upon the realizing of a coin union as a chimera.

But on every hand there will be persons, and there are such now, who, independent of the above-mentioned influences, keep in view the aim of realizing the conception of thus embracing the interests of all countries. An idea so comprehensive will finally surmount all opposition, and so much more successfully, because the material interests of universal nature are at present exerting a powerful influence, and keenly combating all opposition.

The fact that the coin union has already won a foothold, makes it important to reduce all its parts and various significations to a concrete form. The author is of the opinion that the proposals made during the coin conference at Vienna, in 1873, merit a careful attention.

In the following pages the question of a coin-union will be discussed from an economical point of view, the proposed coin system explained and compared with other systems, and, so far as concerns its general characteristics, the way and manner of its introduction examined. The principles of the science of municipal economy, in so far as they serve to strengthen the projected system, and which have not yet been discussed, but which are essential thereto, shall be included, because the discussion of the question can only conduce to the commendation and furtherance of a proposed reform by embracing all the important points of its object. According to the author's opinion, the proposals presented best equalize the various unit coins, include the united ratios of the most calculations, and therefore can soonest be introduced. His only wish is, that careful attention be directed to the projected work, and that, as far as possible, the accomplishment of the same be promoted.

71

COINAGE UPON A COMMON UNIT BASIS.

I.

A characteristic element in the modern form of trade, consists in its efforts to remove the dividing peculiarities of the various countries, and to provide common forms and mediums for its movements. We refer here only to the metric system of weights and measures, which by this time is taken possession of by the entire civilized world, and apart from the special circles where it long ago originated, it has been forced into and established in ordinary trade. A similar state of things exists in the department of coinage.

As early as 1838, the states belonging to the German tariff union (besides the 14 thaler and $24\frac{1}{2}$ gulden standard), adopted as the common silver coin the tariff union thaler (3 florins 30 kreuzers of the $24\frac{1}{2}$ gulden standard, or 2 thalers Prussian currency). The intermediate states collectively, of the former German confederation, with the exception of the Hanseatic cities on the one side, and Austria with Liechtenstein on the other, (besides the 30 thaler, the 45 gulden, and the $52\frac{1}{2}$ gulden standards of the Vienna coin treaty, which closed January 24, 1857), established as the common circulating medium, the 1 and 2 thaler pieces ($\frac{1}{30}$ and $\frac{1}{15}$ zollpfund silver $\frac{9}{10}$ fine), and as a union trade coin, the crown and half crown. (A crown = 10 grams gold $\frac{9}{10}$ fine.) From amid the various contrasting coins there was an effort made to find at least some connecting ligament.

The conference between France, Belgium, Italy, and Switzerland, which closed December 23, 1865, went farther, in that it fully harmonized the weight, the purity, the form, and the circulation of the gold and silver coin issued by these states collectively. In the countries mentioned, gold pieces of 100, 50, 20, 10, and 5 francs circulate, and silver coin of 5, 2, and 1 franc, and of 50 and 20 centimes, of the same fineness. The gold coin and the 5-franc silver pieces are .900 fine, and the remaining silver coins .835 fine.

In consequence of the new form of state laws in Germany, a coin unit between the countries of the present German Empire was created by act of legislature. The basis of this system is the mark (0.35842 gram fine gold). There were issued imperial gold coin of 20, 10, and 5 marks (900 parts gold, 100 parts copper), and imperial silver coin of 5, 2, and 1 mark, and 50 and 20 pfennigen, (900 parts silver, 100 parts copper).

The three Scandinavian kingdoms in a late coin convention adopted a gold coin of 0.4032 gram fine gold, whose subdivisions are 100 oeren.

Now, while great countries individually, are congratulating themselves upon the establishment of uniform coin systems, yet trade and the industries have to encounter in prominent countries, including the above-mentioned groups, fifteen different coin systems. The question therefore is, is the object of an international union coin, from an economical point of view, a proper one; or are the efforts thereto but the outflow of a capricious doctrine, which deserves no further attention? The investigation of this question here cannot appear superfluous, because there certainly are voices raised against an international union coin; indeed, the adoption of the new German coin system, which, through the influences of motives other than those apparent, deviates from the French coin standard, and which is already the adopted basis of several prominent countries, makes it questionable whether a common union coin in the important interests of trade is desired.

Let us consider the present condition of international trade. The establishment of the prices of merchandise, of exchanges, and of loans requires on the part of the receivers, the customers, and often also upon that of the dealers, the merchants, a roundabout calculation. The key—the par coin—must be well understood, and, as a rule, especially by those who are largely engaged in business with foreign countries. This unit necessarily must be varied, and though by culture and practice the calculations may be correctly and quickly accomplished, yet they always occasion a loss of time. The immense and constantly increasing amount of business in international trade sums up, therefore, a considerable amount of time which might be employed in productive labor. Time-saving is an important element in industrial development, but, unfortunately, time is not always properly estimated.

When the citizens of those countries which have various coinage systems travel through these respective districts, they are first obliged to exchange their own legal currency for foreign coin; consequently, this necessitates a business transaction of a peculiar nature, perhaps several; and besides all this, the transaction secures a gain to the vender or money exchanger in a majority of cases; so that, for the sake of this money transaction an expense must be incurred. Even if the traveler finds that his coin legally circulates in the foreign province, where he happens to be, yet the reckoning of its value is not without difficulty, and this is more troublesome in small trade, besides furnishing easy opportunity for errors and damage.

Further, from the nature of the industrial relations of the various countries in international trade, a large number of payments in business operations are not effected through exchange, but by the return of bullion. The equivalent for the merchandise given is a certain amount in weight of precious metal. The respective governments of the several districts establish the coin system, and fix for each coin category the required metal quantity, as well as the allowable limit of variation in weight and purity. The coin form, as such, has the discharging power for past obligations, and very properly no account is taken of the diminishing of the precious metal contents, which results from circulation. The publicity of the coin laws, the authority of the executive power, and the confidence of the citizen in obeying the existing coin rules, as well as in the legal capacity of the coin as a means of transacting business, make this control appear no more than necessary. Naturally, therefore, the same control is not excluded from wholesale trade; and, indeed, the custom of proving and weighing the coin is established, and where important deficiencies of the precious metals are discovered, the absent quantity is taken into account by an average percentage. It is true, this is done indirectly, that is, in the price of the merchandise.

As a rule, a knowledge of coinage prevails in international trade, and the coin values of the several countries are known in the interested districts, but without some of the above-stated exceptions. In the mutual trade between the several countries which do not belong to one of the specified coin-groups, the coin form, as such, with its several attributes, is not used; as a rule, the metal is weighed and assayed, although externally it appears in the form of coin. The buyer of merchandise, being obliged to make his payments in bullion money, either purchases bullion or the legal or admitted coin of the country of his creditors, or he melts coin from which he fashions bullion, or has it done, or else he weighs the coin of his own country in order to remit to his creditors, according to the stipulated price, the legal amount of precious metal. The creditor receiving payment from a foreigner, if he does not receive native or legally-admitted coin, is obliged in many cases to sell the bullion or foreign coin, or carry the same to the mint to be issued in the coin of his country.

In international trade also, as a rule, the equalizing of a business transaction is accompanied with an expense of time and money. The gain derived by bankers, exchangers, metal dealers, &c., from brokerage in coin and precious metal, although to appearances not important, yet in fact amounts to a large sum, which is abstracted from the property of the people. Though this gain accumulates from small parts, yet it would more speedily advance the interests of the people if it remained in their own hands.

It is true, indeed, that the management of the money exchange hitherto has not been of that kind as to cause real interruptions to the progress of industrial pursuits, but the full scope of economy, the acquisition of the greatest possible gain from the smallest outlay of time and energy, is, under the present regulations, really not attained. If the observation is admissible anywhere, it is certainly here, that long familiarity with certain customs finally permits the defects of the same to be altogether overlooked. A mutual coin system for international trade purposes would obviate the inconveniences described, and, by removing the useless outlay of time and money, a new impulse would be given to the healthy development of the industrial life of the people.

II.

An international money system corresponding to the coin systems of the several groups and countries, with a fixed amount of precious metal as a unit, should be established, and for conveniently satisfying the wants of trade, which necessarily only demand large sums, there should be some members containing in themselves the compound of the unit.

The first question touching international money is, whether a double or single standard should be adopted. The same reasoning which recommends the single standard for local money, will serve in a proportionate degree for international money. The legal normal relative value between gold and silver very seldom in the double standard corresponds with the market value. In consequence of the exchange processes thereby effected, the possible introduction of a disturbance in prices, the withdrawing of the less valued metal, and the diminishing of that which is obligated to properly advance or to draw stipulated amounts, appear as disadvantages, which are not compensated for by the one advantage attending a double standard, viz, the prevention of a too great shrinkage in value of the two precious metals. It has been stated that the adoption, respectively the retention, of the double standard, is necessary, or at least judicious, for this reason, that in the market value of that metal from which the pay-medium of the single standard is coined, and from which in the double standard the coin would be principally issued, such important variations are possible that it would appear necessary to rely on the other precious metal, and then it would only be necessary to comprehend the system as expressed in the latter metal.

But this argument is not sufficiently strong. For if it is necessary that the coin which serves as the legal local money of a country should be issued from the other precious metal, there is no loss of time by first adopting this system; there is even a possibility of overcoming the loss of time in the transaction of business. Prices will regulate themselves in the new system, and at any rate, the apparent variations in prices are revolutions, which may be of a transitory nature, while the disadvantages which accompany the double standard are inherent. And even if the point about which the price oscillation takes place should advance, that is, should become, after fixing the advance in prices, a permanent one, yet it would in proportion be less disadvantageous than the double standard.

III.

Now, as concerning the choice of gold material. Gold possesses a large value in a small bulk, for which reason it is especially fitted for the equalization of large sums, and because it is small in volume, is adapted for transportation to distant places. Silver, on account of its small relative value, is less convenient for the payment of large amounts and for transportation; besides, the expense of coinage is greater for silver than for gold. But silver, in consequence of its greater hardness, and its ability to withstand abrasion, can, in proportion to gold, remain longer in circulation without the necessity of recoining.

With reference to these attributes, gold best answers the designs and the nature of international trade; besides, for the traveler and the exchange trader it is a convenient and economical circulating material. The circumstance that silver is declining in value speaks in favor of the choice of gold as an international pay-medium. This decline is independent of the demonetization of silver, which has taken place in various states in consequence of the coin reform, and results from this circumstance, that since the year 1860, the amount of silver produced in America, especially in the western part of North America, has very greatly increased, (from 1868 to 1870, = 476,000,000 thalers), while the exportation to the East, (which formerly produced silver, but which, since the time mentioned, has declined in amount) from 1866, to 1870, = 144,000,000 thalers. Now, notwithstanding this ratio may change, yet gold will not cease, on account of the mentioned advantages, to furnish at least the greater part of the material for international money.

But the international money system will only take fast foothold in the various coin territories, and the above warranted industrial advantages be accomplished, when the coin of the same is made to circulate with the local coin. The international coin will be preferred, if in the requisites of industrial purposes it can be easily employed in any country. The real stipulation is this, that the international coin become an accession to the existing coin system; that is, the international coin, at least the chief member, shall reproduce the more important coin systems for trade with but only slight deviations, more or less; or else represent plural or aliquot parts of the chief member in an easy reckoning ratio. Were this not the case, then the coin, which should serve as international, could not possibly attain that universal circulation which lies within the scope of international money. For in whatever way the attainment of an international money might be contemplated, there ever would be governments which would reject the introduction of the proposed international coin. And in case the introduction of the latter could be secured, the trades-people of the various countries would yet stipulate for payment in the former coin, and manage their books and calculations according to the old money, in which they could not legally be prevented. But, even in a wider sense, such agreement by the legislature in regard to external trade, would be declared ineffectual, if the easy, unhindered extension of international coin in the local trade of a country is thereby checked, and those who do not sell by retail, and with whom, in a majority of cases, the conclusion of the business and the payment do not occur together, would stipulate for local coin. And even if the legislature, with reference to payments, should declare the legal quality equal to local coin, yet the traders and professions in extensive business transactions would only admit those who offer or receive international coin as payment, if at all, under burdensome restrictions, so that at last it would be necessary, perhaps, to satisfy their purchases through the former pay-medium. For this the legislature can present no remedy, at least without damage to private liberty, and thereby to trade itself. If the coin does not present in itself the capacity of circulation, the regulations of the government are not sufficient to insure it; trade with its necessities being stronger than all legislative enactments.

The more the international coin, in the accurate conditions of its accession, corresponds to the existing coin system, the smaller under like circumstances will be the change in prices which is joined inseparably with the introduction of every coin system; and consequently, the smaller the disturbance which in such cases the collective international industrial life, and indirectly, also, the industries of every special district, sustain.

But the continually increasing and complicated forms of trade require an increase in the ease and facility of prosecuting business. If the coin, established for international trade, possesses an equally authorized circulation with that of the national money system, there is naturally established between the two a relation of value which is legally fixed. There must always, however, be a roundabout calculation in payments, which, it is true, is easier if the international coin forms a simple fraction or a complete multiple of the fixed local coin; this, as a rule, however, is more tedious, because the international coin contains, besides the unit, the respective compounds as well as pieces of the smaller category. These inconveniences would be obviated, and trade be unhindered, and fully stimulated, if the various countries had a uniform coin system. If the system, as international, where based upon gold, then even where trade is carried on with other countries through payments in metal, that which corresponds to the actual ratio could be produced from the existing and continually increasing stock of coin, and naturally under the normal condition of money here presumed, the necessity would be less frequent than at present to first purchase a metal pay-medium, and thereby regularly allow a gain to the broker; for, independent of the money coined for the benefit of private persons, the local money, which is also international, would be provided through the regular issue upon the part of the government.

If on account of a changed ratio in the metal market it is necessary to represent the common coin system by silver, then the advantages explained above, so far as payments in silver are necessary or satisfactory, will be equally as great. Only in such a case, there would be at separation between local and international money, for, as has already been shown, gold cannot be dispensed with in foreign trade; however the coin of the latter must take the character of trade coin, where the double standard is not allowed. In such places, however, the advantages of an international coin would be realized only in a small degree, because it circulates in curtailed amounts, and in confined or limited circles.

When, as the result of a universal system, the barriers are removed which the various coin systems always place in opposition to the free exercise of the money exchange between the several countries, at least in certain districts, there will be an activity in the money exchange of the various territories much greater than previously existed. This happens, because, although obstacles of other kinds may exist, there is at least a greater possibility presented of adjusting all interruptions with energy and dispatch which arise in the money circulation of the several countries; also of filling up deficiencies where there is a want, and where too large an amount is collected, of drawing the overplus to other places. It cannot be denied that the greater the mobilization of money, the greater is the danger of a sudden and a too great accumulation of the same in a certain district. Crises have occurred before, and they will from time to time occur again. With a change of circumstances, speculation which now requires great precaution will make broader calculations, and as trade enlivens a better knowledge of existing proportionate ratios becomes possible. It is also presumable, that directly through the greater mobility of money, an easy accumulation of the same can be realized.

IV.

The broader development of the industrial organism, which naturally requires for the full display of its power, especially the removal of obstacles and burdensome difficulties, urgently demands a coin unit. The multiplicity of powers and contrivances in the domains of industry, certainly yields rich developments in regard to trade, and a uniformity, which in the sphere of industry naturally runs contrary to existing conditions, can certainly operate only in a stifling manner, while the centralization resulting from the employment of a unit coin system, is directly surrounded by the natural and necessary conditions of an intense and extensive development of trade.

Before the introduction of the unit system can be effected, it will be necessary to form a connection between the unit coin, and the existing local coin of the several territories, and a longer or shorter time will be necessary to conform the one to the other.

The same results will here follow as those formerly mentioned with regard to the checking of the circulation of the new coin. But if the government rapidly calls in the old local coin, and fills the veins of trade with the new coin, then a further hinderance to the actual circulation would not be possible; and yet the violent revolution in prices and the important consequences to the industries, cannot be entirely prevented.

The amount of precious metal which is allowed in connection with the other material is in the universal exchange medium, determined. This is of value to all coin, and consequently also to that form of money used in trade. As for the alloy in coin, it is only of a technical character, a ligature, a preventive against a too speedy waste of the precious metal. The idea is, that the coin is an inseparable whole, and its gross weight is of secondary consideration. This gross weight, however, serves but to control the purity, any absence of which occasions at once either a direct testing of the gold or silver contents of the coin, or the exact existing purity is determined indirectly by separating the mixed ratios. The example, according to which a certain quantity of metal, generally gross weight, is made the basis of which an aliquot part forms the base contents of the same; in other words, the acceptance of the so-called gold coin or silver coin does not correspond to the nature of the thing, and besides yields nothing to the relief of the money exchange, and which, as will later be explained, can likewise be attained in another way.

The arithmetical plan, the measuring scale, according to which the individual coin category is formed, is fixed through the proportion in which trade most frequently moves, through the requisite qualifications for facility in calculation, and there, where it treats of the establishment of an international, relatively a universal system, also through the necessity of a close connection between the new and the existing coin systems. If a careful examination of the phenomena of trade is made, it is seen that the compound of the unit, the four, five, and ten fold of the same, and the decimal multiplier of the latter, also the half, the fourth, the fifth, the tenth, and the decimal subdivisions are in a certain measure the pay forms of the universal types of trade, in which products everywhere appear most frequently in trade, and in which they are the easiest calculated.

Take for the unit the basis of a coin system, $1\frac{1}{2}$ grams of fine gold; employ for the higher members of the scale 2, 5, 10, and if necessary 20 grams, and insert, if necessary, with reference to the other system, the additional member of $2\frac{1}{2}$ grams, so that gold coin of 3, $3\frac{3}{4}$, $7\frac{1}{2}$, 15, and perchance 30 grams might be issued, then for the lower members of the scale take the $\frac{1}{2}$, $\frac{1}{4}$, $\frac{1}{5}$, $\frac{1}{10}$, $\frac{1}{20}$, $\frac{1}{40}$, $\frac{1}{50}$, $\frac{1}{100}$, $\frac{1}{200}$, even down to $\frac{1}{400}$ ($\frac{1}{4}$, $\frac{3}{8}$, $\frac{3}{10}$, $\frac{3}{20}$, $\frac{3}{40}$, $\frac{3}{80}$, $\frac{3}{100}$, $\frac{3}{200}$, $\frac{3}{400}$, $\frac{3}{800}$ grams) and the following result is secured.

FRENCH MONEY.

Of fine gold:					
$1\frac{1}{2}$ grams	=	5	francs,	16.6	centimes.
3 "	=	10 "		33.3 "	
$3\frac{3}{4}$ "	=	12 "		63. "	
$7\frac{1}{2}$ "	=	25 "		83.3 "	
15 "	=	51 "		66.6 "	
$\frac{3}{4}$ "	=	2 "		58.3 "	
$\frac{3}{8}$ "	=	1 "		29.1 "	
$\frac{3}{10}$ "	=	1 "		3.3 "	
$\frac{3}{20}$ "	=	"		51.6 "	
$\frac{3}{40}$ "	=			25.8 "	
$\frac{3}{80}$ "	=			12.9 "	
$\frac{3}{100}$ "	=			10.3 "	
$\frac{3}{200}$ "	=			5.15 "	
$\frac{3}{400}$ "	=			2.58 "	
$\frac{3}{800}$ "	=			1.29 "	

The 5, 10, and 50 franc pieces, and even the preferred 25 franc piece, are reproduced in the proposed coin system with variations respectively in excess, which is of no growing importance in trade. The franc, the $\frac{1}{2}$, $\frac{1}{4}$, and the $\frac{1}{10}$ of the same, and the son, which is still in circulation in France, and the 1 and 2 centime pieces, are very closely reproduced.

ENGLISH MONEY.

Of fine gold:						
$1\frac{1}{2}$ grams	=	4 shillings	1.16	pence	=	$\frac{1}{8}$ pound sterling.
3 "	=	8 "	2.32	"		
$3\frac{3}{4}$ "	=	10 "	2.9	"	=	$\frac{1}{2}$ pound sterling.
$7\frac{1}{2}$ "	=	20 "	5.3	"	=	1 pound sterling.
15 "	=	40 "	11.64	"	=	2 pounds sterling.
$\frac{3}{4}$ "	=	2 "	.58	"		
$\frac{3}{8}$ "	=	1 "	.29			

Of fine gold :

$\frac{3}{10}$ grams =	9.8	pence.
$\frac{3}{20}$ " =	4.92	"
$\frac{3}{40}$ " =	2.46	"
$\frac{3}{80}$ " =	1.23	"
$\frac{3}{100}$ " =	.98	"
$\frac{3}{200}$ " =	.49	"
$\frac{3}{400}$ " =	.24	"
$\frac{3}{800}$ " =	.12	"

Here the sovereign, the $\frac{1}{2}$, and the 2-sovereign pieces, the 2 shillings, 1 shilling, 10, 5, 2, and 1 penny, and the $\frac{1}{2}$ penny are reproduced, and the pieces in the higher category especially present for reckoning purposes a closely corresponding ratio.

FEDERAL MONEY.

Of fine gold :

$1\frac{1}{2}$ grams =	$0	99.7
3 " =	1	99.4
$3\frac{3}{4}$ " =	2	49.25
$7\frac{1}{2}$ " =	4	98.5
15 " =	9	96.92
$\frac{3}{4}$ " =		49.8
$\frac{3}{8}$ " =		24.9
$\frac{3}{10}$ " =		19.9
$\frac{3}{20}$ " =		10
$\frac{3}{40}$ " =		5
$\frac{3}{80}$ " =		2.5
$\frac{3}{100}$ " =		2
$\frac{3}{200}$ " =		1
$\frac{3}{400}$ " =		0.5
$\frac{3}{800}$ " =		0.25

The 1 and 2 dollar pieces, the eagle and $\frac{1}{2}$ eagle, $\frac{1}{2}$ and $\frac{1}{4}$ dollar, the dime and $\frac{1}{2}$ dime, 2, 1, $\frac{1}{2}$, and $\frac{1}{4}$ cents are represented. The $1\frac{1}{2}$-gram system corresponds more nearly to the Federal-coin system, than to any other.

MONEY OF THE GERMAN EMPIRE.

Of fine gold :

$1\frac{1}{2}$ grams =	4	marks 19	pfennigs (strictly 4 marks 18.6 pfennigs.)	
3 " =	8	" 38	"	
$3\frac{3}{4}$ " =	10	" 47.5	"	
$7\frac{1}{2}$ " =	20	" 95	"	
15 " =	41	" 90	"	
$\frac{3}{4}$ " =	2	" 9.5	"	
$\frac{3}{8}$ " =	1	" 4.8	"	
$\frac{3}{10}$ " =	0	" 83.8	"	
$\frac{3}{20}$ " =	0	" 41.9	"	
$\frac{3}{40}$ " =	0	" 20.9	"	
$\frac{3}{80}$ " =	0	" 10.5	"	
$\frac{3}{100}$ " =	0	" 8.4	"	
$\frac{3}{200}$ " =	0	" 4.2	"	
$\frac{3}{400}$ " =	0	" 2.1	"	
$\frac{3}{800}$ " =	0	" 1.05	"	

$2\frac{1}{10}$, $4\frac{1}{5}$, $10\frac{1}{2}$, 21, and 42 marks, 21, 10, 4, and 1 pfennig are represented in sufficiently close amounts for calculation.

If the ratio of gold and silver, with reference to the condition of the

London market in 1873, and the probabilities of the near future, are taken as 1 : 15.8, then for Austria we have as follows:

AUSTRIAN MONEY.

Of fine gold: $1\frac{1}{2}$ grams = 2 gulden 13 kreuzers.

3	"	= 4	"	26	"
$3\frac{3}{4}$	"	= 5	"	32	"
$7\frac{1}{2}$	"	=10	"	45	"
15	"	=20	"	90	"
$\frac{3}{4}$	"	= 1	"	6.5	"
$\frac{3}{8}$	"	= 0	"	53.25	"
$\frac{3}{10}$	"	= 0	"	42.6	"
$\frac{3}{20}$	"	= 0	"	21.3	"
$\frac{3}{40}$	"	= 0	"	10.6	"
$\frac{3}{80}$	"	= 0	"	5.3	"
$\frac{3}{100}$	"	= 0	"	4.3	"
$\frac{3}{200}$	"	= 0	"	2.15	"
$\frac{3}{400}$	"	= 0	"	1.08	"
$\frac{3}{800}$	"	= 0	"	0.54	"

The amounts here represented are, with small variations, easily calculated in the Austrian coin, $2\frac{1}{10}$, $4\frac{1}{4}$, $5\frac{1}{4}$, $10\frac{1}{2}$, 21, 1, and $\frac{1}{2}$ gulden, and 20, 10, 5, 4, 2, 1, and $\frac{1}{2}$ kreuzer are closely represented. Since 1870, Austria has issued 8 and 4 gulden pieces as trade coin, corresponding to the 20 and 10 franc pieces.

RUSSIAN MONEY.

In Russia, the legal 5 rubles in gold (half imperial), equals 5 rubles 15 kopecks in silver; the legal ratio being as 1 : 15.45.

Of fine gold: $1\frac{1}{2}$ grams = 1 ruble 29 kopecks.

3	"	= 2	"	58	"
$3\frac{3}{4}$	"	= 3	"	$22\frac{1}{2}$	"
$7\frac{1}{2}$	"	= 6	"	45	"
15	"	=12	"	90	"
$\frac{3}{4}$	"	= 0	"	64.5	"
$\frac{3}{8}$	"	= 0	"	32.25	"
$\frac{3}{10}$	"	= 0	"	25.8	"
$\frac{3}{20}$	"	= 0	"	12.9	"
$\frac{3}{40}$	"	= 0	"	6.45	"
$\frac{3}{80}$	"	= 0	"	3.28	"
$\frac{3}{100}$	"	= 0	"	2.58	"
$\frac{3}{200}$	"	= 0	"	1.29	"
$\frac{3}{400}$	"	= 0	"	0.65	"
$\frac{3}{800}$	"	= 0	"	0.33	"

Thus, $1\frac{1}{4}$, $3\frac{1}{4}$ rubles, $\frac{1}{4}$ imperial, $5\frac{1}{4}$ ruble ($\frac{1}{4}$ ruble more than half imperial), $\frac{1}{4}$ ruble, 3, 2, 1, and $\frac{1}{2}$ kopeck are very nearly equalized.

HOLLAND MONEY.

The basis of the coin system in Holland is the gold gulden = 0.60561 grams fine gold. Then—

Of fine gold: $1\frac{1}{2}$ grams = 2 gulden 48 cents.

3	"	= 4	"	96	"
$3\frac{3}{4}$	"	= 6	"	20	"
$7\frac{1}{2}$	"	=12	"	40	"

Of fine gold: 15 grams = 24 gulden 80 cents.

$\frac{3}{4}$	"	= 1	"	24	"
$\frac{3}{8}$	"	= 0	"	62	"
$\frac{3}{10}$	"	= 0	"	49.6	"
$\frac{3}{20}$	"	= 0	"	24.8	"
$\frac{3}{40}$	"	= 0	"	12.4	"
$\frac{3}{80}$	"	= 0	"	6.2	"
$\frac{3}{100}$	"	= 0	"	4.96	"
$\frac{3}{200}$	"	= 0	"	2.48	"
$\frac{3}{400}$	"	= 0	"	1.28	"
$\frac{3}{800}$	"	= 0	"	0.62	"

$2\frac{1}{2}$, 5, 25, $1\frac{1}{4}$ gulden, 50, 25, 5, 2, and 1 cents are in amounts easy to calculate, very closely represented.

SCANDINAVIAN MONEY.

In the new coin system of Scandinavia, the unit is the gold crown = 0.4032 grams fine gold.

Of fine gold: $1\frac{1}{2}$ grams = 3 crowns 72 oeren.

3	"	= 7	"	44	"
$3\frac{3}{4}$	"	= 9	"	30	"
$7\frac{1}{2}$	"	= 18	"	60	"
15	"	= 37	"	20	"
$\frac{3}{4}$	"	= 1	"	86	"
$\frac{3}{8}$	"	= 0	"	93	"
$\frac{3}{10}$	"	= 0	"	74.4	"
$\frac{3}{20}$	"	= 0	"	37.2	"
$\frac{3}{40}$	"	= 0	"	18.6	"
$\frac{3}{80}$	"	= 0	"	9.3	"
$\frac{3}{100}$	"	= 0	"	7.44	"
$\frac{3}{200}$	"	= 0	"	3.72	"
$\frac{3}{400}$	"	= 0	"	1.86	"
$\frac{3}{800}$	"	= 0	"	0.93	"

$1\frac{1}{5}$, 1, $\frac{1}{5}$, crowns, 10, 2, and 1 oeren are very closely reproduced.

SPANISH MONEY.

In Spain 1 gold doubloon (= 100 reals) is equal to 5 duros in silver (1 duro = 20 reals = 5 pesetas = 500 centimes). The legal ratio between gold and silver is 1 : 15.48.

Of fine gold: $1\frac{1}{2}$ grams = 1 duro.

3	"	= 2	"			
$3\frac{3}{4}$	"	= 2	"	10 reals	(250)	centimes.
$7\frac{1}{2}$	"	= 5	"			
15	"	= 10	"			
$\frac{3}{4}$	"	=		10 reals	(250)	centimes.
$\frac{3}{8}$	"	=		5 "	(125)	"
$\frac{3}{10}$	"	=		4 "	(100)	"
$\frac{3}{20}$	"	=		2 "	(50)	"
$\frac{3}{40}$	"	=		1 "	(25)	"
$\frac{3}{80}$	"	=		0.5 "	(12.5)	"
$\frac{3}{100}$	"	=		0.4 "	(10)	"
$\frac{3}{200}$	"	=		0.2 "	(5)	"
$\frac{3}{400}$	"	=		0.1 "	(2.5)	"
$\frac{3}{800}$	"	=		0.05 "	(1.25)	"

For reckoning and exchange the 1½ gram system presents in the most complete manner the coin members, the duro and its compounds, the escudo (= 10 reals), 1¼ pesetas (= 5 reals), the peseta (= 4 reals), the ½ peseta (= 2 reals), ¼ peseta (= 1 real), and the ½ and ⅕ real.

PORTUGUESE MONEY.

Of fine gold:	1½	grams	= 0	milreis,	922	reis.
	3	"	= 1	."	844	"
	3¾	"	= 2	"	305	"
	7½	"	= 4	"	610	"
	15	"	= 9	"	220	"
	¾	"	= 0	"	461	"
	⅜	"	= 0	"	230.5	"
	3/10	"	= 0	"	184.4	"
	3/20	"	= 0	"	92.2	"
	3/40	"	= 0	"	46.1	"
	3/80	"	= 0	"	23	"
	3/100	"	= 0	"	18.4	"
	3/200	"	= 0	"	9.2	"
	3/400	"	= 0	"	4.6	"
	3/800	"	= 0	"	2.3	"

The milreis (1,000 reis) and the coron (10,000 reis) are approximately represented, and the 2 3/10 and 4 6/10 milreis; also the 5 tastoes (500 reis), 2 tastoes (200 reis), 1 tastoe (100 reis), and the ½ tastoe (50 reis), very nearly reproduced.

BRAZILIAN MONEY.

Of fine gold:	1½	grams	= 1	milreis,	824	reis.
	3	"	= 3	"	648	"
	3¾	"	= 4	"	560	"
	7½	"	= 9	"	120	"
	15	"	= 18	"	240	"
	¾	"	= 0	"	912	"
	⅜	"	= 0	"	456	"
	3/10	"	= 0	"	364.8	"
	3/20	"	= 0	"	182.4	"
	3/40	"	= 0	"	91.2	"
	3/80	"	= 0	"	45.6	"
	3/100	"	= 0	"	36.48	"
	3/200	"	= 0	"	18.24	"
	3/400	"	= 0	"	9.12	"
	3/800	"	= 0	"	4.56	"

The 5,000, 500, 400, 200, and 100 reis pieces of the present coinage, the 9,000 and 4,500 reis of the earlier gold coinage by Portugal; also the 20, 10, and 5 reis are very closely reproduced. The crusader piece, 480 reis, of the earlier coinage, equals the present 960 reis in silver.

TURKISH COINAGE.

In Turkey, the jüslik, (medschidie, Turkish lira) the 100-piaster piece in gold is equal to 5 jirmilik (a' 20 piaster) in silver, the legal ratio being as 1 : 14.98.

Of fine gold:	1½	grams	= 22	piasters,	28.8	paras.
	3	"	= 45	"	17.6	"
	3¾	"	= 56	"	32	"

Of fine gold:	7½	grams	= 113	piasters,	24	paras.
	15	"	= 227	"	8	"
	$\frac{3}{4}$	"	= 11	"	14.4	"
	$\frac{3}{8}$	"	= 5	"	27.2	"
	$\frac{3}{10}$	"	= 4	"	21.8	"
	$\frac{3}{20}$	"	= 2	"	10.9	"
	$\frac{3}{40}$	"	= 1	"	5.45	"
	$\frac{3}{80}$	"	= 0	"	22.7	"
	$\frac{3}{100}$	"	= 0	"	18.18	"
	$\frac{3}{200}$	"	= 0	"	9	"
	$\frac{3}{400}$	"	= 0	"	4.5	"
	$\frac{3}{800}$	"	= 0	"	2.25	"

In the 20 and 60 piaster piece (late Mamudic coinage) there is a tolerably near union effected; there are also closely reproduced the 10 piaster (onlik), 5 piaster (beschlik), 2 piaster (ikilik), 20 paras (jirmilik, half, piaster), and the 5 paras.

MONEY IN THE PRINCIPALITY OF DONAU.

Since 1868, money in this principality has been computed by lën to 100 bans; 1 lën = 4½ grams fine silver. But the coinage after this standard is very limited; the old reckoning and the earlier customary currency are still universally valid. In Moldau the old computation is that of the piaster or lën to 40 paras, and the Austrian ducat, which equals 37 piasters (the Austrian ducat equals 3.442 grams] fine gold), and 1 piaster or lën = 0.0930 grams fine gold.

Of fine gold:	1½	grams	= 16	piaster,	10	paras.
	3	"	= 32	"	20	"
	3¾	"	= 40	"	25	"
	7½	"	= 81	"	10	"
	15	"	= 162	"	20	"
	$\frac{3}{4}$	"	= 8	"	5	"
	$\frac{3}{8}$	"	= 4	"	2.5	"
	$\frac{3}{10}$	"	= 3	"	10	"
	$\frac{3}{20}$	"	= 1	"	25	"
	$\frac{3}{40}$	"	= 0	"	32.5	"
	$\frac{3}{80}$	"	= 0	"	16.25	"
	$\frac{3}{100}$	"	= 0	"	13	"
	$\frac{3}{200}$	"	= 0	"	6.5	"
	$\frac{3}{400}$	"	= 0	"	3.25	"
	$\frac{3}{800}$	"	= 0	"	1.6	"

WALLACHIAN COINAGE.

In Wallachia the piaster equals 40 paras, 120 asper; but the unit of computation in trade and the Austrian ducat are equal to 32 piasters or lën. One piaster = 0.1076 grams fine gold.

Of fine gold:	1½	grams	= 14	piasters.	
	3	"	= 28	"	
	3¾	"	= 35	"	
	7½	"	= 70	"	
	15	"	= 140	"	
	$\frac{3}{4}$	"	= 7	"	
	$\frac{3}{8}$	"	= 3	"	20 paras.

Of fine gold: $\frac{3}{10}$ grams = 2 piasters, 32 paras.

$\frac{3}{20}$ " = 1 " 16 "

$\frac{3}{40}$ " = 28 "

$\frac{3}{80}$ " = 14 "

$\frac{3}{100}$ " = 11.2 "

$\frac{3}{200}$ " = 5.6 "

$\frac{3}{400}$ " = 2.8 "

$\frac{3}{800}$ " = 1.4 "

The 1½-gram system furnishes for one country, as well as another, amounts in round numbers, which are not difficult to compute in trade.

In Greece, with the exception of the Ionian Islands, the computation since 1868, has been according to the French standard; the coinage of the same is, however, inconsiderable. The old gold and silver drachme of 100 leptas is the currency after which, although it is seldom met with, the money exchange is regulated. The gold piece of 20 drachmes =5.1984 grams fine gold; consequently 1 drachme in gold = 0.25998 grams.

GRECIAN COINAGE.

Of fine gold: 1¼ grams = 5 drachmes 80 leptas.

3 " = 11 " 60 "

3¾ " = 14 " 50 "

7½ " = 29 "

15 " = 58 "

¼ " = 2 " 90 "

⅜ " = 1 " 45 "

$\frac{3}{10}$ " = 1 " 16 "

$\frac{3}{20}$ " = 0 " 58 "

$\frac{3}{40}$ " = 29 "

$\frac{3}{80}$ " = 14.5 "

$\frac{3}{100}$ " = 11.6 "

$\frac{3}{200}$ " = 5.8 "

$\frac{3}{400}$ " = 2.9 "

$\frac{3}{800}$ " = 1.45 "

For computation, the amounts here given present a convenient ratio.

V.

If the universal coin system here presented were adopted, the 2½-fold of the unit might be abandoned, or next to it the 4-fold of the latter could be coined. Special necessities, which exist here and there in certain territories, and which require the introduction of the one or the other of the new members in the system, will not easily admit the conclusion that for the ratio of prices, either for the present or the future, the division $\frac{3}{100}$ ($\frac{3}{800}$ grams) is perhaps not the lowest point in the descending scale. The insertion of new members, which stand in a conveniently computable ratio to the others, produces no disturbance in the unit coin, for example, the 8, or 20 fold of the unit.

Computation, therefore, proves that the system presented above, and which is based upon the amount of 1½ grams fine gold, furnishes the principal coin of the most preferable coin system, for not only the unit and its compounds, but also the subdivisions, with variations are rendered, that without detriment to the money exchange there is a direct equalizing of the value of the species of coin under consideration, and the difficulties of complicated calculations, as well as the risk of important variations in prices, are removed from trade in general.

Place the French system, for which a universal character is so commonly claimed, beside the foregoing scale ($\frac{9}{2}$ grams fine silver, or $\frac{9}{31}$ grams fine gold=1 franc), and it is evident to all, in comparing it with the English system, that the shilling, the sovereign, and the half-sovereign, are not by far so closely represented as they are by the 1½-gram system (2 francs=1s. 7d.; 20 francs=15s. 10d.; even the combination 25 francs only =19s. 9.5d.; 50 francs only=39s. 7d.). But not only with reference to individual members, but also to that of the respective ratios, is the computation more inconvenient.

Toward United States coinage the French system bears no comparison to the 1½-gram system (10 francs=$1.90; ½ franc=9.5 cents; ¼ franc=4.7 cents).

Respecting Austria and Greece, the 1½-gram system is not inferior to the French system, and for Germany the latter cannot reproduce the mark in as many convenient pieces as can the 1½-gram system (1 franc= 81 pfennige).

With the systems of Russia and Holland, the French system is sufficiently approximate, (1 franc=25 kopeken, 1 franc=50 cents); and also in Spain the peseta, the duro, the 1, 2, $\frac{2}{10}$, and $\frac{1}{10}$ real, are very closely reproduced through the French system. (Since 1871, the peseta=1 franc has been taken as the unit of calculation in Spain, the exact value of the franc being 3.9 reals.) However, without question, the 1½-gram system, as the above mathematical proof exhibits, guarantees the best accession to the coinage of the latter country.

Of minor value, also is the union of the French coin system with the Scandinavian (1 franc=72 oeren), which, especially in the subdivisions, is better accommodated by the 1½-gram system. The same may be said of the Portuguese (1 franc=167 reis); and the Brazilian (1 franc= 352 reis); and the Turkish (1 franc=68 piasters 7.24 paras); as well as that of Moldau and Wallachia (1 franc=3 piasters 4.9 paras; 1 franc=2 piasters 27.9 paras). To all of these coin systems the 1½-gram system bears a closer approximation, or at least, in the combination of the pieces, gives an easier computable value than the French system.

No favorable results either would follow the choice of such an amount in weight of fine gold, which in its purity either approaches the existing coin, or which results from the employment of the above-represented scale upon the basis of the mode of computation as is shown in the following:

The shaping of the franc $29\frac{3}{31}$ centigrams to $\frac{3}{10}$ grams (30 centigrams) would naturally in like manner exhibit great disparity toward other systems, and a system established on this amount of weight would be inferior to other systems which approach nearer to the 1½-gram system.

If the type of value as a basis for a universal coin system be $\frac{3}{8}$ grams (37.5 centigrams), to which the German mark, 0.35842 grams fine gold, (or in round numbers, 36 grams), approaches very nearly, then the 5-. centime piece, the franc, the 5-franc piece, the penny, the United States cent, as well as the Holland 5-cent piece, are but distantly reproduced.

By adopting $\frac{3}{4}$ gram (75 centigrams), which is the basis of the Austrian gulden, then the franc, the penny, the Holland 5-cent piece, and the 2-oeren piece cannot be represented.

By taking a basis of $\frac{9}{10}$ grams (90 centigrams), only the Holland cent, the 1 and 2 oeren, the ½ and ¼ mark, the 1 and 5 pfennige, and the 1 milreis of Portugal would be reproduced.

The basis of 3 grams (300 centigrams), which the 10-franc piece approximates in value, does not represent the shilling or the Scandinavian coin of 10 and 1 oeren.

That of 1 gram (100 centigrams) only approximates in value the 50, 25, 5, 2, and 1 oeren, and the 5, 2, and 1 pfennig.

Moreover, the coin of 1½ grams fine gold has been adopted in Japan, whose trade in the near future promises to be very important. The unit coin is the yen, subdivided into 100 parts called sen.

There has lately special stress been laid upon the adoption of 1 gram of fine gold as the basis of a universal coin system; indeed, it has been asserted that the adoption of this weight quantity must bring with it the historical development of coinage. It has also been observed that the amount of each coin, especially of the unit coin, in the course of time separated from the universally valid scale of weight for the mercantile trade, with which it originally united, and that consequently the union of the coin weight with the universal scale of weight only signified the return to the original naturally measured condition.

But, as has already been proven, 1 gram of fine gold lacks in an important degree the ability to establish a basis for a universal coin system, as an accession to the existing systems. However, if, in estimating the inconvenience which must arise from the immediate adoption of 1 gram of fine gold, it is affirmed that the formation of a universal coin system, through a medium suited to that purpose, for instance, 1½ grams fine gold, would in the course of time lead to the definite formation of the coinage upon the basis of 1 gram of fine gold, then it must be remarked that there exists no intrinsic necessary connection between the system of weights and the system of coinage. It is true that coin may be universally formed according to the scale of weight for mercantile exchange; however, this consideration has largely influenced the determining of the metal value of coin, that in trade certain metal quantities have established themselves, for which preferably the exchange of products took place, furnishing a middle point about which commerce is grouped. But that this metal quantity has coincided or must coincide with the universal scale of weight is by no means the case. The product and exchange ratios of the respective territories generally were determined in reference to the quantity of metal by practical wants. The necessity of leading the coin system back to that of the weight system, that is, by the immediate development of the nature of trade upon the metric weight system, as of universal validity, is not the question here. It might not result in the future development of the coinage; this, in our judgment, is more likely to be attained by the adoption of 1½ grams fine gold as the unit coin, and as was also argued in the Paris conference of 1867.

VI.

The necessities of trade demand such an organization of the coinage as shall secure the easiest computation, and the simplest representation of the members. The first will be gained by securing the adoption of the scale explained above, and the second also corresponds to the proposed system.

The coin of the 1½-gram system, has neither in its unit, nor in its compounds, any difficult fractions, as is the case with most of the actual circulating coin. However, because the coin possesses exact measurement is, as has been shown, no essential requisite. Every one can easily retain in his memory the degree of purity of the proposed coin; it is universally intelligible, and not as formerly only known in certain localities. This prerogative, however, is not confined to its purity, but belongs to the entire coin. If the blended weight between gold and copper is chosen as $\frac{16}{16} : \frac{1}{16}$, against which ratio no objections upon technical grounds can be raised, then coin can be issued of 3.2, 4, 8, 16, and if necessary 30 and 32 grams; consequently, pieces of full value are, on account of their simple and more convenient weight, much more easily controlled, while the management of the present circulating coin is, on account of the many decimal fractions which cleave to the whole, more complicated and troublesome.

In small and local trade the assay of the coin is but seldom practiced, and it would be less frequent in international trade, by the adoption of a universal coin system not closely allied to the former bullion form, or independent of the weight of the precious metal; but apart from that, because weighing is practiced in wholesale trade, then assaying cannot be wholly abolished, therefore, the possibility of its practice being easy at any time is a constant advantage, not too small to be estimated. The representation of a simple coin, therefore, is only possible when the gross weight is made the basis, and a decimal alloy is brought into use. As was mentioned before, first the purity should be fixed, and then the alloy chosen, that the coin may have a weight easy of computation. What relation may in this way exist between the precious and the base metals is of no consequence. The blended ratio of $\frac{8}{10} : \frac{1}{10}$ which is referred to as a rule, may be convenient for calculating the fineness and the alloy, but this computation is of very little importance. All that is necessary is the knowledge of the exact gross weight and the exact fineness, but this knowledge is obtainable through the publication of the coin laws, and, further, through instruction and teaching. The issuing of the coin will be advantageous only so far as the two attributes, namely, the gross weight and the purity, are absolutely expressed, and not merely the gross weight and the relation between the precious and base metals declared.

The unit coin of $1\frac{1}{2}$ grams will, if issued, be too small for commerce, and therefore will remain as a coin for computation only; the parts of this unit * consequently cannot be represented by gold, but by metal of less value, the smaller pieces by silver with copper alloy, and the smallest by copper. Where gold is alone the basis, and the unit but a small amount of gold, then silver cannot form an independent coin, but only a representative of the higher valued precious metal, upon which the concrete coin system rests. Because the metal of low value personates only an aliquot part of the precious metal, it may be issued in a more depreciated value than is developed in the computation of the parts which it represents.

If the coin system is based exclusively upon gold, and the unit in consequence of its small precious metal quantity cannot conveniently be represented by gold, then from a strictly theoretical standpoint, there is an expressed contradiction in the coin, because it is issued from another and a depreciated metal, for the unit coin should outwardly express its inherent character. However, the practical necessities of trade which experiences the want of a middle member between the first subdivision and the higher compound, that is, the unit, will urge the coinage of the unit from silver, although of depreciated value, and with the consciousness that it is handling but a mere representative of the unit coin.

It might be judicious to issue silver coin corresponding to the base and the descending scale, that is, the unit of 100 parts, also of 50, 25, 10, and 5 parts, and copper coin of $2\frac{1}{2}$ (or better, 4), 2, 1, $\frac{1}{2}$, $\frac{1}{4}$ parts. The ratio of gold to silver for the first three members of the category should be as is 1:14, and for the last, because the coinage of the small pieces is relatively more expensive, the ratio should be as is 1:13$\frac{1}{4}$.

Further, the first three kinds should contain one-seventh part alloy (that

---

* The Vienna conference came to no determination regarding fractional coin.

is, 875 parts silver, 125 parts copper); of the two latter the alloy should be equal to the fineness (500 parts silver, 500 parts copper); then there would be silver-coin pieces of 24, 12, 6, 4, and 2 grams, gross weight (21, 10½, 5¼, 2, and 1 gram of fine silver), which bear in themselves all the properties of skillfully designed coin.

The silver coin and the copper coin, should be issued by the government alone, and the amount of the silver coin, as well as that of the copper coin, which must be received in payment, and above which no obligation exists for the acceptance of the same, should be legally and accurately fixed. Likewise the amount of silver coin and copper coin for which the public treasury is, on demand from parties, bound to exchange gold, should be prescribed.

VII.

What name the coin in the proposed system should bear is, in the judgment of the writer, of more than ordinary importance. It is certainly desirable to have one and the same signification in all countries. A selection of one from among the different names would, on account of the large number of the existing coin and their denominations, have its difficulties. It might be practical to make choice of a name already sanctioned by general use, and because of the close resemblance of the proposed system to that of federal money, the unit might be called dollar, and the fractional parts cents, and the characteristic new dollar and new cent added for the sake of apposition.

By this apposition, the new system would be distinguished, in terms sufficiently clear and exact, from the old, and a confusion in coinage prevented, especially in those countries which compute by dollars.* †

VIII.

If a universal coin system is adopted upon the basis of 1½ grams fine gold, should there be a silver coin issued whose value is not fixed, but which is accepted only as a trade coin? ‡

The answer to this question must be confined to the following considerations:

If, after the introduction of a universal system of coinage, as an exclusive trade medium, gold has acquired an expansion over a large extent of territory, there will still be, outside of Europe, districts on the borders of civilization in which silver, on account of its external attributes, is very much valued, and universally taken and given in payment. Coined silver, therefore, on account of its convenient form, and also on account of its external appearance, by means of its coinage, will be received by the nations referred to with satisfaction, and perhaps even valued higher than if it appeared in any other form. By the issuing of silver coin, a service will be performed for commerce in the gold as well as in the silver department.

Although the gold standard is in so many districts accepted as of universal value, yet at the same time, in those countries in which, up to

---

* The denomination metric dollar was proposed in the Vienna conference.
† [Since the translation of this work went to press, Dr. W. W. Hubbell, of Washington, D. C., has patented the alloy process, and has had prepared by the Philadelphia Mint, at the instance of Mr. Stephens, Chairman of the Committee on Coinage, Weights, and Measures, fifteen specimens of the *Metric Goloid Dollar*, the first ever coined.—TRANSLATOR.]
‡ This point was not debated in the conference.

the present time, the double standard, or the silver standard alone was legal, there exists many money obligations which are based upon silver loans, the liquidation of which is to take place at a future time, and after the introduction of the gold standard; large amounts of silver coin are still on hand, accumulated partly from abroad, partly from the remnant of former silver coin, and the calling in of which has not yet been fully accomplished.

Now, if it is declared that the silver loans contracted before the introduction of the new system shall be liquidated in gold, according to the existing ratio between gold and silver on pay day, then certainly there could be, from a correct standpoint, no ground upon which to raise objections. For although the creditor does not receive the object agreed upon in the contraction of the debt, viz, silver, yet he receives another, viz, gold, in such amount that thereby he is in condition at once to supply himself with the original object to the original extent by purchase. It is true, the creditor who has accepted gold in back payments, may, possibly, at some time or other, need silver for foreign remittance, but the value of gold in the mean time may have fallen; while at other times he may hold his silver back, and in this way dispense with a double business transaction. But, on the other hand, the debtor (and this is especially to be considered) may thereby be placed in an unfavorable situation, for if at the time of the back payments, gold has fallen in value, he is obliged to pay over a larger amount of gold as equivalent for the silver received than was required at the time of the accepting of the loan. But if there is silver coin on hand, and a possibility thereby of discharging the debt in the same manner it was contracted, that the original quantity of silver as was received is returned in weight, although in another coin form, then the disadvantages resulting to creditor and debtor through the impossibility of another payment than that of gold, will be obviated.

The payment in silver should include the interest as well as the capital, and in order to secure the interest of both parties it should be stipulated that the payment in silver take peace if the same is demanded by one party only, be it the creditor or the debtor. It is to be understood that the precise stipulations mentioned refer only to simple private loans, in which upon the part of the creditor, as of the debtor, there are present one or more persons legally empowered and obligated to sign the bond. State debts and those of railroads, banks, or other public institutions, especially those loans contracted through a challenge for subscriptions, and whose bonds purport a conveyance, are not included in the arrangement referred to above; for the relief aimed at is for the benefit of private and not of public business transactions. The latter must use the legal pay medium, which is gold, because it would require too large an amount of silver to meet the requirements of trade.

The creditor who received silver, for which he has no necessity, will sell it, thereby effecting a circulation of this kind of coin which will serve the purposes of trade or for the payment of debts. There is no basis upon which to rest a legal prohibition to the use of silver coin, not only for the payment of those loans contracted before the introduction of the gold standard, but also for general local payments. Besides, it is self-evident, that the acceptance of the silver coin, as well as the fixing of the value at which it is taken, is left entirely to the arrangement of the parties concerned; but in default of an expressed agreement, the stock exchange determines the proportion. It must, however, be here explicitly remarked, that silver coin has no fixed value. It is not received at the public treasury, nor used by the government in payments, and is only issued for the benefit of private persons. Where the coin system is based upon gold, the silver coin is different from the gold coin, yet the gold coin based on a silver standard, is reduced to a trade coin. Under such a supposition it is scarcely possible to use silver for other than the precise purposes mentioned, viz, for consignments to certain foreign territories, and for the liquidation of old debts, (silver debts).

On the other hand, gold, on account of its great intrinsic excellence, would be used with pleasure to effectuate payments both at home and abroad. Under the supposition of a universal coin system, based upon silver, the circulation of gold coin would be promoted, through a small addition to silver coin; while, on the other hand, where gold is the governing pay-medium, an addition in the sense referred to does not appear necessary, though for the purpose of facilitating trade, and on account of its universal character, a tangible and exact metal quantity of full weight must be insisted upon. In order to prevent all possible mistakes, and to be able to distinguish externally the relation of the silver trade-coin, it will be practical to impress upon it both the fineness and the gross weight, in which it differs considerably from the silver subsidiary coin. This coin may be both heavier and larger, because it is not used in the ordinary circulation of the country, but only serves to equalize large amounts. A former proposition fixed the highest subsidiary coin at 21 grams fine silver, and 24 grams gross weight, so the silver trade-coin might contain 24 grams fine silver, and 28 grams gross weight (= about 1 new dollar and 51 new cents by rate of exchange as 1 : 15.80).

The issuing of silver coin would check at once, at least partially, the depreciation in value of silver, which is occasioned by the demonetization of a large amount of this precious metal. But this is of too small importance to advance as an argument for the necessity of a double standard. The above discussion only shows the advantages to trade in the use of both metals, and not any necessity for a fixed ratio of one to the other.

IX.

Regarding the introduction of the $1\frac{1}{2}$ gram system, the government should first of all coin sufficient gold for their own purposes as well as for the use of private persons, who might require the same for international as well as for transient trade, and which coin should be exchangeable at the public treasuries for the legal coin of the country, according to the published ratio. The international coin will at all times coincide either with the double or with the single standard, according to the systems of the various countries; with the latter the material out of which the legal pay-medium is coined will be like that of the common coin, either gold or silver. In both these cases the use of the common coin may be only recommended, but according to our opinion there dare exist no hinderance to conform the international coin to the legal pay-medium in regard to all the attributes of the same, and to consider them as members of the national money system under consideration. Because the circulation of the common coin, comes under the same form as that of the local coin, the system of international money has a better guarantee for its continuance, especially for a deeper and more general expansion.

In those districts where silver furnishes the material for the legal coin of the country, the international coin is trade money, because the double standard is inadmissible. In most cases, then, it will coincide with the existing trade-coin of the same precious metal, and, because the international coin seldom stands in an adaptable relation to the national trade-coin, the coexistence of the two for purposes of trade may appear unprofitable or superfluous, and it might be best to dispense with the latter and adopt in its place the international gold coin.

The single standard being established, then the so called trade-coin is issued only for the benefit of private parties; the acceptance as well as the circulating value is committed to the agreement of the parties; but in default thereof, the stock exchange determines the latter, while, after the expiration of a certain time, the government receives this coin in payment at a value different from that originally fixed. The traveler holding international coin, and happening to be in a district where the mentioned condition of things exists, as well as the creditors residing there who are paid from abroad in international money, have consequently coin of depreciated value on hand, whose circulation is limited.

But the government might aid in stimulating the circulation of international money, by issuing the same on its own account, and using it in irregular payments; that is, in such payments in which it appears only as a private party, or by issuing it through the Treasury to persons demanding it, establishing for it a certain value for which it might be exchanged for the legal money of the country.

Furthermore, for the above purpose, rules might be established, so that in purely commercial transactions, that is, transactions between tradespeople, in order to stimulate business, and not for immediate accumulation, or not above a certain amount, the acceptance and the ratio of exchange be left to the choice of the parties concerned; otherwise the acceptance to be made according to the daily quotations. For the benefit of travelers it would, perhaps, be advisable to legally announce that the privilege is granted to strangers of paying their hotel bills in international coin, according to its assessed value, and on the other hand, that the host be obligated to accept such payment without reference to the amount of the bill.

After the introduction of the international coin, business transactions may still, as formerly, be arranged and consummated in the existing local coin; but it would serve to advance the circulation of the international coin, if the civil governments of the states would decide that when it is not by the contracting parties clearly set forth in the agreement, then only the international coin shall be valid as currency, and that in case of a dispute, the decision of the court shall be in favor of international money.

It would certainly conduce to the interests of trade, if the stamp impressed upon the international gold coin included, besides the gross weight and the fineness, the equivalent of the local coin; on the other hand, however, there exists the fear that such an imprint would be a constant reminder of the old local money, and act unfavorably on the circulation of the new; besides, a recoinage would add an additional expense to the founding of a universal coin system.

When once the international coin comes in close contact with the trade-life of the several countries, and groups of countries, then the effort should be to reduce the international money to national money, by gradually calling in the local coin of the country, and allowing the coin of the universal system to take its place. This, at first, might be done formally, viz, by adjusting the value, so that from a certain period, books and calculations might everywhere be conducted in accordance with the new standard.

Now, in order to replenish the numerous veins of trade in the interior of each country, with the coin of the new system, it might be practical to designate by degrees certain departments of public business in which, after a stipulated period, payments must be exclusively made in the new coin. Such departments might first be the post and the telegraph, and later the railroads. Above all, care must be taken that the citizens be provided with the means to carry out these regulations, by having ready to hand at the specified time a sufficient amount of the coined metal from the mint. In order that small, as well as large amounts, be obtainable in the departments of business just mentioned, it will be necessary not only to diligently prosecute the issuing of gold, but to undertake as well the coining of silver and copper. The coined amounts pass into the hands of those who need them for payments in the above mentioned departments, either through disbursements or exchange. As regards the railroads, on account of the large sums there exchanged, it might be possible to arrange in the beginning, that all payments above a certain amount, whether they relate to the public or to the road corporations, be exclusively executed in the new coin. In proportion as the coinage advances, the legal enactments, that payments be performed only with coin of the new system, will extend to the other public business. In this way, and besides, by issuing gold coin for the benefit of private parties, it will be possible to introduce the new coin into the arteries of trade, and at last to fix a period in which all payments in general, resulting from transactions subsequent to this period, can only be liquidated in the new coin, and the payment of former obligations at the public treasury must be by weight, and the officially established price. The old coin which finds its way to the public treasury is recoined, and only the metal diminution which it has suffered during its circulation is subtracted by the treasury, so that the expense of the new coining is partly reduced.

Where the mint is not able to furnish sufficient coin until after a lapse of time more or less, and the financial condition of the country permitting, then the old coin which has found its way to the public treasury in the manner of payments, may be from this time definitely suppressed, and in its stead, state bonds may be issued which correspond to the new standard, and which shall be annulled so soon as a corresponding stock of coin is issued. By this means, the old stock of coin, yet in circulation with the new, will be more speedily lessened, and the desired purpose sooner attained. Because by such a process the circulating medium is only increased so far as the new coin shows an excess in the balance against the old, but which in relation to the already circulating amount, and because the emitted certificates have not to remain for an unlimited time in circulation, therefore, in such a mode of proceeding, there can be no great risk.

In order to prevent all abuse, or at least to render the same difficult, and to establish a moral pressure upon the government for the fulfillment of its obligations, namely, the actual issue of the new coin, the state bonds should bear upon their face the exact date of their redemption. Nevertheless, if the finances are not in good condition, there is foundation for apprehension, that by such proceeding the floating debt may be converted into a funded debt, especially if much paper money is already in circulation, and that, in consequence, an aversion to paper currency will be engendered in the public mind; therefore, it is more judicious, especially if the coinage progresses slowly, to cautiously preserve the credit of the state through this transition period, while the demands upon it are extraordinary, instead of resorting to the measures above spoken of.

In those countries where trade is not based upon a metallic currency, but where state paper and bank notes are the ruling circulating medium, the mode of introducing the $1\frac{1}{2}$ gram system is essentially the same. It is true, owing to the anomalous money condition, the international coin is not able in the same degree to take fast foothold, as in other countries, but the converting of the international money into local money will first furnish to the new system a solid basis and proper life power. In such cases the regulating of the ratio of value can be accomplished in connection with the introduction of the new system. But first of all, only the amount of the individual category of the existing state certificates and notes in circulation is to be superseded by the new standard, to which, as has already been stated, a relatively small addition may be given. However, later, the government and the banks which issue notes, may, by concerted action, and by loans and purchase, introduce gold into trade.

In those states where at present only paper money circulates, but where formerly the silver standard legally and actually existed, and because of the unfavorable contingencies for the furnishing of gold, which the suggested reform in money affairs readily brings with it, there is not the least necessity to first restore the money circulation to a silver basis, and subsequently to introduce the gold standard in the form of the $1\frac{1}{2}$ gram system. On the contrary, the cost of a twofold change, and the inconveniences and disturbances to trade, necessarily combined therewith, are so important that it appears more judicious yet for a time to bear the evils which attend the anomalous money condition, and which, besides, have generally long existed, than to effect but a temporary relief. If favorable junctures arise, they should be taken advantage of without delay, and the introduction of the gold standard be at once begun. The sacrifice is not greater, but the results are most favorable for the immediate attainment of a regularly defined money system. Evidently the governments of such countries must closely observe the proportionate appearances of trade, in order to take advantage of the propitious time, and also display sufficient steadiness to withstand all efforts which proceed from the circles of industry and speculation, which, for the attainment of selfish aims, would still further protract the irregular conditions of trade.

If circumstances occur to cause a rise in the value of gold, then the new gold coin, especially where it circulates with the silver coin, the standard of the country, cannot be retained in circulation. In such cases, as was mentioned before, payments in the various circles of public trade, being restricted to the new coin, prove a preventive against a too large outflow of gold. To realize these payments, amounts, at least really necessary, are retained in every country, and by means of this arrangement the efforts to secure a gain by the sale of gold are paralyzed.

To prevent the inconveniences mentioned, it might be well, in the valuation of the new coin over against the coin of the various systems, without detriment to the connection, to place a higher estimate upon the former, than, according to the precise calculations, belongs to it. This could be in the form of an imposition of the seigniorage, and the result effected would be to retain the gold in the respective districts. This effect would naturally be permanent, if the definite appearance of the universal coin system is the immediate result, and then first a rise in the value of gold would ensue. For although the rise in value is characteristic of the coin, there is always, at least up to a certain point, a corresponding rise in the price of merchandise, so that a small quantity of gold will purchase the same amount of products.*

---

* The form of its introduction was not closely discussed in the conference.

X.

It is not in our opinion an absolute necessity to realize the idea of a universal coin system, through a coin convention of the several states. The idea of a national, relatively, a universal coin union, as explained above, should first be presented to the various districts throughout all, or, at least, the most prominent business countries. Those who are interested in the accomplishment of this project should unite and discuss the questions germain thereto in a common council, and through a chosen central standard organ, bring to the knowledge of the governments which are prepared to join them in official intercourse, the resolutions adopted. The idea, through its inherent power, and its intrinsic value, will beat a path for itself; and the examination of the subject represented will convince the governments that while on the one hand, the question is one which corresponds to the demands of modern trade in the highest degree, on the other, it can be prosecuted without exposing the industrial organism to abrupt and penetrating disturbances.

Many beneficent institutions, and measures of a universal character, have, in modern times, been projected through the activity of confederations, and carried to completion by the governments without any mutual and positive obligations having been entered into between them for their perfection. The governments, indeed, can, what alone is advantageous in the case, exercise a care over the various matters referred to in points of discussion, and with regard to the measures for carrying out the object, place themselves one with the other, in proper understanding, but the form of a strict compact appears non-essential to the attainment of the end contended for. If the most prominent industrial and commercial countries take the initiative in the introduction of a universal coin system, then the force of circumstances, which is stongest felt in the departments of business, and the natural interest in the advancement of their own material welfare, will necessitate the remaining states to follow the path opened up by the principal countries.

XI.

The coin of the international, relatively of the universal system, should contain, besides the denomination and the designation of value, (the latter positive), in its imprint such peculiarities as shall designate the country by whose government it was issued. But in whatever territory this coin is issued, its circulation in all countries belonging to the international coin league, will be complete and unhindered.

In order strictly to maintain the regulations of coinage, it will be necessary to call in such coin, which, through long circulation, has suffered a loss of precious metal exceeding the legally admitted minimum of its imprint, and to replace the same with pieces of full value, because the money exchange is sensitive, and the reckonings of the same, immediate and strict.

It is in accordance with the nature of the business, that every government which issues coin, and, which in consequence of its circulation, loses any considerable part of its value, should call in and recoin the same, because the Administration is under obligations to exercise care over the proper condition of its coin. It may easily happen, however, that coin of depreciated value, may remain a long time in circulation, and therefore, the regulations of coinage be interrupted, because this coin does not reach the treasury of the country from which it was issued. This inconvenience will be obviated, if the governments control the issued coin pieces without distinction as to their origin, either forcing those which are depreciated out of circulation, and returning them to the governments which issued them, or by an especial agreement entered into among the states concerned, have them recoined at the expense of the latter, and impressed with their own peculiar coin stamp. The latter regulation is necessary, because, otherwise the controlling government, by retaining worn-out coin in order to superintend its recoinage, may very easily, in this way, increase the power of its own treasury.

The depreciated pieces should be received at the public treasury without any reduction of their value, and recoined, because the creation, and therefore the careful preservation of the universal circulating instrument is properly a real, and in its first features, a public matter. It is true, it is the citizens, especially, who by use have worn the coin, but the share in this loss can never be determined. Besides, in the standard laws there exists a provision that coin shall be taken at its full value without reference to the depreciation it may have sustained. So long as the international gold coin is only trade coin, its quality, like that of merchandise, is in the small pieces subject to a diminution in value, yet in this case the acceptance of the same at their full value might be accomplished, by reflecting that the government has as much interest in the existence and the circulation of such coin, on account of its extraordinary advantage to trade, as it has in the coinage of the legal local coin in general.

If coin is lessened in its value through any other means than protracted circulation, then, in that event, by its acceptance at the public treasury, it suffers a reduction, for only those expenses which are occasioned by the ordinary use of the coin, and not those occurring through premeditated, or careless damage, are provided for out of the state treasury; besides, there exists no obligation on the part of private individuals to accept such coin, therefore, those who receive it must bear the loss.

Silver and copper coin, when called fractional currency, are only issued for the benefit of the state, and it has already been remarked, that the amount of this fractional coin, which is exchangeable at the public treasury for gold coin of full value, should be legally fixed. The obligation for the redemption is based upon the nature of the fractional coin, which is, indeed, properly only the sign of a practically unrepresented part of the principal coin, (current base coin), a bill of exchange for the latter. The exchange, which altogether can be equalized by a current coin beginning from the smallest sum, should be strictly stated. But practical considerations are opposed to this, because the necessities of trade demand a corresponding amount of fractional coin to be held in circulation, therefore, the exchange of a somewhat higher amount should be allowed. Besides, the current coin is most necessary to those who accumulate large amounts of fractional coin. The duty of each government to redeem, naturally, only extends to its own issue of fractional currency.

MONEY REFORM,

BY

AUG. EGGERS.

WITH ONE COLORED COIN MAP OF THE WORLD, AND THREE OTHER LITHOGRAPHIC CHARTS.

[Translated from the German by Mrs. C. P. Culver.]

PREFACE.

Man must work in harmony with the Divine will.

A universal coin, based upon a pure unadulterated gold standard, is the noble object referred to in the above apothegm. May the following arguments promote the understanding of the same, and do their part to the accomplishment of the German Money Reform.

A. E.

BREMEN, November 1, 1872.

99

I.

INTRODUCTORY.

Through a communication of the 5th of November, 1871, the plan of a law concerning the issuing of imperial gold coin was laid before the Imperial Diet, and after a mere debate, in full session from the 11th to the 25th of November, and without the deliberation of a committee upon the nature of its contents, it was accepted, and on the 4th of December established as a law.

Perhaps there never was an act of such immeasurable importance so speedily consummated, by an august body. To introduce a new coin system which affects 40,000,000 of people under the German Empire, dwelling apart in various cities, boroughs, villages, and hamlets, is a work which, according to one financial authority, requires from 8 to 10, and to another from 20 to 30 years.

Many laws are changed by the imperial power by the mere stroke of a pen, without producing material disadvantages. But the consequences of a mistake in the choice of a new coin regulation, extends through a generation. After Germany has fully consummated her gigantic labor, it cannot be reconsidered for from 50 to 100 years. Questions in domestic economy are discussed at length by the learned, before they are actually determined upon. On the 5th of November, the practical business men first saw themselves, through the introduced preliminaries, invited to an earnest consideration of the coin question. They expected that the plan of a committee, or at least a brief report, would be submitted, by which means, during the winter, the various opinions could be presented for deliberation. Neither the one nor the other occurred.

As regards the special part I took in the coin question, touching the propositions presented, my first treatise bears date 21st of March, 1871. The Weser Gazette published the first part of my second on the 12th of April, and refused, in a singular manner, to accept the remainder. It is true, I was allowed space for more extensive treatises in the Bremen Trade Journal, but not one word of my labors in the Conference has by this party been given a place. Mr. Camphausen explained to me in an interview about the 10th of October, that it was useless to develop my opinions; that he had a plan which he considered available to the purpose. The chambers of commerce, generally, asked for the mark of 100 pfennigen; Mr. Mosle acknowledged that the Bremen chamber did, because Mr. Delbrück demanded it. Base servants, who withhold the truth from their masters! It is a false idea that the chambers of commerce represent the entire commercial interest. Upon the authority of these, and some few men, who the high chancellor, the confederate council, and the Imperial Diet believed understood the question of coinage, and with actual suppression, or a premeditated plan to ignore opinions existing outside of the prescribed circle, the coin law of the 4th of December was enacted. The opinion which appeared in a communication in September of that same year, by Peiser of Berlin, and in which he opposes the mark of 100 pfennigen, is to a certain degree correct—"the provisional adoption of the coin system of the mark upon the part of the Imperial Diet, looks to the introduction of the new gold coin, for whose speedy creation the most urgent necessity existed."

101

I desire nothing more than, that an official reconsideration of the coin laws, and a careful examination of my propositions, should take place.

There have been added to the foregoing formal-arguments, observations and practical knowledge which are more decisive than all theoretical presumptions, for on July 1 we had the opportunity of introducing the mark into Bremen.

An experienced and wise statesman examines every new step taken forward in an important matter, that he may be certain he is on the right road. In Bremen they have presented the following objections to the mark :

1. That a coin of the size of a centime or pfennig, as a hundredth, is not practical. A centime is seldom used. For example, if 1 loaf costs 3 centimes, 2 loaves costs 6 centimes, &c., then it is first necessary to change 3 sou into centimes, and all coffers and pockets would overflow with centime pieces. For that reason 2 loaves of corresponding size are sold for 5 centimes ; but thereby it is necessary for the customer to purchase *two*, for in the purchase of a single loaf ½ centime is lost. Almost everywhere in France, calculations are made by the sou of 5 centimes as a unit, whilst the copper centime is used scarcely anywhere. It is very singular that we say 5 centime and mean 1 sou. The division of 100 centimes has, in France, for a long time, been considered a mistake ; and in the Universal Coin Conference of 1867, the French Government recommended the 5-franc thaler of 100 sou as a common reckoning unit, instead of the franc.

As with the centime, so it is with our pfennig. The movement (originating in favor of the husbandry), which divided the mark into 100 pfennigen, dates from the time when the French coin regulation adopted the division of the franc into 100 centimes, a complete coin regulation.

For Germany, a centesimal coin of the size of 1 cent, which, in case of necessity, can be divided into halves and quarters, is proper enough. A pfennig, of which, instead of 4 or 6, it requires 5 to make a half groschen, is almost useless. The retail dealers speak unanimously, "We do not reckon by pfennigen," while formerly the half groat (something less than ¼ groschen), circulated largely. The wholesale dealers recommend that calculations be made by 5 pfennigen, a rule, however, which is not much followed ; consequently, book and cash accounts present cumbersome entries and irregularities, which would be otherwise, if the calculating unit were formed of 100 cents. It is evident that the mark of 100 pfennigen has proved itself impracticable in Bremen.

2. If, as was the case in Bremen, a coin regulation is established, to legally take effect upon a certain day, then the necessary coin should be ready. But there was a deficiency, and there is still, at this time (the latter part of October), a deficiency in half groschens and pfennigen. The first is a convenient coin for many purposes where pfennig pieces are not practical. But there being a deficiency of half groschens, a groschen must be paid out, being the smallest silver coin at hand. The drier = 2½ pfennigen, while, to be sure, it is legal in Bremen, yet it does not belong to the mark system, and on account of its fractions, occasions manifold disputes between retailers and small purchasers. It is calculated that at least 2,000,000 pfennigen would be necessary to effectively introduce the coin regulation of the mark into Bremen. A retail dealer requires hundreds, and a large employer thousands. At the rate of 2,000,000, then Germany would need nearly 600,000,000 pfennigen, the furnishing of which, certainly, as well as the issuing of 2-pfennig pieces, and the existing copper coin, must be taken into account. So that by doubling the capacity of the mint, it would require at least one year to prepare

the requisite amount of coin for the introduction of the mark. A precipitate introduction, which, in spite of expostulation, took place in Bremen, dare not be repeated, for example, in South Germany. At first trade will desire them, and afterward not be able to use them, just as it was with the centime in France. Besides, there are persons to whom the existence of the decimal pfennig pieces is inconvenient or disadvantageous, who often, by common consent, will accumulate and then retire them. Between *them* and the division of the groschen into 4-drier pieces a great difference in this respect exists, because, while the latter are truly needful and desirable, the removal of the useless decimal pfennig would, in the opinion of many persons, be a serviceable work.

The fact that after the pfennig has been in circulation for one year, it will be called in as useless, is enough to make the sure retention of the mark of 100 pfennigen impossible. In the eyes of Germany, the imperial power would be disparaged.

3. A large advance in the price of all kinds of food took place in Bremen. The groschen is valued at something above 8⅔ per cent. of what was the former value of 2 groats. The retail dealers immediately took advantage of this, and by requiring 1 groschen for every 2 groats, raised their goods that much more. A rounding off of prices is characteristic of small dealers. Upon the one side, it is not feasible to oppose the retail price; the continual fluctuations are submitted to, for example, in the case of bread, to determine whether a loaf at a certain time shall cost 10 or 11 pfennige, but on the other side, it is as troublesome for the dealer to return 4 or 9 pfennige, as it is for the customer to pay 11 of the same. Bread often falls 10 per cent. in the course of a month, and the price in both cases is 10 pfennige, at one time to the advantage, and at another to the disadvantage, of the buyer.

Trade always endeavors to assimilate itself to the coin system, by seeking the easiest mode of making payments. A variation in prices takes place with the introduction of every new coin system, and this the system brings with it, entirely independent of the excellencies or disadvantages of the same.

But, as yet, there is no effort made in Bremen to assimilate prices; instead of that, the merchants use the opportunity to force their prices even higher than 8⅔ per cent., so that the united advance averages about 15 per cent. Merchandise will be slow to accommodate itself to the system, because its exchange unit diminishes or increases in quantity or quality. Until to-day (the last of October) there has been an antagonism between sellers and buyers, and as yet no agreement has been established.

Those who understand the Bremen coin reform should take the opportunity, at a proper time, to explain how extremely critical, indeed perilous, would be the introduction of the mark of 100 pfennigen into South Germany. In place of the 3-kreuzer pieces, 10 pfennige = 3½ kreuzers are substituted. To the customary letter-postage of 3 kreuzers, the government will add 16⅔ per cent., and, following the example of the government, the retail dealers will raise their prices in a corresponding manner. It will be found that the calling in of the gulden and kreuzer, and the replacing of the same with the mark and decimal pfennig, cannot be as suddenly accomplished as in a single trading city. For a long time, therefore, there will exist in South Germany a suspicious ferment, which cannot be quieted by the explanation that every new coin system brings with it inconveniences and variations in prices. The South Germans will reply: "In the mark of 100 pfennige you have by a majority established the most faulty centesimal coin system that could have been chosen. Apart from its division into hundredths, our gulden of 60 kreuzers of 4

pfennige is much more practical. Our 3-kreuzer piece is nearly equal
to the 4-kreuzer piece of Austria, which = 2 sou = 1 penny = 2 cents."
The official organs of the governing party protest that the new coin system must accurately correspond to the silver groschen, and the laborers
and peasants have not the judgment to understand a new coin regulation.
Remarkably tender solicitude, after introducing your deep and lofty
measure, whose consistency is all on the top! You yourselves would
not submit to the small variation of the Wilhelm's thaler, and yet have
obliged your allies of South Germany, and the inhabitants of Alsace
and Lorraine, to accept an advance of from 16⅔ to 23½ per cent. . And
after all the pain and labor which you have imposed upon us, we find a
new Chinese wall of from 50 to 100 years erected around Germany to
favor the trader and speculator.

All Germany will one day discover that the coin law of 1871, was a
grave mistake, and this discovery will produce, especially in South Germany, important political results.

II.

WHAT ELSE IS ACCOUNTABLE FOR THE NEW COIN-LAW?

He who enters upon the study of a subject through incorrect propositions, wastes his powers. The conscientious inquirer, if confronted by
opposing arguments, carefully reflects and examines his own anew.
This can be said of but the fewest authors upon the subject of coinage.
The incorrect propositions in reference to the German coin reform, which
have found expression in the movements and different publications of
the government, consist—

1. *In the idea that the new gold standard must necessarily be based upon
the existing silver standard; that the chosen coin system must stand in a
complete and easy calculating ratio to the former silver standard, and that
a computation of the ratio of obligations must be made in the new standard.*

To this is joined the question, According to which relation of value is
this computation to be made? According to the average for a certain
term of years? According to the relative value at the time of the first
introduction, or establishment of the coin-law? Shall debts be paid
according to the relative value at the time of their contraction, or of their
payment? Shall the computation be a voluntary one, that is, appear a
mere day's quotation? &c.

There should be a reckoning of silver in the gold standard. The two
metals, as is known, fluctuate continually toward each other. Each quotation is arbitrary, and must affect either the creditor or the debtor. The
government, which calls for the exercise of justice toward all, dare not incur
the possibility of the reproach that it would enrich one class of its citizens at the expense of another. There is no Gordian knot which must
be cut with a sword. A parallel standard, effectively introduced, is
adapted to open it. Besides, the establishment of a new gold standard,
upon the existing silver standard, is to be rejected upon other grounds,
as I will endeavor to explain in a subsequent chapter.

As to what concerns the choosing of the coin system, it is desirable,
certainly, that the established coin of the new gold standard stand in
close relation to the existing money conceptions of the groschen, the 3-
kreuzer piece, and the sou. But the necessity of erecting upon the
former silver standard of an easy calculating ratio, a computation of the
existing debt ratio, and an interference with the same, is entirely obviated if the new gold standard is introduced in parallel standard, because

then the silver debts are not to be recalculated, but to be discharged by the payment of silver. The establishment of a coin system after the manner recommended by me, first, for public receipts and disbursements, then for retail, and finally for wholesale trade, makes it easy to secure a new practical unit coin to serve the purposes of a universal coin.

The erroneous propositions which lie at the base of the coin-law consist—

2. *In the idea that a universal coin is for the special benefit of bankers and wholesale dealers, and that the other classes have little or no interest in it.*

The facts are just the contrary. The bankers and wholesale merchants are opposed to a universal coin, because, through long practice, they understand the money systems of the various countries, and use tables and books of reckoning, a vantage-ground which they would lose if the exchange trade were placed upon a par basis, a universal coin saving a computation. The agriculturist, for example, would easily understand the foreign grain-price. The retail and traveling trade would be delivered from the tribute of the money exchanger.

3. *In the supposition that by a universal coin the average value of the circulating coin of Germany would be dependent upon the fineness of the inflowing foreign coin, which does not possess the same guarantee.*

Other countries have hitherto not understood why Germany is under obligation to accept in full the coin which has lost in value by circulation. This difficulty, however, might be easily met by the assurance that with us none but our own coin shall be legal money. Then foreign coin would not be employed in the interior in wholesale trade, and would only circulate among retail and traveling dealers; a universal coin, however, would advance it, and produce a gain of a hundred-fold. The same gain would accrue to the retail and traveling trade, by the bank-notes of foreign issue, which otherwise can have no extensive circulation, as they have not the same protection as is accorded to the domestic paper money. The same circumstances would attend the foreign fractional coin.

All these objections are bagatelle against the advantages of a universal coin agreement, and which outweigh the disadvantages a thousand-fold. The advantage to the industries, which, through a universal coin, would accrue to Germany, would be worth from 40,000,000 to 60,000,000 thalers yearly, representing a capital of from 800,000,000 to 1,200,000,000 thalers, to which the insignificant cost of 100,000 thalers, for recoining the mark, is not to be compared.

Another mistake is—

4. *That coin conventions are necessary for the establishment of a universal coin.*

Because, such conventions stipulate certain mutual obligations, which can only be annulled after undoubtedly known violations of the same, therefore they are nothing less than a guarantee against inaccurate coin of foreign states; but the legal, universally valid measure of value, in the coin, is better secured through the well-understood interests of a government, than through conventions. Over this, each citizen, for whose benefit they are issued, watches. A mutual uninterrupted control, which exists already, is satisfactory.

The erroneous suppositions, with regard to the coin reform, consist—

5. *In presuming that a common measure of value is of no importance to the exchange trade between two countries; that the course of exchange, from various causes, must continually fluctuate, and that the equalization of the balance of trade can be effected through easily calculated metal remittances.*

The answer to that is this: that there is an essential difference, whether the exchange trade rest upon a par-basis, which every one understands, or whether it is established upon an unequal ratio of value, known only to the exchanger and wholesale merchant. In the London Exchange list there are quotations represented from 37 places, 15 of which are called chief places (small places like Bremen are not specified). Multiply the latter number by itself, and you have in these various chief places 225 quotations. It is true, many of these quotations are of no practical significance, there being no exchange which can show as large a quotation list as London. At all events, the circulation of bills is a complicated business, which is simpler between Paris and Brussels, London and Edinburgh, New York and San Francisco, because they have the same measure of value, and because the variation is represented by but a small balance, for or against, of $\frac{1}{8}$, $\frac{1}{4}$ per cent., &c. Each of the chief factors of computation is of like value, and in this way variations in quotations of other persons are easily understood and calculated.

The present diversity of coin systems forms an enigma, whose solution is in the hands of the exchanger and wholesale merchant, by means of which their wealth is much more rapidly increased, at the expense of other people, than would be possible without it. The telegraph net-work tends to centralize the business world. The gulf between poor and rich in favor of the exchange princes is greater from year to year. The large money powers absorb the small, which formerly had an independent existence, and the large exchanges draw the business of the small to themselves. The summit of the exchange is a new dominion which threatens to overwhelm and devour everything. A yearly income of 1,000,000 thalers at 5 per cent. compound interest, amounts in 50 years to upwards of 200,000,000 thalers, but the same in 100 years is upwards of 2,500,-000,000 thalers; 1,000,000 thalers is only $\frac{1}{10}$ per cent. of 1,000,000,000 thalers, the amount of the yearly exchange of Germany. One per cent. of this sum, which is the amount flowing yearly into the pockets of these privileged persons, on account of the various coins used in international trade, will at compound interest in 100 years amount to upwards of 25,000,000,000 thalers.

The entire wealth of Germany is estimated at but little more than double the latter sum. To the sum of 25,000,000,000 thalers, the profit is yet to be added which the broker realizes from the actual international securities especially, because the various coins are not understood by other people. Thus, from year to year, there is an imperceptible impoverishing of other classes, and finally, a social revolution must ensue. In the interests of the existing governments, and as a discretionary social regulation, there is an obligation to meet the evil as far as possible, by timely reform of the present arrangements. A universal coin is one of the means thereto.

6. *It is feared that the easy ebb and flow of precious metal, induced by a universal coin, will cause frequent disturbance to the metal basis of the Prussian bank-notes ; and it is believed that there is no right to resign the privilege of a note emission with one-third remittance in the interest of the state.*

The Prussian bank is a business company of the Prussian state, with bank stockholders. The two hundred principal stockholders choose a central committee, and this committee choose three deputies and three representatives. In 1871, the deputies were the bankers, Messrs. E. Conrad, Mendelssohn-Bartholdy, and Gelpke ; and the representatives were Warschauer, Plant, and Zwicker. These constitute the board of managers of the principal bank, with the exception of the place of president; the head of the bank is obliged, in his judgment, to obey the central committee. The deputies exercise uninterrupted control, as well in generals as in particulars, over the management of the bank. They are privileged to be present at all conferences of the board of managers of the principal bank. They present arguments and resolutions, but do not vote. They can at any time call an extra convention of the board of managers of the chief bank.

Notwithstanding all the officials appointed by the government, and the principal stockholders through their deputies are not allowed to assist in governing and in passing resolutions, but only in directing and advising, yet in the bank the latter form a decided element; for (a) they have through their bank stock a material interest in the dividend; (b) they possess paper value whose price, through the rise and fall of bank discounts, through the circulation of bank notes, and other bank operations is influential; and (c) they have a greater experience and knowledge in the routine money matters than the directors.

Such in fact is the manner in which the principal stockholders, the central committee, the deputies and their assistants, manage the Prussian bank, and in whom the influence of the bank upon the exchange and the money affairs of almost all Germany center. The Prussian Government draws from the bank a dividend of only 1,250,000, to 1,750,000 thalers, which it is able to dispense with or produce in some other way. On the other hand its financial operations are interwoven with those of a few money princes and exchange monopolists. The Prussian minister of finance, and the imperial chancellor, would be more independent if the business of the company were abolished, and by free competition could maintain themselves better under the money power.

The privilege of the bank to regulate the money market, through expanding and contracting the note circulation, through increasing and diminishing the discounts, prevents the equilibrium which trade would bring with it in free exchange of production and consumption, and, in fact, according to the nature of the thing, only the stockholders of the bank are benefited; and if in time of peace the Prussian bank is not placed upon a pure metal basis, that is, for every 10-thaler bank-note issued has 10 thalers of precious metal in her vaults, she is not prepared for war. If at the outbreak of war she has a large amount of unsecured notes in circulation, the dread is easily disseminated, that in the event of defeat she must suspend payment. Ready money disappears from trade, and step by step she goes with increasing note circulation downwards to forced circulation, and all its fearful financial domestic and social disorders and ruin. To prevent this, there is but one means which secures full provision for time of peace and time of war.

If for the purpose of averting the first shock of a crisis it is necessary to grant an exception to this rule, a certain amount of bank-notes or treasury loans upon treasury bonds might be held ready, and issued by special permission, in order to relieve the money market for the first four to six weeks, but which should be called in through an interest-bearing loan, in order to re-establish a pure metal basis. In England the bank act is suspended for that same purpose. If subsequently the government again restores the pure metal basis, she will purchase her war necessities cheaper, and give to her army and officers what belongs to them, viz, full money value instead of money whose value is affected at the will of the government, or which is arbitrarily subject to a discount.

The existing privilege of an almost unlimited note issue is unfortunate for Prussia's financial manager and the high chancellor, and it conceals within itself great disadvantages to domestic industries in peace and great disasters in war. If completely secured, we need fear no outflow of our precious metals. An increased discount protects us from an excessive outflow. If money is tight abroad, and the prices of goods and merchandise are proportionately low, then by cheap purchases we can reimburse ourselves from two to three fold for the interest lost in ordinary times upon a large metal treasure.

The false idea unfortunately exists, that, as the high chancellor must maintain for the Prussian bank the right of issue, that is one reason why a universal coin upon a variable metal basis is not desirable.

It is further incorrectly maintained:

7. *That if Germany calls in her inconvenient silver coin, the high price of gold abroad will prevent the gold coin from flowing out.*

But Germany has, properly speaking, a bank-note standard. Her currency consists of gold coin, silver thalers, and paper money. If gold abroad is above $15\frac{1}{2}$, then under favorable circumstances the most profitable results accrue; that is, gold will flow out.

On the other hand, a favorable balance of trade will bring to us no gold if it is not under $15\frac{1}{2}$. The government, after deliberation, will not buy until a certain price is legally established, because she can easily perceive that the reproach might be made that her brokers manipulate the coin reform for their own purposes of speculation.

III.

A UNIVERSAL COIN.

I have already proven that the brokers, banks of issue, and wholesale merchants are opposed to a universal coin; that the mark in their hands will be a new implement of gain, and that its actual introduction threatens to impoverish the other classes. However, the ethical side of the question is far more important than the material. The 20 mark piece = 24.69 francs = 19s. 7d. = 476.4 cents. The foreigner who has no scale by which to translate our mark into his own money value, will not understand us. A universal coin is part of a universal language. It appeals to a sense common to all people, and is therefore a medium of peace, to employ which Germany is now in immediate position—I might say in duty bound, independent of the fact that it would be a work of wise political forethought.

The bankers belonging to the Liberal party call the mark a German national coin, and assert that the Germans must have a special coin regulation. However, it might rather be called a Jewish national coin, because an exclusiveness in coinage is of special advantage to the Jews, as a class, and would accord with their other exclusiveness. I esteem the Jews very highly in many respects, but I wish Germany to remain true to her German spirit. She has no inducement to place her light under a bushel.

IV.

THE WILHELM'S THALER.

The object of a universal coin is to get clear of roundabout calculations and exchanges. For instance, the division of one gold gulden=

Chart II.   THE CHIEF COINS OF

5 Wilhelms-Thaler.	= 7 Thaler (exactly)	= 12¼ S. G. Guld. (exactly)	= 25
50 Cents.	= 21 Sgr. (exactly)	= 1¼ S. G. Guld.	= 2½
25 Cents.	= 10½ Sgr. (exactly)		= 1¼
20 Cents.	= 8 Sgr.	= 30 S. G. Kreuz.	= 1
10 Cents.	= 4 "	= 15 " " "	= 10
2½ Cents.	= 1 "		
2 Cents.	= ⅝ " (nearly)	= 3 " " "	= 2
1 Cent.	= ⁵⁄₁₂ " (nearly)	= 1½ " " "	= 1

ɔɜ	= 10 Austr. Guld.	= 1£ Sterling.	= 5 Dollars.
	= 1 " "	= 2 Shillings	= 50 Cents.
	= ½ " "	= 1 "	= 25 "
	= 40 " Kreuz.	= 10 Pence	= 20 "
	= 20 " "	= 5 "	= 10 "
	= 5 " "		
	= 4 " "	= 1 "	= 2 "
	= 2 " "	= ½ Penny	= 1 "

$2\frac{1}{2}$ francs, into 100 kreuzers, is either beyond comprehension or purposely ignored. Such a kreuzer would $= 2\frac{1}{2}$ centimes, 1 centime would be equal to $\frac{4}{10}$ kreuzer. Now translate $6\frac{1}{4}$ or 23 kreuzers into centimes; most persons would have brain-splitting calculations.

In order to assimilate with France, Germany must accept the franc of 100 centimes. I have already explained, that because the centime is so small it is defective for calculation, which even the French Government herself has acknowledged as not to be recommended.

Again, Germany can agree no better with England than with France, as her penny is not decimal.

Germany can only, in any reasonable manner, harmonize with the United States, because her unit coin equals $1\frac{1}{2}$ grams.

As the standard measure of the unit coin is not a pound of gold, but a fixed weight of precious metal, and as coin does not circulate in pounds, but in separate pieces, therefore the fineness of every piece must contain a round weight in grams, and not consist of unretainable and endlessly progressive decimals. Besides, a means of improvement or culture exists in a weight retainable in the memory, in that it facilitates the explanation of the idea of money. The franc and sovereign form fractional weights, and for this reason in the Paris Coin Conference of 1867, a motion was presented by the United States to dispense with the 25-franc piece. The dollar of the United States contains but $\frac{1}{10}$ per cent. more than $1\frac{1}{2}$ grams fine gold, and very closely corresponds to a practical basis for an international coin. This small plus quantity is, however, favorable for Germany's choice of $1\frac{1}{2}$ grams, because in it lies an extra guarantee for the entrance of coin of full weight. Besides, the choice of $1\frac{1}{2}$ grams would win for Germany a place in complete harmony, for all practical purposes, with the United States, an advantage which would make it necessary for England to recoin her sovereigns for her foreign trade $2\frac{3}{4}$ per cent. higher, at first only to be taken at the value of each day's quotation, but subsequently, by forced circulation. Four shillings of the new sovereign of 100 half pennies would exactly equal our $1\frac{1}{2}$-grame thaler of 100 cents.

The "dollar" originated in the specie thaler of the old German Empire, and which wandered from Germany into the wide world, and the scale of whose value I proposed, after the re-establishment of the Empire, that it might be again introduced under the name of Wilhelm's thaler.

The manner of computation, according to population, is as follows:

In sovereigns	35,000,000
In francs	77,000,000
Gold dollar, entirely or partly	80,000,000
Silver dollar	521,000,000

Last year Japan introduced the gold dollar of $1\frac{1}{2}$ grams. In the Chinese Empire, including Mongolia, &c., 1,000 Mexican dollars of full weight are calculated at 717 taels. A small coin-chart of the world accompanies this work, which represents to us in general outlines the four most important coin departments.

I present the following specification. The estimate of the number of inhabitants, with the exception of the Chinese Empire, is taken from the table by von Hübner; but the prevailing money systems are prepared from other sources, so far as incomplete materials previously arranged could assist me:

The sovereign of 20 shillings, of 12 pence.

Great Britain and Ireland	31,817,108
Bermuda Isle	11,796
Saint Helena, Ascension, Seichellen, Socotra, Perim	25,000
Cape of Good Hope	566,158
Natal and Bosuts land	193,103
Mauritius	340,664
Australia; New South Wales	503,900
Queensland	96,172
Victoria	647,589
South Australia	178,500
Tasmania	97,368
West Australia	21,065
New Zealand	256,400
	34,754,823

The franc of 100 centimes.

France	36,800,000
Belgium	4,984,451
Switzerland	2,669,095
Italy	24,368,787
Greece	1,457,894
Wallachia	2,400,921
Moldau	1,463,927
Algiers	2,921,246
Cayenne	24,432
Martinique	139,109
Guadeloupe and dependencies	151,594
	77,381,456

The gold dollar of 100 cents altogether or partly.

United States	38,650,000
Upper and Lower Canada, New Brunswick, New Scotland, Prince Edward Island, Hudson's Bay	3,989,800
Newfoundland	130,000
British Columbia and Vancouver's Island	82,000
Antigua, Barbadoes, Dominica, Grenada, Montserrat, Nevis, Saint Kitts, Saint Lucia, Saint Vincent, Tobago, Barbuda, Virgin, Arguilla, Trinidad	461,487
Jamaica	441,255
Bahama, Turk's Island, Caicos Island	39,900
Saint Pierre and Miquélon	3,799
Liberia	718,500
Sandwich Islands	62,995
Japan	35,000.000
	79,579,736

The silver dollar of 100 cents altogether or partly.

Mexico	9,173,052
Gautemala	1,180,000
St. Salvador	600,000
Honduras	350,000
British Honduras	25,700
Nicaragua, with Greytown and Mosquito	400,000
Costa Rica	135,000
New Granada	2,794,473
Venezuela	1,565,000
Guiana (British)	162,000
Ecuador	1,300,000
Peru	2,500,000
Bolivia	1,987,352
Chili	2,084,945
Argentine Republic	1,852,110
Paraguay	1,337,439
Uruguay	400,000
Falkland Islands	662
Cuba and the neighboring dependent islands	1,369,642

Porto Rico and dependencies.	615,547
St. Domingo	136,500
Hayti	572,000
Spain	16,835,000
Gibraltar, Malta	163,683
Goza, except Heligoland	3,000
	160,683
Morocco	3,000,000
Sierra Leone, Gambia, Gold Coast	199,966
Senegambia and Gabun	803,865
Guinea Coast (Dutch)	120,000
Senegambia (Portugal), St. Thomas Island, Principe	27,000
Angola, Benguela, Mopamades, Ambriz	2,000,000
Zanzibar	800,000
Abyssinia	3,000,000
Nubia and Kordofan	3,100,000
Isle of Bourbon	207,886
Straits settlements (Singapore, &c.)	282,831
Siam and Cochin-China	8,299,000
Philippine and Suluk Archipelago	4,348,456
Presidio and Guinea Island	35,000
Timor and Cambing	850,000
Marquesas Island and New Caledonia	54,000
Society Island, Tahiti	11,000
Hong-Kong and Labuan Islands	128,000
Macao	100,000
China, with Hainan and Formosa	419,000,000
Mantchooria, Mongolia, Thian, Thibet, Corea, Licoukhicou Islands	27,500,000
	521,404,109

In my former writings, prepared for the purpose of solving the German coin question, I have examined the system more in detail. No other system has the proper conciliating and harmonizing power between North and South Germany, and Alsace-Lorraine, as that of the Wilhelm's thaler. The $\frac{1}{10}$ part of the thaler=$2\frac{1}{2}$ cents, is only $\frac{1}{2}$ pfennig more than the silver groschen. The $\frac{1}{50}$ part=2 cents, very nearly $\frac{5}{8}$ silver groschen, and 2 per cent. less than 3 South German kreuzers. That is intelligible to everybody. The equalization of the principal coin of the system is represented upon the accompanying chart, No. 2. The introduction is safe and proportionately easy when the way is opened up. This, as has previously been stated, I have in detail, through these publications, been recommending for a year and a half.

I will take this opportunity to remark that many objections have been made to the gold coin at present issued. The Numismatisch-Spagistische Anzeiger (Numismatic Philological Advertiser), of Hanover, contains several hints worth noticing.

V.

STANDARDS.

The gold standard is preferable to the silver standard, for this reason, viz, the value and density of gold, which, proportionately, is about 1:28, makes it better adapted to money purposes. In order to place herself in immediate exchange operations with the other civilized countries, Germany must introduce the gold standard, the circulating volume of which is about 4,500,000,000 thalers, currency.

As it is not possible to replace at once the silver coin with gold coin, therefore the entering gold standard must for a time mutually circulate with the existing silver standard, which can be done either in *optional standard* (called, also, double standard), or in *parallel standard* (contemporaneous standard).

In order to an understanding in any department of science, it is of special importance to securely fix the terminology of the same, that there may be no misconception of words which designate certain things. This is the case now, for example, with the *double standard*, which is sometimes understood by persons to mean optional standard, and then again parallel standard; two terms which really differ from each other, as is symbolically shown by the lithographic chart No. III.

1. The pure *silver standard* is a standard in which a certain weight of silver, in a coined or an uncoined condition, forms the calculating unit. A pure silver standard exists, for example, in Hamburg in the banco-mark, of which 59⅓ are produced from 1 pound of silver. A characteristic feature of a pure silver standard is expressed in the connection of the same with the whole volume of silver of every country; that its increase is not dependent upon the pleasure of a privileged power, but that every private person, as in Hamburg, can deposit silver in the bank, or send it to the mint to be coined.

2. The pure *gold standard* is a standard in which a certain weight of gold forms the calculating unit. To this standard silver only serves as fractional currency; and in order to prevent its being melted down, it is coined with just so much silver as will secure to it a depreciated value in the coin system.

3. The *parallel standard* (a standard which is alongside, in addition to, or contemporaneous with another standard).—For this term, parallel standard, and its definitions, we are indebted to Dr. Grote. It is a standard established in a country adjoining, by the side of, or contemporaneous with, another. For example, in North Germany, horses, real estate, &c., are exchanged for pistoles in sums of 5 thalers and upward in gold, and which by a continually varying exchange, as merchandise for gold, and gold for merchandise, are used as currency thalers. Moreover, a standard is first made vigorous through fractional coin.

The parallel standard is altogether independent of the standard by the side of which it circulates.

4. The *optional* or *alternative standard* (called, also, *double standard*), consists of two standards existing together in the same country; as, for example, in France, where the debtor is allowed to pay, according to his pleasure, either in silver or in gold francs, the purity of which is legally established at a ratio of 15.5:1. Fig. 4 of Chart III delineates the French optional standard. The out and in flow of precious metal is entirely independent of the balance of trade, and occurs as often as one metal exhibits a better reckoning in payment than another. Two pounds of coined gold, and 31 pounds of coined silver, furnish an equal number of francs, viz, 3,100; nevertheless, 6.90 francs are abstracted from the gold, and 23.25 from the silver, as the cost of coinage, to reimburse which the price of gold must be under 15.46, and that of silver above 15.62. This exchange designates the boundary, beyond which one metal takes the place of the other. But in case of a necessity for metal money, the medium price of 15.54 is established between 15.48 and 15.62, as a turning point, about which the optional standard moves.

In case *a*, gold is 15.58. Payments are made in gold or silver coin, but silver coin is preferred.

In case *b*, gold is 15.52. Payments are made in gold or silver, but gold coin is preferred.

In case *c*, gold is 15.40. Payments are made in gold; gold is imported and coined; silver is at a premium, which is denoted by undulating lines, and is exported.

In case *d*, gold is 15.50. Payments are made either in gold or silver, but gold is preferred.

Chart III.   STANDAI

STANDARDS.

1. Pure Silver Standard.   2. Pure Gold Standard.

3. Grote's Parallel Standard.

A standard alongside, in addition to, or contemporaneous with another standard.

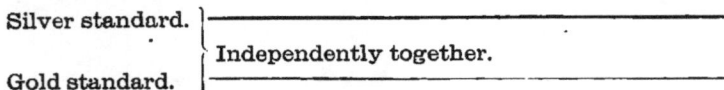

Silver standard.

Independently together.

Gold standard.

4. Optional or Alternative Standard.
(Also called double standard.)

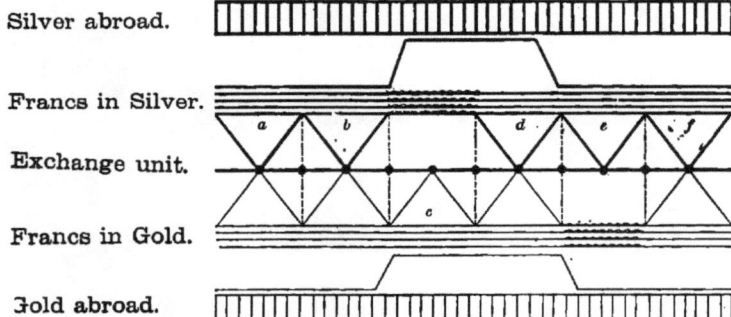

Silver abroad.

Francs in Silver.

Exchange unit.   *a*   *b*   *d*   *e*   *f*

c

Francs in Gold.

Gold abroad.

C. My mode of Introd

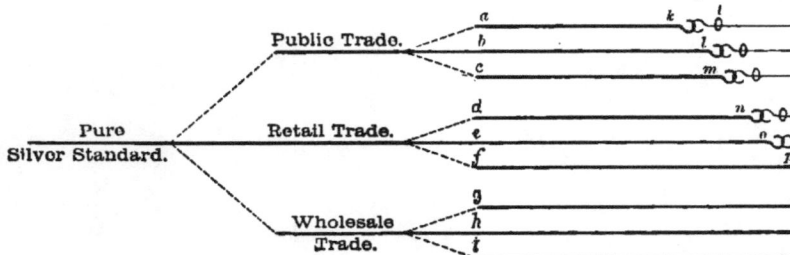

Public Trade.   *a*   *k*   *l*

  b   *l*

  c   *m*

Pure   Retail Trade.   *d*   *n*

Silver Standard.   *e*   *o*

  f

  g

Wholesale   *h*

Trade.   *i*

MODES OF INTRODUCTION.

A. Mode of the Coin Law of Dec. 4, 1871.

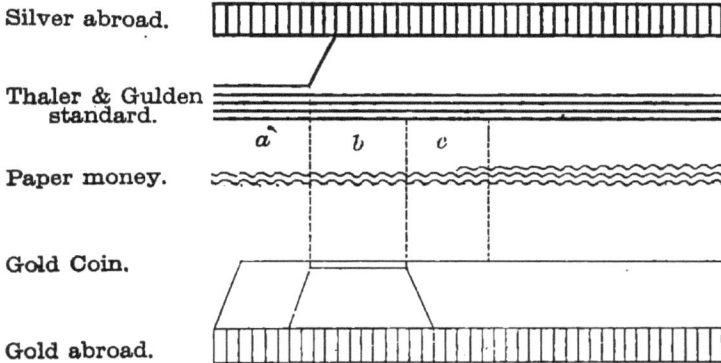

Silver abroad.

Thaler & Gulden standard.

a b c

Paper money.

Gold Coin.

Gold abroad.

B. Mode suggested by me.

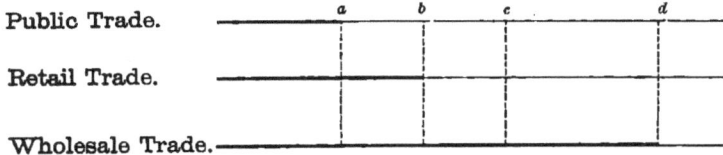

Public Trade.

a b c d

Retail Trade.

Wholesale Trade.

ion specifically represented.

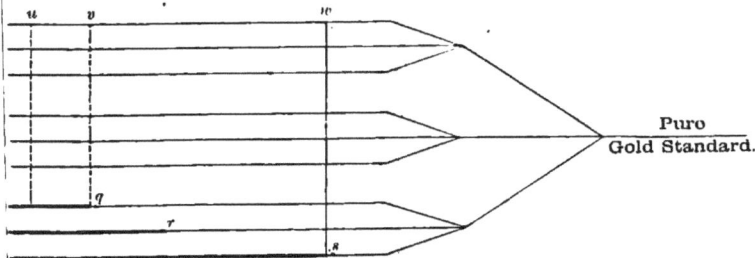

u v w

Puro
Gold Standard.

q

r

s

Eggers, Money Reform.

In case e, gold is 15.70. Payments are made in silver, and silver is imported and coined; gold is at a premium and is exported.

In case f, gold is again 15.50.

These are but the outlines of the peculiarities of the French optional standard; but there are besides other attributes of importance. For example, the temporary popularity of the one or the other metal; the question whether the metal must be brought from England, liable to freight and costs, or whether it can be imported direct from the country producing it; the domestic consumption of metal; the French coin drifting abroad, which finds its way back to France; the bank-notes, which circulate behind both metals, &c.

The French optional standard is the most intricate and difficult to understand. Since 1870, a genuine bank-note standard has been adopted.

A, in Chart III, shows no form of standard, but delineates the introduction of the gold standard, under the coin law of December 4, 1871.

The debtor has the choice of payment in gold or silver, but cannot, as in France, have coining done for his own benefit. A private person cannot exchange one coined metal for the other, or effect an increase of our coined money. The price of gold and silver for importation from abroad is to him of no consequence. On the other hand, by the entrance of an unfavorable balance of trade, which may occur suddenly at any time in the course of the year, it is known that the three months' exchange between Berlin and London, including three months' interest, and 6 per thousand costs, advances 6 thalers 25½ silbergroschen. Gold is exported if it stands above 15.50.

In the four kinds of standard delineated above, private persons have the privilege of having coin issued, and whether the balance of trade be favorable or unfavorable, the precious metals flow freely in and out, according to circumstances and the wants of trade. But the coin-law of December 4, 1871, committed our exchange between gold and silver entirely to the arbitrary judgment of the imperial power, which cannot dispense with the more than doubtful advice of the brokers.

In the accompanying explanations, gold is designated by light lines, silver by heavy, and paper money by undulating lines. Each line represents 100,000,000 thalers. Originally the volume of money consisted of 5 of silver and 2 of paper.

In case a, gold is 15.50. The government imports gold, whereby freight and cost of coinage raises the price above 15.50. The money volume stands at 5 silver, 2 paper, and 1 gold.

In case b, gold is 15.65. In this case there is no doubt that the government exchanges silver for gold at a great disadvantage. The money volume stands, 4 silver, 2 paper, and 2 gold.

In case c, gold is 15.70. An unfavorable balance of trade is the result, which carries off gold without filling its place with silver. Bank-notes take the place of gold. The volume of money is 4 silver, 3 paper, and 1 gold, while originally it was 5 silver, 2 paper, and 1 gold. We have 100,000,000 thalers silver less, and just that much more paper money.

In the above cases the danger is designated in large outlines (and this was brought about by the passage of the coin-law of December 4), which shows Germany entering yet deeper into the paper-money inflation. The government has assumed therewith an immense responsibility.

As concerns the amount of gold hitherto obtained by us, the records of the Imperial Diet, at the beginning of last May, makes the following exhibit: The profit acquired in the course of the past year, from an amount of gold in round numbers of 35,870,000 thalers, under favorable price conjunctions, after deducting the cost of coinage, was more

H. Mis. 8——8

than 600,000 thalers. Nevertheless, according to the London quotations, which in 1871, averaged 15.58, the lowest, viz, 15.47, being in December, the ordinary business premium, at which the record hints, would, independent of the coinage cost of 4 marks per pound for silver, cause a loss of 288,000 thalers.

The profit is perhaps influenced in some way by the payment of the money for war damage, and the gain of 600,000 thalers is undoubtedly based upon a more or less arbitrary calculation.

In whatever way it may be possible to retain the mentioned gain of 600,000 thalers, there are undoubtedly, as the record shows, no favorable circumstances awaiting our future gold acquisition.

The usually accepted ratio of $15\frac{1}{2}$ of the French coin law, is referred to. But at this time the ratio is entirely different. According to the Economist, the yearly average united production of precious metals is, from 1849 to 1863, 226,000,000 thalers gold, 111,500,000 thalers silver; from 1864 to 1868, 200,000,000 thalers gold, 130,000,000 thalers silver.

The entire production of silver increased from 33 to $39\frac{1}{2}$ per cent., while that of gold decreased.

On the contrary, the demand for gold increases and that for silver diminishes. Germany requires for her exclusively pure gold standard 800,000,000 thalers gold, and she will release her silver. Holland and Scandinavia are also making efforts to introduce the gold standard. Since 1861, Asia has received proportionately more gold than silver. By the English and French steamers there was carried from Europe to Egypt and Asia, on an average—

	Thalers gold.	Thalers silver.		Thalers gold.	Thalers silver.
From 1851 to 1860 ..	7, 300, 000	60, 000, 000	From 1851 to 1866 ..	19, 100, 000	47, 100, 000
1861 ..	9, 500, 000	59, 100, 000	1867...	11, 000, 000	13, 700, 000
1862 ..	22, 700, 000	97, 300, 000	1868...	43, 500, 000	23, 700, 000
1863 ..	53, 500, 000	100, 900, 000	1869...	17, 500, 000	42, 900, 000
1864 ..	46, 500, 000	113, 700, 000	1870...	13, 900, 000	14, 900, 000
1865 ..	29, 000, 000	64, 900, 000	1871...	21, 900, 000	25, 900, 000

The large exportation, from 1862, to 1865, is explained by the high price of cotton. Fair Dhollerah stood from January 1, 1863–'66, at $17\frac{1}{4}$, $23\frac{1}{2}$, 20, and $17\frac{1}{4}$ pence.

For the equalization of the balance of trade with Asia, standard silver had from 1851, to 1866, the high price of $61\frac{3}{8}$ pence=15.37 : 1. From 1851, to 1866, French silver for the benefit of England flowed into Asia, and it is reported that England gave France, on an average, for every 15.38 pounds of silver, 1 pound of gold. It is easy to translate the English price of silver, since $60\frac{7}{8}d.=15.49$; and $\frac{1}{8}d.$ amounts to a little more than .03 pound.

For Germany the matter assumes a shape entirely different. From 1867, to 1871, gold averaged $60\frac{3}{8}d.=15.61:1$. From 1871–'72, silver varied as follows:

	Average price.	Highest price.		Average price.	Highest price.
1871.	d.	d.	1871.	d.	d.
January	$60\frac{9}{16}$	$60\frac{5}{8}$	November	$60\frac{7}{8}$	61
February	$60\frac{9}{16}$	$60\frac{5}{8}$	December	$60\frac{5}{8}$	$60\frac{7}{8}$
March	$60\frac{3}{8}$	$60\frac{1}{2}$	1872.		
April	$60\frac{1}{4}$	$60\frac{1}{4}$	January	$60\frac{7}{8}$	$61\frac{1}{8}$
May	$60\frac{1}{4}$	$60\frac{1}{4}$	February	61	$61\frac{1}{8}$
June	$60\frac{3}{8}$	$60\frac{7}{16}$	March	$60\frac{1}{4}$	$60\frac{7}{8}$
July	$60\frac{9}{16}$	$60\frac{5}{8}$	April	$60\frac{9}{16}$	$60\frac{7}{8}$
August	$60\frac{11}{16}$	$60\frac{3}{4}$	May	$60\frac{1}{8}$	$60\frac{1}{4}$
September	$60\frac{3}{4}$	$60\frac{13}{16}$			
October	$60\frac{7}{16}$	$60\frac{5}{8}$			

Silver stood but a short time at a favorable price for exportation. According to the English import lists, the price fell rapidly in those months in which large consignments of silver from Germany were received.

It is evident that the coin reform will encounter almost insurmountable difficulties in accepting the coin law with a ratio of 15.50 : 1.

There must be found a way which will safely lead to its attainment. Such a way is represented at B in the drawing, through a periodically progressive introduction of the gold standard. The entire money circulation is divided into three departments; public trade, retail trade, and wholesale trade. a denotes 1st July, 1874; b 1st October, 1874; and c 1st January, 1875. Left of the line, a represents only the silver standard. Between a and b the gold standard has taken possession of the public trade.

The silver standard still exists in retail and wholesale trade. Between b and c the gold standard has also been introduced into retail trade, and the silver standard still is maintained in wholesale trade. At c the gold standard enters into the wholesale trade and effectually displaces the silver standard. d represents the period at which the displacement is complete. To the right of d the gold standard governs in all three departments.

This mode of introduction is practically illustrated in Hamburg coinage, where, as is known, the banco-mark is used in wholesale trade, while computations in retail trade are made in the currency mark and shillings; and in public trade. in thalers and groschens. The groschen was first effectively introduced in 1866, for postage, telegrams, &c. If the province of the groschen were enlarged, then practically the next step would be to introduce it into retail trade. In that event, a considerable amount of the groschen standard would come into circulation, upon which basis wholesale trade would gradually tend to the same result.

In Hamburg the groschen did not formerly exist. Just as the introduction of the groschen was accomplished in Hamburg, so have I recommended for the last year and a half that the coin and computation rules, in harmony with the United States, could be introduced through the Wilhelm's thaler of $1\frac{1}{2}$ grams fine gold throughout Germany, first in public trade and afterward in retail and wholesale trade.

In the next chapter I will explain the mode of introduction in detail.

VI.

THE MODE OF INTRODUCING THE GOLD STANDARD.

In C, chart III, the mode of introducing the gold standard is represented in detail, according to the common outlines as given in B.

By doubling the capacity of the mint, we would be in from one and a half to two years able to produce about 600,000,000 pieces (equaling, say, 25,000,000 thalers) fractional currency of the Wilhelm's thaler. As soon as three-fourths of the amount is finished, the introduction of the same as a computation unit can commence, first in public trade, then in retail trade, and in the course of a half year the work will be complete throughout Germany.

After the half year mentioned, the present coin, the currency thaler and gulden standard, might for a time circulate in conjunction with the new coin of the Wilhelm's thaler. but it should be gradually displaced by the coin of the Wilhelm's thaler. According to the ratio of value of $15\frac{3}{8}$ pounds silver equaling 1 pound of gold, it would rate as follows:

Thalers.	Florins.	Wilhelm's thalers.	Cents.
$14 =$	$24\frac{1}{2} =$	10	
$7 =$	$12\frac{1}{4} =$	5	

Silver groschen.	Kreuzers.		
$42 =$	$2 - 27 = 1$		
$31\frac{1}{2} =$			75
$21 =$			50
$10\frac{1}{2} =$			25
$5\frac{1}{4} =$			$12\frac{1}{2}$

Besides the above exact equivalents, there are yet 1 florin and 15 kreuzers $= 51$ cents. At first the new coinage for South Germany need be no higher than 25-cent pieces, and for North Germany, up to 5 and 10 cents.

The present issue of 10 and 20 mark pieces contain 7.6846 grames fine gold, and are worth in the $1\frac{1}{2}$ gram standard 2.39 and 4.78 Wilhelm's thalers. They are mostly deposited in the coffers of the reserved war-fund and in the Prussian bank, and during the period of the introduction they could be rated at $2\frac{1}{2}$ and 5 Wilhelm's thalers, and after the introduction is complete they could be remelted into gold pieces of $3\frac{3}{4}$ and $7\frac{1}{2}$ grams. In this way, during the transition period, they would be protected from the risk of exportation, and their remelting completely secured.

The introduction should first be effected in public trade, because in that the state has not only the undisputed right to fix the medium of the money trade, but all persons who come in contact with public business will be obliged to furnish themselves with the new coin and familiarize themselves with it. The introduction of a new *coin system* is much easier than is that of a new *long* and *dry measure*, for this reason, that in the latter, only private parties trade one with the other, and many prefer to retain the old, and will not take the trouble to become familiar with the new.

An introduction by districts is recommended, because it is neither possible to meet the demands of the entire circulation of Germany at once with the gold standard, nor practical at a single stroke to replace the existing standard of calculation in the many cities and villages, consisting as it does of the thaler of 30 silvergroschen, of 12 pfennige, and of the gulden and kreuzer. Besides, a knowledge of a standard must precede its introduction. Then, again, as a different rate of postage cannot be charged, for example, in Munich, in the new standard, from that which at the same time obtains in Würzburg, therefore after the entire amount of fractional coin presumed to be necessary is prepared, it will be known in what sums to dispense the same in the several places, in order to supply at once the public, retail and wholesale trade.

I separate the departments of public trade into three divisions:

a. Post and telegraph trade and revenue collections.

b. Passenger and freight trade, &c., upon railroads.

c. Tolls and taxes everywhere and of all kinds, as well as all other public incomes and disbursements.

After a sufficient amount of small coin is prepared, it may, together with a certain amount of gold coin, be distributed according to the population throughout the empire. At each railroad station and post-office there should be prepared a distributing coffer, or subtreasury, charged with the apportionment.

The first distribution should be according to the tax or voting-list; the after distributions of the introductory coin, and the distributions of the subsequent coinage, may be made according to the actual necessities. The best way to introduce the new coin into retail trade is to pay it out in salaries, and other disbursements; 25,000,000 thalers fractional coin would soon find its way into the hands of millions. Thus the introduction would be gradually accomplished by these departments.

For example, in the drawing C, *k* signifies 1st July, *l* 1st August, and *m* 1st September, 1874. The first department is usually filled with persons of culture who serve as educators to the others. During the introduction, the subtreasury holds in reserve a sufficient supply for the department in which the gold standard has been introduced. The aggregate from the post, telegraph, and revenue, amounts to about 30,000,000 thalers. In 1870, the passenger trade of the German railroads yielded 50,267,951 thalers, and the freight trade and other sources of income 108,906,645 thalers. The amount of income from all other public sources can be ascertained beforehand.

As soon as all business in public trade throughout Germany is conducted in the new gold standard, travelers will carry none other with them. Very soon it will prevail exclusively in restaurants and hotels, and from thence find its way into retail trade. The latter will endeavor to get rid of the double standard of coinage, and adopt the new standard as soon as the government can furnish an adequate amount of coin, which is in course of preparation. The distribution is similar in manner to that employed in public trade. The cities have precedence, and the country districts follow. In the drawing C—

d represents Berlin, Munich, Stuttgard, Dresden, and other chief cities.

e represents the remaining cities.

f the country districts.

n represents, for sake of example, 1st October, 1874.

o represents, for sake of example, 1st November, 1874.

p represents, for sake of example, 1st December, 1874.

It is self-evident that the data furnished here are only for the sake of example. As has already been remarked, the introduction into retail trade may be accomplished all at once, if it is exactly known how much is needed in each city and in every district. In any case, however, let there be a large and amply sufficient reserve.

The links in the lines at *k*, *l*, &c., denote that the existing coin will for a time be preferred to the new gold standard. By the circle *t* is understood that as soon as the new standard exists in sufficient amount, the government determines to use it only in its public transactions. But, besides, the circle indicates an inherent necessity in trade, to discontinue the use of the old silver coin, and to give preference to the new standard as soon as a change in the form of computation becomes imperative. The person of the most limited intellect will find it easy to exchange 42 silver groschen, or 2 florins 27 kreuzers, for 100 cents at the distributing coffer, and then, for example, pay 2 cents for a letter and 10 cents to the next railroad station. Those who have no direct use for the coin of the gold standard will yet have no difficulty in paying out 100 cents, in place of 42 silver groschen, or 2 florins 27 kreuzers.

At the introduction of the gold standard of the Wilhelm's thaler into public and retail trade, it will rest entirely upon the existing silver standard. The railroads will carry their net receipts in gold, for which they at first have no other use, to the distributing coffer, and again exchange 14 thalers, or 24½ florins, for 10 Wilhelm's thalers. The same privilege in certain minimum amounts may be allowed to private persons; for example, country people who have received gold standard in the market before it has been introduced into their places of residence.

The introduction of the Wilhelm's thaler in the post-office will be gratifying from the first for this reason: that in North Germany 1 silvergroschen=3⅓ kreuzers, while in South Germany it only=3 kreuzers; this, in any event, will be equalized. An estimate of 2 cents will furnish an international postage basis, because 2 cents=3 kreuzers=2 sou=1 penny. The coin of the new standard will be desirable in North Germany on account of the gain in postage which is united with it.

In order to introduce the gold standard of 1½ grms into public and retail trade, there should be ready: 1. 25,000,000 thalers in new coin; 2. 175,000,000 thalers in 20 and 10 mark pieces, presuming that the coinage under the law of December 4, 1871, is retained as at present until April 1, 1873. 3. The present silver and paper money of the existing currency, and gulden standard should be allowed as valid.

In order that the latter be not missed, in any event, there should be enough of the new standard on hand to supply the entire public and retail trade, with silver fractional coin, in the new method of calculation, within from a year and a half to two years after commencing the issue. After the introduction has been accomplished, the mint should use its entire power in preparing 20, 25, and 50 cents, and should call in the old coin according to the measuring scale of the new coinage.

Until now, the question has been with regard to public and retail trade. The first is the special province of the government, the latter requires the assistance of the former. Fractional coin is used in large amounts. The next question is as to the introduction of the new standard into wholesale trade, which demands gold coin almost entirely, and which should be allowed the issue of coin for its own advantage. So soon as the public and retail trade are fully supplied with coin of the gold standard, the calling in of the 20-mark piece and the replacing it with gold coin of the 1½ gram standard of full weight, should ensue, and which coin should be issued also in pieces containing 15 and 30 grams; then there would be, in the existing silver standard, in conjunction with the gold standard of the Wilhelm's thaler, which until now rested upon the silver standard, a complete parallel standard introduced into wholesale trade, in which silver answers for gold, and gold for silver, as merchandise does for money, as has been shown in a former chapter in which the kinds of standards were treated of.

VII.

THE WILHELM'S THALER IN PARALLEL STANDARD.

In the delineation C, *u* designates 1st January, 1875, as the day upon which the introduction into the public and private trade is provisionally accomplished, and on which it is obligatory to completely supply the same with the coin of the new system, and to replace the 10 and 20 mark pieces with the new gold coin of full weight. For this purpose it is presumed that from one to one and a half years is necessary. This period is designated by the space between *u* and *r*, and *r* represents the 1st January or the 1st July. From this period private persons might exercise the privilege of having coin issued for their own benefit.

Henceforward German coinage presents a new appearance. Our gold standard enters into exchange operation with the entire volume of gold in foreign countries, and between their silver standard and ours there is established a ratio of value corresponding to the ratio between gold and silver in London. This forces the effectual introduction of the gold standard into wholesale trade, because otherwise it has to deal with various inconvenient standards, while both public and retail trade are carried on through a gold standard of a common unit, and which, in relation to foreign trade, is more agreeable and comprehensible.

For example, the manufacturer who pays his workmen in gold standard is glad to regulate his prices in gold by America and England, and these unconditionally give the preference to our gold standard. The farmer prefers to sell his produce for gold, because he only desires this, and it is immediately carried to the exchange to be traded for in gold. Bills of exchange payable in the gold standard circulate together with those payable in the silver standard, and the latter are discounted in the gold standard. There arises a special discount for such gold exchange, whose advance is adjusted according to the demand for the same and the supply of the gold standard. For example, if gold discount at 5 per cent., and the discount point for exchange in the silver standard is 3 per cent., it is especially so because silver is abundant and gold is scarce. Then silver flows out and gold enters; thereby the two points of discount are equalized; that is, are presumably 4 per cent., so that the other factor is not proportionately changed.

But transactions in gold, impelled by the natural power of the expansion of the gold standard in public and retail trade, are again quickly increased, and the circumstance of a rise in gold discount and of an exchange of silver for gold is again repeated.

But apart from the fact that the introduction of the gold standard into wholesale trade, is through the natural power of the material, there is nothing to prevent a number of head firms upon opportunity anywhere, from occupying a place as a chamber of commerce, and constituting a banking-house to operate in gold. The first proceeding would be a branch introduction of the gold standard, because the latter takes possession only of certain branches of business in the same place, as in New York, certain products are exchanged for gold dollars and cents, and others for paper dollars and cents, and where day-book and ledger are carried and the yearly balance made in cash of two values. The latter proceeding would be accomplished in a local manner, and in many cases is to be recommended.

When neither the hypothecated debtor, nor the creditor is engaged in wholesale trade, and consequently does not operate with the silver standard, it would be foolish for the one to exchange his gold obtained through business for silver which he would pay over to his creditor, and then for the latter to take the silver thus received and carry it to the broker, to again trade it for gold. There would be no difficulty in calculating the interest according to the day's quotation, and adding the capital to the average quotation. There would be an effort to pay off mortgages, or to convert them into the new gold standard. Besides, other debts would be liquidated by the payment of silver.

It is a very hazardous undertaking for the state to interfere with the debt ratio. In whatever way this is done, the accusation of partiality will be made; and this reproach may be avoided, because the state has in the mode explained by me a safe means of entirely preventing the doubtfully authoritative encroachment upon the circumstances of debts. Every debtor pays his silver debts in silver, but may, if he chooses, pay them in gold. By this means the superabundant silver flows out of the country.

VIII.

MODES ENTIRELY DIFFERENT.

The government, in its argument upon the coin laws, declares:

That it is impossible to fill the arteries of trade at once with the gold standard and as speedily to call in the existing silver currency coin, because, in such an event, a condition of things must take place corresponding to the so-called double standard in so far as the silver currency coin, previously issued, and the new gold, as equally-constituted pay mediums, with fixed ratios of exchange, circulate together.

The assertion, "in such an event a condition of things must take place," &c., will become weakened as soon as the entire trade is divided into separate departments, and one department after the other is supplied with the gold standard, according to the scale of amount to which the place is entitled.

The declaration, section 8 of the coin law, that the silver currency coin and the gold coin shall exist together as equally-constituted pay mediums, is of small consequence to the public and retail trade, because they deal only in small amounts and in cash payments, but of great importance to the wholesale trade.

The coin law had reference to the entire trade, and of this especially to wholesale trade. My mode of introduction, as previously explained, is entirely different; that is, introducing the gold standard first into public and private trade, and upon this there would naturally be constructed a way to accomplish the same for wholesale trade.

The mode traced out by the coin law has the following defects:

1. The more valuable metal can flow off in the same way as it disappeared in a former period of the German money history, somewhere about 150,000,000 thalers gold. The optional, or double standard which the coin law will use during the transition period, may become a *Danaiden vessel.*

2. To regulate the probable outflow of gold through the circulation of Prussian bank-notes, is a means of gain in the hands of the deputies of the bank.

. 3. The privilege which is granted to the debtor to pay his debts in that metal which is cheapest at the time of their contraction, places the wholesale trade for many years upon a fluctuating basis.

4. The mode of the coin law comprehends the debt ratio only under forced necessity. After the introduction of the pure gold standard, the debtor will be forced to pay in imperial gold coin.

While the present legal mode of reckoning is of no benefit to him, as the 20 gold-mark, according to the present quotation, 15.70, is worth .2½ silvergroschen more than 6⅔ thalers, and gold in the next year will fall heavily below 15.50, he would be, after the entrance, forced to bear at the farthest a great loss by yielding to the computation.

The farmer, for example, whose estate is burdened with a mortgage of 4,650 thalers, owes in this sum, taking 30 thalers to the pound, 155 pounds in coined silver thalers. The thaler is but the measure and is only the form in which he owes the substance of 155 pounds of silver. This debt of 155 pounds of coined German silver, he subsequently discharges by the payment of 10 pounds of coined German gold = 13,954 gold-marks, or ¼-thaler pieces. In 1847, and 1848, gold had a value of nearly 16:1. At that price, 10 pounds of gold would = 160 pounds of silver, and he must pay 5 pounds of silver more, = 150 thalers, than he owes.

5. The mode designated by the coin law originates the question, how

to secure a reasonable price for our silver: Shall it remain in the hands of Mr. von Bleichröder, and his associates, through their almost unlimited power to establish what price is suitable to choose?

The mode recommended by me for the introduction avoids all the obstacles in the above points:

1. Gold is to us fully secured, if we make the gold standard the exclusive medium of a fixed department of trade, which then, unlike a *Danaiden vessel*, will securely retain the gold coin. Besides, the high tariff during the introduction will make the outflow impossible.

2. Upon the second point I will take the opportunity of speaking in detail when treating of the bank question.

3. The pure silver, or the pure gold standard, and, for the transition period, the parallel standard, establishes a stable basis for trade. Where the debtor has a choice of metals, many kinds of business are impossible.

4. A forcible interference with the debt ratio would be avoided. Each one would be able to discharge his silver debts by the payment of silver. The introduction of the gold standard into the public and retail trade, and then extended gradually into wholesale trade, from that time on enables contracts to be made in gold. At last, but few debt contracts in silver would be left, especially the unlimited mortgages. The question whether an unspecified time shall be fixed for the same is united with the fifth proposition.

5. In the fourth part of my treatise on Domestic Economy, I explicitly stated that Germany can best realize on her stock of silver by issuing it in piasters of 22½ grams fine silver with 2½ grams copper alloy. This is the value of a 5-franc thaler, and which forms the dollar of Central America and Ecuador. Our piaster would soon take equal rank by the side of the same, and it would assist us to introduce it elsewhere. Eight piasters 1½ inches in diameter (=37½ millimeters), laid one by another, is a metric foot. Ten almost equals the long measure of China, which equals 0.37464 meter. A tael, which in China, is equal in weight and value to silver of 898 fineness, weighs 37.573 grams; therefore 3 piasters are very nearly equal to 2 taels. As Mexico sends her silver over the earth, utilizing it everywhere, so Germany, by the use of her piaster, would gradually be able to put her silver into circulation, and therefore the issuing of the same would be advantageous. Besides, she would possess in the piaster a common measure of value with other countries. After the gold standard has for the most part taken possession of wholesale trade, a conversion of the remaining debt ratio of the silver standard into the piaster may take place. The piaster is equal to 40½ silvergroschen=2 florins 21¾ kreuzers=54 shillings currency. Nine pounds of fine silver are equivalent to 200 piasters=270 currency thalers=472½ South German gulden. The debtor, who owes 155 pounds of coined silver in 4,650 currency thalers, would not then be forced, according to the arbitrarily received ratio of 15½:1, to pay 10 pounds of coined gold, which, perhaps, at that time is worth 160 pounds of silver, but he would be able to liquidate his debt by the payment of 3,444½ piasters. Moreover, as has been stated, there exists an inherent tendency in most private obligations, to convert by voluntary agreement. The period of a complete supplanting of the silver standard by the gold standard is represented in drawing *C* by *s*; it will depend, however, upon the progress of events and upon our future judgment.

In the same measure as my proposed unit coin is distinguished from the mark, so is my proposed manner of introducing the gold standard essentially distinguished from the view taken by the coin law.

IX.

THE DANTZIC CONGRESS AND THE BANK QUESTION.

In the commercial trade convention, assembled at Dantzic, from the 23th to the 29th of August of this year, the three following resolutions on the bank question were offered:

I.—*Resolution by Böhmert, Gensel, Lammers, and Dorn.*

1. The privilege of issuing bank-notes shall depend alone upon the performance of stipulated terms.
2. These stipulated terms are mainly for the purpose of securing the actual redemption of the notes, &c., and to make possible the continual cognizance of the business condition of the bank.

II.—*Resolution by Dr. Wolff.*

In the fifth German trade convention, which assembled in Leipzic from the 13th to the 15th of May, the following resolutions were adopted:

1. The right to issue bank-notes for the whole German Empire, shall in the future only belong, *in principia* to one great central bank.

The note privileges now existing, may continue, but no new ones shall be allowed, and the present ones shall not be enlarged. So far as a bank possesses the privilege of unlimited issue, the same shall be reduced to the actual sum corresponding to the present business trade of the bank.

2. According to resolution 1, which recommends the creation of a central bank, it actually in all its essential parts belongs to the Prussian bank organization. It is, therefore, a recommendation to change the Prussian bank into a common German imperial bank.

3. After Germany has fully accepted the gold standard, no more bank-notes of less amount than 100 marks (= $33\frac{1}{3}$ thalers = $58\frac{1}{3}$ gulden) shall be issued, and those already in circulation shall be called in,

With this restriction, that—

4. The authority of the bank shall be prevented from pronouncing such notes irredeemable which have been called in, but unseasonably presented; that—

5. The bank be obliged to redeem all counterfeits, if, on presentation, it is not able to prove that the party presenting them for redemption did know their true character, or did not take due precaution to become acquainted therewith.

6. A note circulation, not based upon specie, shall be subject to a tax corresponding to its exchange value, and if that is impracticable, it shall be secured by a contingent fund.

III.—*Resolution by the author.*

The trades congress recommends that the note circulation, not resting upon a specie basis, be curtailed from year to year, until a complete specie basis is reached.

The three foregoing resolutions were discarded. The first, as is seen, by the adherence of the middle and small banks of issue; the second, by the friends of the Prussian bank, or the future imperial bank of issue; against the third motion many persons spoke, who acknowledge a specie basis as

Chart IV. CHART C

I. EX

a. *Scale of 80 Thalers.*
b. *80 Exchange units.*
c. *100 " "*
d. *60 " "*

II. EX

The Earth's complete scale of 12,0

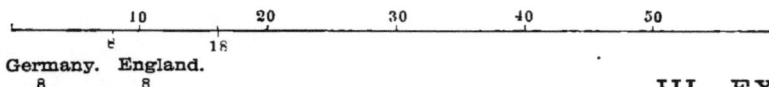

| | 10 | 20 | 30 | 40 | 50 |

Germany. England.
8   8

III. EX

Scale of 80 (ten millions) Thlr. (Germany).

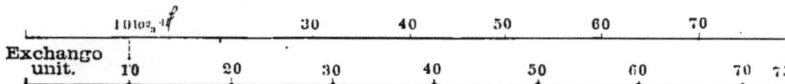

Exchange unit. 10   20   30   40   50   60   70

IV. EX

Scale of 77½ (ten millions) Thlr. (Germany).

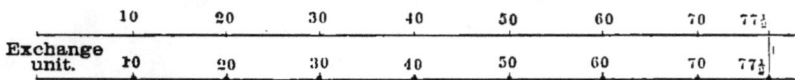

10   20   30   40   50   60   70   77½

Exchange unit. 10   20   30   40   50   60   70   77½

V. EX.

a. The Earth's complete scale of 12,

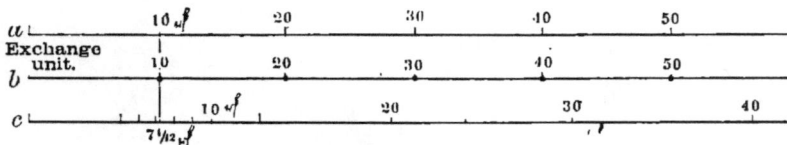

a
Exchange unit.
b
c

10   20   30   40   50

10   20   30   40   50

10   20   30   40

7 1/12

c. The Earth's complete scale estin

IPLE.

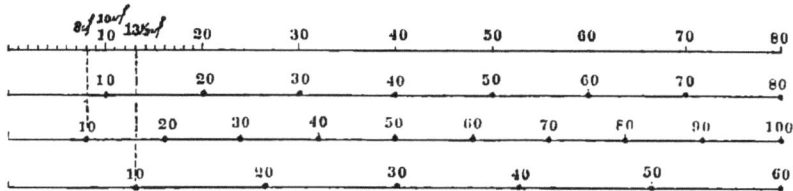

MPLE.

,000,000 Thalers mixed standard.

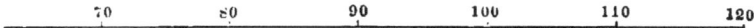

MPLE.

Scale of 80 (ten millions) Thlr. (England).

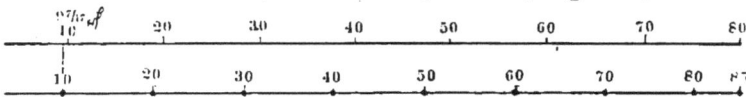

MPLE.

Scale of 82½ (ten millions) Thlr. (England).

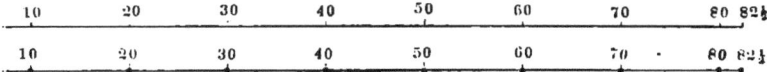

IPLE.

0,000,000 Thalers mixed standard.

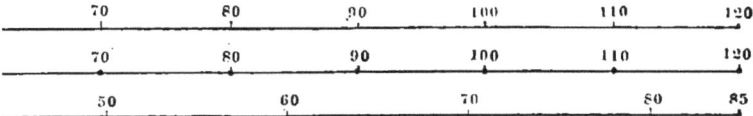

ed at 8,500,000,000 Thalers metal.

the most beneficial, but who have not confidence in the clear perception and ability of Germany to place her coinage upon a complete metal basis, in opposition to the material force of the interests of the banks of issue.

But Germany has sufficient time to acquire this clear perception and ability, because the definite regulations of the bank question, on account of the entangled contested interests, cannot be fully enforced for a term of years. The imperial bank of issue conquered the trade convention of Leipsic, and supported the domestic industrial congress of Dantzic. The combat will fluctuate here and there for a long time. Some honest men, but who are erroneously influenced by dogmatical propositions, maintain that the unsupported bank-notes are of actual benefit to the domestic industries. But the question is based upon the interest drawn from the sum of about 150,000,000 thalers of bank-notes without a metal basis. The medium and small banks do not wish to lose the half which hitherto fell to them, and the imperial bank of issue endeavors to seize the whole. The industrial interests of the people, as well as that of the state, demand deliverance from the conduct of banks of issue; and I, for my part, foster the firm confidence that the few men who have already spoken in favor of establishing the German coinage upon a complete specie basis, and who are opposed to an insecure government paper money—Tellkampff, Hübner, Kämmerer, Dannenburg, Hirth, Schneider, Engel, von Unruh, Auspurg, Geffcken, Eggers, and others, will, at no distant period, grow into a great money-reform party.

X.

METAL AND PAPER MONEY—SCALE OF VALUE AND EXCHANGE UNIT.

Gold and silver are the substances which almost universally form the basis of exchange and the estimate of value. A fixed weight of precious metal serves, in a coined or uncoined condition, as a common medium of exchange, and as a scale of value. The thirtieth part of 1 pound of silver forms the fineness of 1 thaler, and by the united sum of thalers (into which category the circulating paper thaler also comes), is measured the value of that placed opposite, and which stands against it for the purpose of exchange. These opposite values consist, for example, in 100 pounds of cotton of a certain quality, an amount of corn, wool, iron, labor wages, shares in stock, &c., of equal value, but varying from time to time—only considered here so far as they actually are exchanged for the thaler.

For example, suppose A has 1,000 thalers to pay to B for merchandise received and to receive upon the same day the same amount for goods delivered; or suppose an arrangement by a certain number of persons is made with a clearing-house to be accommodated with exchange payments, and the balance announced; the thaler only serves as a measure of value, and not as an exchange or pay medium. Only so far as other opposite values are actually returned for the thaler is the price ratio of one to the other influenced.

The money against which a value is actually placed, to be exchanged, we will call the exchange unit. Chart IV, example I, represents money by a scale in long measure.

Germany requires for her money circulation about 800,000,000 thalers. Upon the scale (a) is registered the $\frac{10}{10000000}$ part, viz: 80 thalers; b represents the same exchange unit, while c has 100, and d 60. The measuring scale is drawn upon a graduated line of equal distances, and upon this the measure of value is accurately laid. The more plentiful the exchange unit is, the smaller is its value, and the scarcer the amount of the exchange unit is, the greater is its value. An exchange unit whose value in case *b* is 10 thalers, is reduced by 100 exchange units to 8 thalers, and rises by that of 60 to the value of $13\frac{1}{4}$ thalers.

The ratio between the amount of money upon the one hand, and the exchange unit upon the other, and the rapidity with which money performs the functions belonging to it, are objectively equal to the price at the same fixed time. I say objectively, for the subjective estimate, which influences the fixing of the price, does not belong to the department of the theory of money.

Every country which employs the precious metals as a pure measure of value, or as a basis for paper money, needs a certain amount of the whole sum of the commerce of the world. This is estimated at 12,000,000,000 thalers, against which the united exchange units of the world stand. Of that, England has an amount which Germany very nearly equals, viz: 800,000,000 thalers.

Example II, of Chart IV, shows a scale of 12,000,000,000 thalers by which the amount of money of all countries is represented. For example, Germany 8, England 8, &c. The ratio of the amount of money in each country to the whole volume of money is constant, so long as no country imports more than she exports. Money only serves to equalize when the equipoise between imports and exports, that is, when the balance of trade, is disturbed.

I will illustrate such a circumstance in example III, in which I have placed upon a scale together the amount of money of Germany and England, 80 times 10,000,000 thalers, and under is placed the exchange units, viz: for Germany 75 times 10,000,000 thalers, and for England 85 times 10,000,000 thalers.

In the former, 10 thalers are worth $10\frac{2}{3}$ thalers, and in the latter $9\frac{7}{17}$ thalers. Merchandise is held at a reduced rate in England, and in Germany at an advanced rate; and, besides the usual trade, the amount of 25,000,000 thalers is imported, in place of which 25,000,000 thalers of precious metal, as a universal equivalent, are returned. The ratio which now enters is represented in example IV, in which Germany stands recorded at 77,500,000, and England at 82,500,000 thalers, against each of which is placed an equal amount of exchange units, viz: $77\frac{1}{2}$ and $82\frac{1}{2}$, whereby it is perceived that the amount of the exchange units of the two countries taken together, is the same, and that, consequently, the value of each individual unit remains unaltered.

Moreover, the amount of the exchange units in the united districts of the commercial world, as well as the ratio of the same in individual countries, is continually changing. Abundant harvests of grain, cotton, &c., produce in some years larger amounts of objects of value than in others, and therefore less money is required to purchase them.

Then, too, the amount of money is not constant, but varies; 1, by the newly acquired gold and silver, which is coined into money; 2, by the instability attending a forced circulation of paper money; and, 3, by the to-and-fro movements upon trade by paper money, or the calling in of the same.

According to the London Economist, from 1864, to 1868, of the existing united product of gold and silver averaging 330,000,000 thalers yearly, by far the greater part was coined into money. But at the same time, apart from the new clearing-house regulations, &c., increasing from year to year the exchange unit of the whole commercial world, the ratio of the existing scale of value would not essentially alter the exchange unit placed opposite, if the two latter factors were wanting. A measure of value, consisting entirely of gold and silver, is the equalization of a scale of metal members, and to which, in consequence of new productions in gold and silver, new members are added. But it is entirely different with the scale of the whole commercial world adjusted at 12,000,000,000 thalers. Of this 12,000,000,000, thalers, only about 8,500,000,000 thalers is metal money. The bank-notes unsupported by specie and the government paper money, are estimated at 3,500,000,000 thalers. To establish the latter sum, (but which, according to Dr. Otta Hübner, by adding the whole amount of bank-notes and paper currency amounts to 4,300,000,000 thalers), the paper money burdened with a discount was scaled according to its value in specie, and adjusted to the provisions of a fixed metal basis.

For all the ordinary purposes of internal local trade, this 3,500,000,000 thalers of paper money has the full capacity of money without actually being money. But for international trade, it differs very materially from the universally necessary valid money; that is, money in the widest sense of the word.

The word money, originally, was only applied to the thing possessing value, gold money, silver money, &c. But for a long time Germany has accepted the mere representative of money for the substance. By this the German language is falsified. But until the word money is restored to its proper position, when only metal money is used, we must submit to comprehend paper money as money.

In example V, the measure of 3,500,000,000 thalers in paper money is changed, and represents in the given scale 8,500,000,000 thalers precious metal. Now this mixed standard of 12,000,000,000 thalers (a) stands against as many exchange units, and these again stand opposite a scale representing 8,500,000,000 thalers of pure metal money. In the latter case, 7½ thalers will purchase what in the former will require 10 thalers.

But, as has been plainly proven, the scale of 12,000,000,000 thalers is constantly changing through the variableness in value and volume of paper money. It is a scale of value, not of metal links, but of gum-elastic. For example, the United States has in circulation about 1,000,000,000 thalers in paper money. If gold stands at 115 per cent. premium, then the amount upon gold is reduced nearly to 870; whereas, if gold is 110 per cent., then the amount upon gold is 909,000,000 thalers. From that day on, in which gold fell from 115 per cent. to 110 per cent., the value of the money circulation of the country advanced 39,000,000 thalers, which, in a short time, established changes in the scale of value in the United States equaling more than 4 per cent., which is of great influence upon all merchandise imported, or upon that which is in close exchange operations with imported merchandise. When gold is low, importations are generally large, because a better market is found and the superfluous gold flows out.

In Russia, Austria, Italy, &c., there are constant variations in the scale of value, from the same causes which are especially great in a crisis. For example, from the 22d May to the 18th June, 1866, gold advanced in New York from 130 to 155—167¾ per cent., and remained from 18th June until 25th August between 147 and 155 per cent., averaging 151 per cent. The difference between 130 and 151 per cent. upon 1,000,000,000 thalers amounts to 107,000,000 thalers. If the worth of the volume of paper money of the other European and American countries should vary in like ratio, the value of the whole amount of money would thereby be changed many per cent.

The influence upon the scale of value, which originates through the increase or diminishing of bank-notes and paper money, unprotected by specie, was brought to light during last year, especially in France, where the amount of notes unprotected amounted to about 430,000,000 thalers more than on 1st July, 1870, lowering the value of the entire amount of the commerce of the world about $3\frac{1}{2}$ per cent.

Moreover, although the coinage of Germany is affected by the prevailing misfortunes of other countries, yet she may exert an influence upon the same by giving an example of a sound, restricted, and pure money circulation, in which it is to her own advantage to take precedence of all other countries.

Of the previously mentioned 800,000,000 thalers which circulate in Germany, 600,000,000 thalers are specie, 150,000,000 thalers bank-notes, unsupported by specie, and 50,000,000 thalers government paper money. Bank-notes and government paper money are associated, being both upon one piece of paper, whereby they differ from all other circulating mediums. For example, bills of exchange, checks, &c., in that they circulate for the purposes of common exchange as money. Metal money supplies nothing, as the bank-note and paper money does that in times of confidence. Exchange makes the transportation of specie unnecessary, but it is not a par currency; that is, it is not paid at its full nominal value. It purports an order; the discount is bargained for; it is sold and indorsed. When it is due, it is paid for in the usual way, viz, with money (metal money, bank-notes, or government paper money). The more exchange is discounted in a place, the dearer is money. Only the payable exchange represents money. The check is only a bill of exchange upon money and circulates but a short time.

In order to place herself upon a complete metal basis, Germany needs, of the 7,900,000,000 thalers metal money abroad, 200,000,000 thalers. By annihilating 200,000,000 paper money, the whole amount would be reduced from 12,000,000,000 to 11,800,000,000 thalers, which would perform the same functions as the present 12,000,000,000 thalers.

According to the ratio of 118 to 120, the value of 1,000 thalers would increase about 17 thalers.

The tribute which, for example, an officer has to pay yearly from his salary to the German bank of issue, and to the assessed and emitted state paper money, amounts for this reason to about 1.7 per cent. Every pure money claim, and money in almost every form, is now subject to this tribute. But if we adopt the gold standard, and our 200,000,000 thalers uncovered paper money is replaced by gold, which forms about the half of the entire amount of money, the 1.7 per cent. is nearly doubled.

If the entire commerce of the world was obliged to be carried on by means of 8,500,000,000 thalers, instead of 12,000,000,000 thalers, the value of the thaler would be increased about $12\frac{1}{2}$ silvergroschen. It is to be assumed that mankind, at no distant period, will throw off the illusion of paper money. Then, apart from all other agencies, the value of specie would augment from year to year, and Germany draw a large gain from a stock of gold of 800,000,000 thalers.

XI.

SPECIE, BANK-NOTES, AND REPRESENTATIVE MONEY.

It is maintained that bank-notes are more convenient than coin, because they can be more speedily paid out and better transported. As to the first, gold pieces are more quickly paid out than bank-notes of ordinary size. This was proven by Consul Meier, in the decision which took place in the Bremen common council, upon the acceptance on the 18th February, 1857, of the notes of the Bremen Bank by the public treasury. The 100-thaler bank-notes, which are referred to on this occasion, do not economize time, if, as is the custom in France, gold is done up in sealed and verified rolls.

In the counting of large sums of gold, pieces of the size of the American double-eagle are the most convenient. A dozen pieces thrown upon the counter are seen in a moment. In traveling, 200 thalers in gold takes up about as much room as 7 silver thalers. Gold pieces, also, are not as easily lost as paper money. For transportation by mail, gold pieces are as practical as paper money.

The Prussian bank, according to the official report, spent, during the year 1869, for the manufacturing of bank-notes the sum of 72,577.18 thalers, and for 1870, 21,670.27 thalers. In 1870, the Bremen bank paid for their new currency notes, which were introduced into trade in 1871, 10,887 gold thalers, 71 grt. = 12,055 currency thalers. According to a statement by Roscher, which I have at hand, the yearly average loss in weight of the English half sovereigns amounts to 0.0581 or 0.0325 per cent. of the whole. It is admitted that the waste of gold pieces of the value of double eagles or sovereigns, especially if they are used in large sums, or, as is customary in France, in rolls, including the cost of coinage, would make gold a not more costly pay medium than bank-notes, presuming that no torn bank-notes are again given out, and the cost of protecting the specie covering and the labor of their occasional redemption is included.

One advantage, however, which cannot be denied to a bank-note, is, that it can be treated as a piece of paper, and that it is lighter than gold. But the cases in which this advantage is taken into consideration do not often occur. Besides, a bank-note has this attribute entirely independent of its metal basis. A bank-note resting upon a complete metal basis is just as light as one not enjoying this distinction.

But now if no bank had any interest in the issuing of bank-notes fully protected by specie, then, as soon as the attainment of a final, sensible money reform was contemplated, all bank-notes would gradually disappear from trade, and then would be considered whether in place thereof a new regulation should be adopted to provide for wholesale trade in order that the citizens be not deprived of a large amount of mere representative money. It has been shown that the government issues from its mint, subsidiary coin of a depreciated metal fineness. The cost of the same, which is defrayed by the state, and the cost of preserving the metal would be outweighed by the saving of coinage and the use of the coin.

XII.

BANKS OF ISSUE, SCARCITY OF DWELLINGS, AND STRIKES.

In the commercial trade convention at Dantzic, Drs. Alex. Meyer and Eras, took occasion, in a resolution offered by them looking toward a remedy for domestic distress in regard to rents, to trace back, among other things, the irregular enhancement of the price of residences to the unjustly practiced increase of the circulating medium, which had in an especial manner raised the price of land, and expressed a determination to strive with all possible power against this hidden cause of the evil.

Every bank-note unprotected by specie (for only these can be meant) assists to lower the value of money, and, therefore, from the standpoint of the question on dwellings, it is unjust.

Chapter X illustrates what ratio the amount of money in Germany bears to the whole amount in the world. A silver thaler in Germany is of that value of which the one-thirtieth pound of silver abroad, for example in England, invariably seeks the equalization, which is effected in its natural circulation through the out and inflow of precious metal.

But if the pay medium, through a large amount of unsupported bank-notes, is suddenly augmented, from that time forward there exists no equalization with foreign countries, but there is thereby effected a mere enhancement of prices at home.

A speculator, for example, wishes to operate in corn. He has his note discounted at the bank, and receives therefor bank-notes with which he purchases corn here and there throughout the country. The bank-notes thus scattered over the country, enhance the price of all merchandise. The foreigner can purchase more cheaply outside of Germany, and foreign merchandise finds with us a good market. Exports diminish, imports increase. Before many months an unfavorable balance of trade appears, to the equalization of which, precious metal is demanded from abroad, as the universally valid compensation.

But, then, our banks of issue have need of their gold and silver in order to satisfy the growing liabilities of their unprotected bank-notes; therefore, they seek to prevent the outflow of specie by an exorbitant discount and a large curtailment of their note circulation. In consequence of this, merchandise again falls. The increased circulation had morbidly increased prices. The laborer must suddenly be put upon half-time, and the resulting misery from the demoralization of labor, affects the workman.

The effect which the bank-notes not based upon specie have upon the house question, and upon that of strikes, is brought about chiefly from the fact that they, as tools to increase interest and dividends, are always ready to enter into trade as soon as a business confidence is awakened; that they frequently increase the value of all necessaries, and that the unavoidable reaction of a period of labor demoralization is the result.

Drs. Meyer and Eras voted in the congress for an imperial bank of issue. In their proposals concerning the wants of dwellings, they pointed out the unjust increase of the currency as one of the hidden causes of the evil. Perhaps these gentlemen also belong to the modest friends of a complete metal protection. We have seen that, from the standpoint of the question on dwellings, an increase of the currency through the issue of notes, not based upon specie, is not just. We will investigate whether it can be considered just from *any* standpoint.

XIII.

BANKS OF ISSUE AND CHAMBERS OF COMMERCE.

In the Introduction are given the resolutions which were adopted by the trade convention at Leipzig upon the bank question. The minority of the chambers of commerce had their delegate pledged to favor a banking privilege with restrictions. As in the commercial trade congress at Dantzic, so also at Leipzig, those gentlemen voted, who hold a specie basis as the best, either for an imperial bank or for banking privileges with restrictions. Indeed, they voted according as they looked upon the one or the other as the smaller evil. In Leipzig, also, there were really men who entertained the opinion that banks of issue are of great advantage to trade and manufactures. Besides, it may be said of the debate on banks in Leipzig, as was said when the railroad question was under consideration, viz, during an opportunity in the debate upon the latter question, one of the speakers exclaimed, "Is this a convention of railroad directors, or of the representatives of commerce and manufactures?" So, too, of the congress at Dantzic, it might be asked, "Are these bank directors, or the agents of the people?" We have seen that the banks of issue increase misery and augment strikes. The manufacturer has to bear as much therefrom as the workman. We will now investigate whether reliable manufacturers and merchants, as reported in the chambers of commerce, and in the trade convention, in any way whatever, derive an advantage from the existence of the banks of issue.

From our examinations thus far, we are satisfied that, if all bank-notes· and all state paper money were annihilated, the world would not be deficient in precious metal to accommodate her money trade; 8,500,000,000 thalers, specie, would, in the absence of paper money, accommodate the same volume of trade as the present 12,000,000,000 thalers of mixed standard does. There is no other result possible; 85 thalers would have the same purchasing power as the present 120 thalers have. Whenever the trade of any country is lively, money will be in demand, and increase in purchase power. If this is more the case in one country than in another, then money will flow out of the latter into the former, for which the latter will receive merchandise and things of money value, as we have seen in Examples III and IV.

If in Germany, 8,000,000 thalers bank-notes were added to the present amount of money of 800,000,000 thalers, then 101 thalers would have no more purchase power than 100 thalers have at present, without the extra 8,000,000 thalers of new bank-notes. In the latter case, 100 thalers must discharge the same functions as the 101 thalers, and its purchase power would relatively be 1 per cent. higher. A lively trade makes money valuable and sought for. Not only every private gentleman, clerk, soldier, laborer, and widow—they who are obliged to live upon a certain sum—but also every merchant and manufacturer, every bank depositor, in short, every one who has a certain sum lying in cash, or who, as long as the effect of the 8,000,000 thalers of the new emission continues, finds it impossible to meet his expenses, secures, when business is in a flourishing condition, a gain of 1 per cent. Of this legitimate gain they are robbed by the banks of issue, through the introduction of 8,000,000 thalers of new bank-notes into the market. They take 8,000,000 thalers exchange from which the discount is subtracted, and gain actual interest upon a seeming capital. If, when money is discounted at 4 per cent., the sum of 800,000,000 thalers is sufficient, and in consequence of a revival in trade there is a demand for money, then by the continuation of the store of 800,000,000 thalers, money becomes scarcer and the discount rises. The business man who receives bank-notes would, in the absence of banks of issue, have to pay to a bank of deposit, based upon specie, a little more interest. Every reliable business man, however, will gladly submit to this, when, on the other hand, a pure specie standard is carefully preserved upon an unadulterated basis, and upon which rests all business in merchandise, stocks, exchange, &c. He does not desire that the purchase and interest power of his neighbor's money shall be damaged through unprotected bank-notes, in order to work to his advantage. In having any new business in view, he will simply ask himself if he is able to bear the high standard of interest; otherwise he will not enter upon it.

A higher discount diminishes the profit in mercantile business, &c., and the result is a restriction of the same. In this, however, lies the corrective of a too great expansion. With a pure metal standard, the discount only denotes the condition of business trade, as quicksilver in a thermometer. This natural corrective is wanting, when on account of a lively trade there is a demand for money, and banks are permitted to increase their issue of notes, unsupported by a specie basis. Regular reports of the bank cannot supply the natural corrective, because from them it is not evident whether an increase of currency has its origin in an increase of solid business, or in a desire on the part of the bank for dividends. In no case does a report of the status of the bank accomplish what an advanced discount does, because the latter is palpable, while by an increase of note circulation, the discount generally remains unaltered, and no one•has any material motive, because of restriction, to re-establish his ordinary business level, as every solid business man makes efforts to do.

Besides, if an increased demand for money justifies an increase of unprotected note issue, then under similar circumstances a second increase is justifiable. Once loosed from the safe anchorage of a pure specie-based circulation, and we are abandoned to the arbitrary limit of an unprotected paper money, and hurried step by step, ever deeper, into a mere paper standard. Then, by a business crisis, a heavy loss is occasioned to trade and manufactures.

Nearly all the discount business is associated with the banks of issue, and they have in their notes generally the customary pay-medium, or money, with which, without trouble, they can discount exchange. Mere banks of deposit must generally pay interest for their deposits, and cannot compete with notes exempt from interest and use their money in other advantageous ways. In a crisis they have double reasons for so doing, because then all exchange and the price of stocks are more than usually disarranged, and better opportunities for business which secures a profit are offered than is allowed by mere discount. They have, therefore, at the time of a crisis, no inducement to offer assistance to business people who are not their customers. They must, however, keep in view the possibility of a forced circulation occurring, and that for the paper money which they have given in exchange, they retain money which is burdened with a tax. They dare not at least endanger their own with specie of equal capital.

Discount operations lean upon the banks of issue in times of prosperity, and they direct the business world during a crisis. However, at such times the banks of issue must immediately curtail their circulation, and if they do not wish to be exposed to the danger of suspending specie payment, they will use their power to increase their stock of specie.

The bank of Darmstadt, in its report for the year 1866, conceded that in July and August, of 1870, it was for this reason obliged to limit its discounts. It spoke as follows:

We discontinued (at the beginning of the crisis) entirely all large disbursements and discounts, denied ourselves of those parts of our exchange portfolio which, according to man's judgment, might be difficult for us, and drew therefor larger amounts of cash. We very soon had the amount of our yet circulating notes in ready money. We voluntarily, and by way of precaution, withdrew our bank-notes from trade.

The Prussian bank, and the other banks of the North German Confederacy, had in the year 1870:

	End of June.	End of July.	End of August.
	Thalers.	*Thalers.*	*Thalers.*
Metal, Prussian bank	87,370,000	93,404,000	98,773,000
Metal, other banks	41,217,000	42,481,000	43,237,000
Treasury bills and bank-notes, Prussian bank	2,267,000	1,873,000	2,989,000
Treasury bills and bank-notes, other banks	4,232,000	13,142,000	7,562,000
Bills of exchange, Prussian bank	97,770,000	121,153,000	106,232,000
Bills of exchange, other banks	85,671,000	89,013,000	75,854,000
"Lombards," Prussian bank	20,136,000	22,069,000	23,762,000
"Lombards," other banks	23,283,000	26,191,000	25,977,000
Sundries, Prussian bank	13,023,000	19,989,000	18,476,000
Sundries, other banks	28,757,000	20,229,000	28,142,000
Bank-notes in circulation, Prussian bank	167,965,000	201,483,000	195,772,000
Bank-notes in circulation, other banks	67,779,000	63,675,000	50,221,000
Deposits, Prussian bank	21,717,000	20,163,000	18,290,000
Deposits, other banks	19,273,000	20,980,000	21,183,000
Indorsements, &c., Prussian bank	3,039,000	11,509,000	6,446,000
Indorsements, &c., other banks	33,218,000	52,773,000	40,745,000
Bank-notes without a specie basis, Prussian bank	80,595,000	108,059,000	96,999,000
Bank-notes without a specie basis, other banks	20,562,000	21,194,000	15,984,000

From this comparison it is evident, that—

1. As the trading class most need the assistance of the banks, that the Prussian bank, as well as the remaining banks of the North German Confederacy, of that time, spent a part of their power, in order to be able to recuperate at the close of the war, already in progress, and of the business crisis; doing that which they had neglected in time of peace, viz, by large stores of metal to be ready for time of war.

2. That the medium and small banks essentially curtailed their note circulation and their discounts.

3. That the Prussian bank expended largely, especially in the first pressure.

It is a great calamity to trade and manufactures when a sudden crisis nearly destroys the source from whence they were accustomed to draw their supply of money. Many are forced to employ other means, because their merchandise and goods are squandered at panic prices.

In 1870, prices stood as follows:

	July 1.	August 1.	September 1.
	d.	*d.*	*d.*
Cotton, Orleans middling	10$\frac{7}{16}$	8$\frac{1}{4}$ – $\frac{1}{4}$	9$\frac{1}{4}$
Spirits, at home, Berlin	16$\frac{1}{4}$	14$\frac{1}{16}$	16$\frac{1}{4}$
Rape-seed oil	14	13$\frac{1}{4}$	14
Rye	49$\frac{7}{8}$	44$\frac{1}{4}$	51$\frac{1}{4}$
Prussian 4$\frac{1}{2}$ per cent. state's loan	93$\frac{1}{2}$	81$\frac{1}{4}$	89$\frac{1}{4}$
Cologne-Mindener Railroad	134$\frac{1}{2}$	111	127
Lombardy Railroad	114$\frac{1}{2}$	90$\frac{1}{4}$	105$\frac{1}{2}$

The panic prices occurred immediately at the time in which the banks of issue employed a large part of their power to strengthen their metal basis.

As a rule, in ordinary times, a complete metal basis is a security against heavy losses, because Germany, in a crisis, is, above all, furnished with a substance in demand from the whole world, viz, precious metal.

So great, however, was the loss sustained by trade and manufactures, in the summer of 1870, through the banks of issue, that the management of the Prussian bank at that time, which differs from that of the other banks in an expansion of its note circulation, gained favor, it is true, but also threatened Germany with the fearful danger of a forced circulation, which, by less favorable events of the campaign, might easily have occurred, and which, for trade and manufactures, would have been a calamity ten times greater than the losses which grew out of the sudden restriction of the other banks.

From a forced circulation, and the other misfortunes specified above, the trade and manufactures are defended, when there are no banks of issue. The other unemployed money of the country would then be collected into a bank of deposit, in which henceforth is concentrated the business of discount, upon the basis of a pure specie circulation. It is true that a somewhat higher interest would have to be paid, by trade and manufactures during lively business seasons, but in a crisis there will not be a scanty price given. Then the vaults of Germany will be filled with metal, and then, instead of sacrificing merchandise and goods in order to import metal, metal can be exported to purchase foreign values at panic prices. By the emission of unprotected notes, the banks of issue acquire interest, while the trade and manufactures suffer loss. A crisis in the commercial world of the nations will be a harvest of gain to us if we possess a pure metal basis. This we shall draw from our metal which other people are in want of. Every million thalers paper money, then, which we have in circulation, unprotected, is a loss to us.

But why is it that many merchants and manufacturers regard the banks of issue as advantageous to their position? Many of these gentlemen are mistaken as to their real nature. Others stand in close relation as directors. The banks of issue, especially the Prussian bank, influence, through their note emissions, rates of discount, and other operations, the price of merchandise, foreign exchange, and stocks, and to know this beforehand, or to assist in determining, is a source of great advantage in the exchange, as we have already shown. The position of director secures this advantage, that even before the outbreak of a crisis many banks discount in the most extensive manner, and at a relatively cheap rate, which is divided among the nearest friends at hand. The immediate recipients acquire by this means the money medium, which saves them from sacrificing their merchandise, and are only slightly affected by a future forced circulation. That portion of the traders and manufacturers who stand at a distance from the banks of issue, especially the independent element whose paper is not discounted by the bank, or who are unfairly repulsed, because they oppose the banks of issue, are threatened by two evils. Many other business people who need banks, blow, from mere fear of loss, into the horn of the bank of issue party.

The stockholders of the banks of issue, however, prefer to yield their privilege of issue, and gradually change into banks of deposit. It is a fact long known, that the latter, nearly throughout, yield a larger dividend, and that from interest the stockholders should desire a change; but the directors find in the interchange of their bank-notes, for exchange, a business without care or trouble, and in the influencing of the money-market through bank-note circulation, a source of gain. They govern, through material means, intelligence, and fear, the most of the commercial board; and for that reason the commercial convention is partly a convention of bank adherents. The independent element despair of being able to lift the commercial convention and the industrial congress, above the power of bank interests, to the standpoint of a true, sound, money circulation, and which would be one of the public benefits of the German Empire. But of that we will not despair.

XIV.

BANKS OF ISSUE AND THE STATE.

We have seen how Dr. Alex. Meyer, secretary of the standing committee of the Commercial Trade Convention in Dantzic, in connection with Dr. Eras, drew attention to the increase in the rents of dwellings as the result of the emission of notes unsupported by specie. For that reason we hoped to greet him as a modest friend of a complete metal basis. But we were left in doubt by an expression which the doctor made in the debate on banks. He spoke of *the power which the state needs in the issue of certificates of deposit in order to control trade.* Is this for the benefit of trade, or for that of the state? We have already shown how trade suffers when a bank controls it by the issue of certificates of deposit, but now forsooth the state must do the same. The doctor appears to be the "*enfant terrible*" of the Liberal Bank Party.

The scale of value of the precious metals is the natural basis of all coinage, or of all money affairs. No genuine domestic economy is disposed to permit any one to arbitrarily adulterate the same, and thus to abolish the natural corrective compensation. The idea, especially, that the state with her certificates of deposit controls trade, must be rejected as monstrous, so much the more as the state occupies a peculiar position on the money question. The state has pronounced the $\frac{1}{30}$ pound of fine silver, equaling 1 thaler currency, as the scale of value. As we have seen, the value of 1 thaler depends upon its quantity. The state receives the service of her officers, her military, and she owes money. Dare she adulterate the scale of value established by herself by creating an amount of paper money to perform the entire money functions of the silver thaler, when, by the increase of the whole amount of money, the value of the thaler is lessened? Dare the state pay her soldiers and her debts with thalers thus depreciated?

A perverted financial economy in times of peace permits the issue of thalers of unreliable paper money. A war breaks out and a money dilmema ensues. To satisfy the violent demand for supplies, new unprotected paper is issued and enters into trade. The fortunes of war are variable. In order to negotiate a war loan, at a high figure, the treasury must assist by new paper money. Suddenly the military situation becomes doubtful. The creditor refuses to accept paper money, and insists upon specie, which has long since been withdrawn from trade, and in part forced out of the country. In order to prevent, in the midst of the war, a panic, and a sudden high discount upon paper money, a forced circulation is declared. The specie, which no longer is needed in trade, leaves the country entirely. The banks of issue, taking advantage of these favorable circumstances, entirely dispense with all concern as regards a metal basis, in order to increase their dividends. Only a small amount of specie is retained, in case the state should make a demand for a resumption of specie payment.

Golden times for bankrupts and stock-jobbers! In the United States, the Eldorado of the Manchester school, the status of the paper dollar (bank-notes as well as state paper money, greenbacks so called) was:

1861. December 31	= 100	cents specie.
1862. December 31	= 75	" "
1863. December 31	= 66	" "
1864. June 20	= 50	" "
1864. July 20	= 35–36	" "
1864. December 31	= 44	" "

1865. March	1 = 50	cents specie.
1865. April	1 = 66	" "
1865. December 31 = 69		" "
1866. June	18 = 60–64	" "
1866. December 31 = 75		" "
1867. December 31 = 75		" "
1871. December 31 = 90		" "

A widow, who loaned $1,000 gold in 1861, must in 1864 be content to receive from her debtor $1,000 paper money, whose value is less than $500 in gold. A merchant, A, in 1861, entered into partnership with B in the mercantile business; A's capital is $10,000 in gold, B's is nothing. At the close of 1863, there is an overplus of the active amount over the passive amount of $15,000, paper money, of which $5,000 is regarded as business profit, each partner claiming $2,500. Now the $15,000 paper money is worth no more than was the $10,000 gold, so that the business has brought no gain. Nevertheless, at the close of 1863 B possesses $2,500 paper money = $1,667 in gold, which A must pay him, although of his original $10,000 he has but $8,333 in gold.

The fluctuations of the paper standard form a lottery. If a business man sells for paper money, on open account, he may secure the amount of the same by a fixed balance; in many instances, however, only through great difficulty. In the United States, this is called the gold profit, and it always costs, according to the height of the special existing interest standard for this purpose, from ½ to 1 per cent. monthly. In times of trouble or excitement, it has been from ¼ to ½ per cent. per day. To avoid paying the tax upon exchange, many business people became speculators. In New York there exists an express gold exchange for the paper money swindle. A business man, who on January 1, 1862, sold $1,000 worth of merchandise, on six months' credit, received therefor only $857 in gold. One thousand dollars in gold, borrowed 31st December, 1861, could on the 31st December, 1862, be reimbursed by $1,000 bank-notes, worth only $750. A tailor, who on the 20th June, 1864, furnishes his customer with a suit of clothes, from imported cloth, to the amount of $100 in paper money, which at the time was worth $50 in gold, must on the 12th July accept $100 paper money, worth only from $35 to $36 in specie, which does not pay the cost of the cloth, whereby he loses more than the value of his labor. The soldier is cheated out of his pay. In 1864 a barrel of flour cost $15 paper money, or $7.50 gold. The laborer received his wages in paper. He demanded and extorted, where he formerly received $1 in specie, $2 in paper, and wages have generally kept at this height in the United States, although paper dollars very soon rose again to 90 cents. A social revolution is the result, and the high wages in the United States, proceeding from the perverted financial economy, causes a significant ferment in the social democratic movements of Europe.

If the United States had desired to do justice to her officers and soldiers, she would have formed a new budget with every change of premium, or gauged all her receipts and disbursements according to the specie standard. *Many functionaries seek to indemnify themselves in other ways.*

We have also seen that an interference of the state with the sign of value in trade, is not only of great disadvantage to the same, but exposes the state itself to great danger. Let us investigate whether the state needs a bank of issue independent of itself, or of the state paper money, for its financial operations.

That it is convenient for a minister of finance who requires money, to furnish it by the disbursement of paper money, no one will deny. But because such disbursements are united; (1,) with a disturbance of the natural conditions of trade; (2,) with the enrichment of the bankers, whom the government consults, and who by their knowledge of the operation secure business advantages; (3,) with injustice toward all officers, the army, the government creditors; in short toward all who live upon a fixed salary; (4,) with the fearful danger of a forced circulation, therefore the small inconveniences with which a fixed stable proportion of a pure specie basis is united, are not to be taken into consideration.

Dr. Wolf broke a lance in the congress, in favor of the imperial bank of issue, and said, "The danger of a forced circulation is certainly not made impossible by a central bank." I maintain that it is greater with a central bank, because such a bank is especially exposed to the risk of serving the financial projects of the moment. We can make a forced circulation impossible, by annihilating all banks, except the Prussian bank. If Germany, on engaging in a war, has a pure metal basis of 800,000,000 thalers, and besides, has in her war treasury 40,000,000 thalers gold in cash, then we are safe against a forced circulation. With such a metal production, we would find ourselves in an entirely different condition than if we should enter into a war with a deficit of about 200,000,000 thalers bank-notes, and state paper money, unsupported by specie, as happened in 1866-'67. The war tax of from 20,000,000 to 25,000,000 thalers monthly, helps us at first. From four to six weeks after the outbreak of a war the commercial world has, through various means, recovered, and where there is confidence money is cheap.

The only effective money of Germany, therefore, is specie. Consequently, it is not necessary to flood the market with paper money, at a discount of from 3 to 4 per cent., in order to make it cheaper. The state will negotiate a loan with England in legal money, that is, specie, if it can there obtain it cheaper. A country which in war pays a heavy interest, is considered more solid from the highest standpoint, than when, for convenience sake, it grasps at an interest-saving paper-money circulation, which leads step by step to a forced circulation. The state will, with the specie which it receives, purchase its necessary munitions, provisions, &c., cheaper than with unprotected paper money, and it will give to its officers and army what belongs to them, viz, specie of full value.

The duties of a reliable financial minister, in the event of a war, are so clearly defined, and the financial condition of the country resting upon a complete metal basis, at the outbreak of a war, is so secure, that, in reference to the critical condition in which, by the outbreak of war, the joint interests of trade and manufactures, and especially of the laborer, are placed, I unhesitatingly hold, the exception to a complete metal basis, for the first four to six weeks after the opening of hostilities, to be allowable; as I explained in Chapter II.

XV.

ADAM SMITH ON SPECIE AND PAPER MONEY.

On account of the interest which the Manchester school is exciting at this time, that which Adam Smith, in his "Wealth of Nations," chap. ii, says in regard to its most essential elements, is given a place here.

In order to create materials for the sustenance of life, certain things, as fixed capital, are requisite, viz, landed estate, machinery, &c. For the purpose of improving and enlarging the means of livelihood, products not convertible can be used as fixed capital. Money is the only part of the circulating capital of a society of which the maintenance can occasion any diminution in their neat revenue.

The fixed capital and that part of the circulating capital which consists in money, so far as they affect the revenue of society, bear a very great resemblance to one another in three ways:

1. A certain quantity of very valuable materials, gold and silver, and of very curious labor, instead of augmenting the stock reserved for immediate consumption, the subsistence, conveniences, and amusements of individuals, is employed in supporting that great but expensive instrument of commerce, by means of which every individual in the society has his subsistence, conveniences, and amusements regularly distributed to him in their proper proportion.

2. When we talk of any particular sum of money, we sometimes mean nothing but the metal pieces of which it is composed; and sometimes we include in our meaning some obscure reference to the goods which can be had in exchange for it. When we say that a man is worth fifty or one hundred pounds a year, we mean commonly to express not only the amount of the metal pieces which are annually paid to him, but the value of the goods which he can annually purchase or consume. A certain income in money includes rather what may be purchased by it than the money itself.

Thus, if a guinea be the weekly pension of a particular person, he can in the course of the week purchase with it a certain quantity of subsistence, conveniences, and amusements. In proportion as this quantity is great or small, so are his real riches, his real weekly revenue. His weekly revenue is certainly not equal both to the guinea and to what can be purchased with it, but only to one or the other of those two equal values; and to the latter more properly than to the former, to the guinea's worth rather than to the guinea.

If the pension of such a person was paid to him not in gold but in a weekly bill for a guinea, his revenue surely would not so properly consist in the piece of paper as in what he could get for it. A guinea may be considered as a bill for a certain quantity of necessaries and conveniences upon all the tradesmen in the neighborhood. The revenue of the person to whom it is paid does not so properly consist in the piece of gold as in what he can get for it or in what he can exchange for it. If it could be exchanged for nothing, it would, like a bill upon a bankrupt, be of no more value than a useless piece of paper.

The same guinea which pays the weekly pension of one man to-day may pay that of another to-morrow, and that of a third the day thereafter. Money is indeed a very valuable part of capital, but it makes no part of the revenue of the society to which it belongs.

3. The machines, instruments of trade, &c., which compose the fixed capital, bear this further resemblance to that part of the circulating capital which consists in money, that as every saving in the expense of erecting and supporting those machines, which does not diminish the productive powers of labor, is an improvement of the neat revenue of the society, so every saving in the expense of collecting and supporting that part of the circulating capital which consists in money is an improvement of exactly the same kind.

The substitution of paper in the room of gold and silver money replaces a very expensive instrument with one much less costly.

When the people of any particular country have such confidence in the fortune, probity, and prudence of a particular banker as to believe that he is always ready to pay upon demand such of his promissory notes as are likely to be at any time presented to him, those notes come to have the same currency as gold and silver money, from the confidence that such money can at any time be had for them.

Let us suppose, for example, that the whole circulating money of some particular country amounted at a particular time to one million pounds sterling, that sum being then sufficient for circulating the whole annual produce of their land and labor. Some time thereafter, different banks and bankers issued promissory notes, payable to the bearer, to the extent of one million, reserving in their different coffers two hundred thousand pounds for answering occasional demands. There would remain, therefore, in circulation eight hundred thousand pounds in gold and silver and one million of bank-notes, or eighteen hundred thousand pounds of paper and specie together. But the annual produce of the land and labor of the country had before required only one million to circulate and distribute it to its proper consumers, and that annual produce cannot be immediately augmented by those operations of banking. One million, therefore, will be sufficient to circulate it after them. The goods to be bought and sold being precisely the same as before, the same quantity of money will be sufficient for buying and selling them. The channel of circulation will remain precisely the same as before. One million was sufficient to fill that channel. Whatever is poured into it beyond this sum must overflow. One million eight hundred thousand pounds are poured in; eight hundred thousand pounds therefore must overflow. This sum cannot be employed at home; it is too valuable to be allowed to lie idle; it must be sent abroad to be employed. But the paper cannot go abroad, because at a distance from the banks which issue it, and from the country in which payment for it can be exacted by law, it will not be received. Gold and silver therefore to the amount of eight hundred thousand pounds will be sent abroad, and the channel of home circulation will remain filled with a million of paper instead of the million of specie which formerly filled it.

But though so great a quantity of gold and silver is sent abroad, we must not imagine that its proprietors make a present of it to foreign nations. It is a new fund created for carrying on a new trade.

If they employ it in purchasing foreign goods for home consumption, they may either, first, purchase such goods as are likely to be consumed by idle people who produce nothing, such as foreign wines, silks, &c., or, secondly, they may purchase an additional stock of materials, tools, and provisions, in order to maintain and employ an additional number of industrious people.

As employed in the first way, it is a disadvantage to society, by promoting prodigality and increasing expense without increasing production.

So far as it is employed in the second way, it promotes industry; for, though it increases the consumption of the society, it provides a fund for supporting that consumption. It is, however, not only probable, but almost unavoidable, that it must be employed in purchasing that of the second kind. For though some particular men may sometimes increase their expense very considerably though their revenue does not increase at all, we may be assured that no *class* or *order* of men does so; because, though the principles of common prudence do not always govern the conduct of every *individual*, they always influence that of the majority of every class or order. But the revenue of idle people, considered as a class or order, cannot, in the smallest degree, be increased by those operations of banking. Their expense in general, therefore, cannot be much increased by them, though that of a few individuals among them may, and, in reality, sometimes is. The demand of idle people therefore for foreign goods being the same, or very nearly the same, as before, a very small part of the money which, being forced abroad by those operations of banking, is employed in purchasing foreign goods for home consumption is likely to be employed in purchasing those for their use. The greater part of it will naturally be destined for the employment of industry, and not for the maintenance of idleness.

When paper is substituted in the room of gold and silver money, the quantity of the materials, tools, and maintenance which the whole circulating capital can supply may be increased by the whole value of gold and silver which used to be employed in purchasing them.

What is the proportion which the circulating money of any country bears to the whole value of the annual produce circulated by means of it, it is perhaps impossible to determine. It has been computed by different authors at a fifth, at a tenth, at a twentieth, and at a thirtieth part of that value. If but four-fifths of the circulating gold and silver is added to the funds which are destined for the maintenance of industry, it must make a very considerable addition to the quantity of that industry, and consequently to the value of the annual produce of land and labor.

An operation of this kind has, within these five and twenty or thirty years, been performed in Scotland, by the erection of new banking companies in almost every considerable town, and even in some country villages. The effects of it have been precisely those above described. The business of the country is almost entirely carried on by means of the paper of those different banking companies, with which purchases and payments of all kinds are commonly made. Silver very seldom appears, except in the change of a twenty shillings bank-note, and gold still seldomer. But though the conduct of all those different companies has not been unexceptionable, and has accordingly required an act of Parliament to regulate it, the country, notwithstanding, has evidently derived great benefit from their trade. I have heard it asserted that the trade of the city of Glasgow doubled in about fifteen years after the first erection of the banks there. That the trade and industry of Scotland have increased very considerably, and that the banks have contributed a good deal to this increase, cannot be doubted.

Although the circulating gold and silver of Scotland have suffered so great a diminution, its real riches and prosperity do not appear to have suffered any. Its agriculture, manufactures, and trade, on the contrary, the annual produce of its land and labor, have evidently been augmented.

It is chiefly by discounting bills of exchange that the greater part of bank and bankers issue their promissory notes. The payment of the bill, when it becomes due, replaces to the bank the value of what had been advanced, together with a clear profit of the interest.

The first two banks of Scotland, which were founded in 1695 and 1727, would have had but little trade had they confined their business to the discounting of bills of exchange. They invented, therefore, another method of issuing their promissory notes; by granting what they called cash accounts, that is, by giving credit to the extent of a certain sum (two or three thousand pounds, for example), to any individual who could procure two persons of undoubted credit and good landed estate to become surety for him that whatever money should be advanced to him, within the sum for which the credit had been given, should be repaid upon demand, together with the legal interest. The easy terms of these cash accounts have perhaps been the principal cause both of the great trade of those companies and of the benefit which the country has received from it.

Whoever has a credit of this kind with one of those companies, and borrows a thousand pounds upon it, for example, may repay this sum piecemeal, by twenty and thirty pounds at a time, the company discounting a proportionable part of the interest of the great sum from the day on which each of those small sums is paid in, till the whole be in this manner repaid. All merchants, therefore, and almost all men of business, find it convenient to keep such cash accounts with them, and are therefore interested to promote the trade of those companies by readily receiving their notes in all payments, and by encouraging all those with whom they have any influence to do the same. The merchants pay them to the manufacturers for goods, the manufacturers to the farmers for materials and provisions, the farmers to their landlords for rent, &c., until the merchants again return them to the bank to balance their cash accounts or to replace what they may have borrowed of them.

By means of these cash accounts a merchant in Edinburgh, without imprudence, can carry on a greater trade, and give employment to a greater number of people, than a London merchant. The London merchant must always keep by him a considerable sum of money, either in his own coffers, or in those of his banker, who gives him no interest for it, in order to answer the demands continually coming upon him for payment of the goods which he purchases upon credit. Let the ordinary amount of this sum be supposed five hundred pounds. The value of his goods in his warehouse must always be less by five hundred pounds than it would have been had he not been obliged to keep such a sum unemployed. His annual profits must be less by all that he could have made by the sale of five hundred pounds' worth more goods; and the number of people employed in preparing his goods for the market must be less by all those that five hundred pounds more stock could have employed. The merchant in Edinburgh, on the other hand, keeps no money unemployed for answering such occasional demands. When they actually come upon him, he satisfies them from his cash account with the bank, and gradually replaces the sum borrowed with the money or paper which comes in from the occasional sales of his goods. With the same stock, therefore, he can, without imprudence, make a greater profit himself than the London merchant, and give employment to a greater number of people.

The whole paper money of every kind which can easily circulate in any country never can exceed the value of the gold and silver of which it supplies the place, or which (the commerce being supposed the same), would circulate there if there was no paper money. Should the circulating paper at any time exceed that sum, it must immediately return upon the banks to be exchanged for gold and silver. When this superfluous paper was converted into gold and silver, they could easily find a use for it by sending it abroad. There would be an immediate run upon the banks, and if they showed any backwardness in payment, the alarm which this would occasion necessarily, would increase the run.

A banking company which issues more paper than can be employed in the circulation of the country, and of which the excess is continually returning upon it for payment, ought to increase the quantity of gold and silver in its coffers, not only in proportion to this excessive increase of its circulation, but in a much greater proportion, its notes returning upon it much faster than in proportion to the excess of their quantity. If, for example, a bank with a circulation of 40,000 pounds sterling in notes has 10,000 pounds sterling in specie, then if she would increase her circulation to 44,000 pounds sterling, she must keep in her coffers, not 11,000 pounds only, but 14,000 pounds sterling specie. She will thus gain nothing by the interest of the 4,000 pounds excessive circulation, and will lose the expense of continually collecting 4,000 pounds of specie which will be continually going out of its coffers as fast as collected.

Every particular banking company has not always understood or attended to its own particular interest, and the circulation has frequently been overstocked with paper money.

By issuing too great a quantity of paper, of which the excess was continually returning, in order to be exchanged for gold and silver, the Bank of England was for many years together obliged to coin gold to the extent of between £800,000 and £1,000,000 a year, or at an average about £850,000. For this great coinage the bank was frequently obliged to purchase gold bullion at the high price of £4 an ounce, which it soon after issued in coin at £3 17s. 10½d. an ounce, losing in this manner between 2½ and 3 per cent.

The Scotch banks, in consequence of an excess of the same kind, were all obliged to constantly employ agents at London to collect money for them, at an expense which was seldom below 1½ or 2 per cent. with an additional three-fourths per cent. expense for carrying. Those agents were not always able to replenish the coffers of their employers so fast as they were emptied. In this case the resource of the banks was to draw upon their correspondents in London bills of exchange to the extent of the sum which they wanted. When these correspondents afterward drew upon them for the payment of this sum, together with the interest and a commission, some of those banks, from the distress into which their excessive circulation had thrown them, had sometimes no other means of satisfying this draft but by drawing a second set of bills, either upon the same or upon some other correspondents in London; and the same sum, or rather bills for the same sum, would in this manner make sometimes more than two or three journeys, the debtor bank paying always the interest and commission upon the whole accumulated sum. Even those Scotch banks, which never distinguished themselves by their extreme imprudence, were sometimes obliged to employ this ruinous resource.

The Scotch banks, no doubt, paid all of them very dearly for their own imprudence and inattention, but the Bank of England paid very dearly, not only for its own imprudence, but for the much greater imprudence of almost all the Scotch banks.

The overtrading of some bold projectors in both parts of the United Kingdom was the original cause of this excessive circulation of paper money.

What a bank can with propriety advance to a merchant or undertaker of any kind, is not either the whole capital with which he trades, or even any considerable part of that capital, but that part of it only which he would otherwise be obliged to keep by him unemployed, and in ready money for answering occasional demands. If the paper money which the bank advances never exceeds this value, it can never exceed the value of the gold and silver, which would necessarily circulate in the country if there was no paper money.

When a bank discounts to a merchant a real bill of exchange, drawn by a real creditor upon a real debtor, and which as soon as becomes due is really paid by the debtor, it only advances to him a part of the value which he would otherwise be obliged to keep by him unemployed and in ready money for answering occasional demands. The payment of the bill when it becomes due replaces to the bank the value of what it had advanced, together with the interest. The coffers of the bank resemble a water pond, from which, though a stream is continually running out, yet another is continually running in fully equal to that which runs out.

A merchant, without overtrading, may frequently have occasion for a sum of ready money, even when he has no bills to discount. When a bank, besides discounting his bills, advances him likewise upon such occasions such sums upon his cash account, and accepts of a piece-meal repayment as the money comes in from the occasional sale of his goods upon the easy terms of the banking companies of Scotland, it dispenses him entirely from the necessity of keeping any part of his stock by him unemployed and in ready money for answering occasional demands. When such demands actually come upon him, he can answer them sufficiently from his cash account. The bank, however, ought to closely observe the accounts. If in the course of four, five, six, or eight months the sum of the repayments is fully equal to that of the advances, it may safely continue to deal with such customers. In other cases it must discontinue.

The banking companies of Scotland accordingly were for a long time very careful to require frequent and regular repayments from all their customers, and did not care to deal with any person, whatever might be his fortune or credit, who did not make what they called frequent and regular operations with them. By this attention they gained two very considerable advantages.

1. They, by this attention, were enabled to make some tolerable judgment concerning the thriving or declining circumstances of their debtors, without being obliged to look out for any other evidence besides what their own books afforded them; men being for the most part either regular or irregular in their payments, according as their circumstances are either thriving or declining. A bank which lends money to perhaps five hundred different people can have no regular information except what its books furnish.

2. By this attention they secured themselves from the possibility of issuing more paper money than what the circulation of the country could easily absorb and employ. When they observed, that within moderate periods of time the repayments of a particular customer were upon most occasions fully equal to the advances which they had made to him, they might be assured that the paper money which they had advanced to him had not at any time exceeded the quantity of gold and silver which he would otherwise have been obliged to keep by him for answering occasional demands; and that, consequently, the paper money, which they had circulated by his means, had not at any time exceeded the quantity of gold and silver which would have circulated in the country had there been no paper money.

When, partly by the conveniency of discounting bills and partly by that of cash accounts, the creditable traders of any country can be dispensed from the necessity of keeping any part of their stock by them unemployed and in ready money for answering occasional demands, they can reasonably expect no further assistance from banks and bankers, who, when they have gone thus far, cannot, consistently with their own interests and safety, go farther. A bank cannot, consistently with its own interest, advance to a trader the whole or even the greater part of the circulating capital with which he trades; because though that capital is continually returning to him in the shape of money and going from him in the same shape, yet the whole of the returns is too distant from the whole of the outgoings, and the sum of his repayments could not equal the sum of its advances within such moderate periods of time as suit the conveniency of a bank. Still less could a bank afford to advance him any considerable part of his fixed capital; for example, the capital which the undertaker of an iron-forge employs in erecting his forge and smelting-houses, &c. The returns of the fixed capital are in almost all cases much slower than those of the circulating capital; therefore, the necessary money therefor should not be borrowed from a bank.

It is now more than five and twenty years since the paper money issued by the different banking companies of Scotland was found fully equal, or rather was somewhat more than fully equal to what the circulation of the country could easily absorb and employ. They had overtraded a little and thereby lost, or at least diminished their profits. Those traders, and other undertakers, having got so much assistance from banks and bankers, wished to get still more. The banks they seemed to have thought could extend their credits to whatever sum might be wanted without incurring any other expense besides that of a few reams of paper. They complained of the contracted views and dastardly spirit of the directors of those banks, which did not, they said, extend their credits in proportion to the extension of the trade of the country. The banks, however, were of a different opinion, and upon their refusing to extend their credit, some of those traders had recourse to an expedient which, for a time, served their purpose though at a much greater expense, yet as effectually as the utmost extension of bank credits could have done. This expedient was no other than the well-known shift of drawing and redrawing—the shift to which unfortunate traders have sometimes recourse when they are upon the brink of bankruptcy. The practice of raising money in this manner had been long known in England, and during the course of the late war, when the high profits of trade afforded a great temptation to over-trading, is said to have been carried on to a very great extent. From England it was brought into Scotland, where, in proportion to the very limited commerce and to the very moderate capital of the country, it was soon carried on to a much greater extent than it ever had been in England.

The trader, A, in Edinburgh, we shall suppose, draws a bill upon B, in London, payable two months after date. In reality B, in London, owes nothing to A, in Edinburgh; but he agrees to accept of A's bill upon condition that before the term of payment he shall redraw upon A, in Edinburgh, for the same sum, together with the interest and a commission, another bill payable likewise two months after date. B, accordingly, before the expiration of the first two months, redraws this bill upon A, in Edinburgh, who again, after the expiration of the second two months, draws a second bill upon B, in London, payable likewise two months after date; and before the expiration of the third two months B, in London, redraws upon A, in Edinburgh, another bill, payable, also, two months after date.

The bills which A, in Edingurgh, drew upon B, in London, he regularly discounted two months before they were due with some bank or banker in Edinburgh; and the bills which B, in London, redrew upon A, in Edinburgh, he as regularly discounted either with the Bank of England or with some other bankers in London. Whatever was advanced upon such circulating bills was, in Edinburgh, advanced in the paper of the Scotch banks, and in London, when they were discounted at the Bank of England, in the paper of that bank. Though the bills upon which this paper had been advanced were all of them repaid in their turn as soon as they became due, yet the value which had been really advanced upon the first bill was never really returned to the banks which advanced it; because, before each bill became due, another bill was always drawn to somewhat a greater amount than the bill which was soon to be paid; and the discounting of this other bill was effectually necessary towards the payment of that which was soon to be due. This payment, therefore, was altogether fictitious. The stream which, by means of those circulating bills of exchange, had once been made to run out from the coffers of the banks was never replaced by any stream which really ever run into them. The greater part of this paper was over and above the value of the gold and silver which would have circulated in the country had there been no paper money, and upon that account immediately returned upon the banks for redemption. It was a capital which those projectors had very artfully contrived to draw from those banks, not only without their knowledge or deliberate consent, but for some time, perhaps, without their having the most distant suspicion that they had really advanced it. In order to avoid discovery the speculators formed a ring and discounted their bills sometimes with one banker and sometimes with another. The difficulties which the Bank of England, the principal bankers in London, and which even the more prudent Scotch banks began, after a certain time, and when all of them had already gone too far, to make about discounting, not only alarmed but enraged in the highest degree those projectors. Their own distress they called the distress of the country; and this distress of the country they said was all owing to the ignorance, pusillanimity, and bad conduct of the banks which did not give a sufficiently liberal aid to the spirited undertakings of those who exerted themselves in order to beautify, improve, and enrich the country.

In the midst of this clamor and distress a new bank was established in Scotland for the express purpose of relieving the distress of the country. It met the views of the speculator and drew the business of the other banks to itself, but in two years it was obliged to stop operations. The distress was only aggravated, and heavier than it would have been two years previous.

That the industry of Scotland languished for want of money to employ it was the opinion of the famous Mr. Law. His plan was afterward adopted by the Duke of Orleans. The idea of the possibility of multiplying paper money to almost any extent was the real foundation of what is called the Mississippi scheme. The splendid but visionary ideas which are set forth in that and some other works upon the same principles still continue to make an impression upon many people, and have, perhaps, in part, contributed to that excess of banking which has of late been complained of, both in Scotland and in other places.

The Bank of England is the greatest bank of circulation in Europe. It was incorporated, in pursuance of an act of Parliament, by a charter under the great seal dated the 27th of July, 1694. It at that time advanced to the government £1,200,000 sterling for an annuity of £100,000 sterling, or for £96,000 a year interest at 8 per cent. and £4,000 a year for the expense of management. The credit of the new government established by the revolution, we may believe, must have been very low when it was obliged to borrow at so high an interest.

In 1696 her bank-notes were discounted at 25 per cent.* In 1746 the bank had, upon different occasions, advanced to the public £11,686,800 sterling, and its divided capital had been raised by different calls and subscriptions to £10,980,000. In those different operations its duty to the public may sometimes have obliged it, without any fault of its directors, to overstock the circulation with paper money. It has upon different occasions rendered great service. Upon other occasions this great company has been reduced to the necessity of paying in sixpences.

The gold and silver money which circulates in any country is a very valuable part of the capital of the country which produces nothing to the country. The judicious operations of banking by substituting paper in the room of a great part of this gold and silver enables the country to convert a great part of this dead stock into active and productive stock.

The commerce and industry of the country, however, it must be acknowledged, though they may be somewhat augmented, cannot be altogether so secure when they are thus, as it were, suspended upon the Dædalian wings of paper money, as when they travel about upon the solid ground of gold and silver. Over and above the accidents to which they are exposed from the unskillfulness of the conductors of this paper money, they are liable to several others from which no prudence or skill of those conductors can guard them.

An unsuccessful war, for example, in which the enemy got possession of the capital, and consequently of that treasure which supported the credit of the paper money, would occasion a much greater confusion in a country where the whole circulation was carried on by paper than in one where the greater part of it was carried on by gold and silver. The usual instrument of commerce having lost its value no exchanges could be made but either by barter or upon credit. All taxes having been usually paid in paper money, the prince would not have wherewithal either to pay his troops or to furnish his magazines. A prince anxious to maintain his dominions at all times in the state in which he can most easily defend them, ought upon this account to guard not only against that excessive multiplication of paper money, which ruins the very banks which issue it, but even against that multiplication of it which enables them to fill the greater part of the circulation of the country with it.

The circulation of every country may be considered as divided into two different branches, the circulation of the dealers with one another and the circulation between the dealers and the consumers. Though the same pieces of money, whether paper or metal, may be employed sometimes in the one circulation and sometimes in the other, yet each requires a certain stock of money. The retail business frequently requires but small coin. Where bank-notes are issued for so small sums as twenty shillings—as in Scotland—paper money extends itself to a considerable part of the circulation between dealers and consumers.

It were better, perhaps, that no bank-notes were issued for a smaller sum than five pounds. Paper money would then, probably, confine itself to wholesale trade.

To restrain private people, it might be said, from receiving in payment the promissory notes of a banker, for any sum whether great or small, when they themselves are willing to receive them; or to restrain a banker from issuing such notes when all his neighbors are willing to accept of them, is a manifest violation of that natural liberty which it is the proper business of law not to infringe, but to support. But those

* The original says 20 per cent. See Wealth of Nations, vol. 2, p. 74.—[Translator.]

142   THEORY OF THE COIN, COINAGE, AND

exertions of the natural liberty of a few individuals which might endanger the security of the whole society are, and ought to be, restrained by the laws of all governments; of the most free, as well as of the most despotical. The obligation of building party-walls in order to prevent the communication of fire is a violation of natural liberty, exactly of the same kind with the regulations of the banking trade which are here proposed.

The increase of paper money, it has been said, by augmenting the quantity, and consequently diminishing the value of the whole currency, necessarily augments the money price of commodities. But as the quantity of gold and silver which is taken from the currency is always equal to the quantity of paper which is added to it, paper money does not necessarily increase the quantity of the whole currency. From the beginning of the last century to the present time, provisions never were cheaper in Scotland than in 1759, though from the circulation of ten and five shilling bank-notes there was then more paper money in the country than at present.

It would be otherwise, indeed, with a paper money of which the payment was not exigible till after a certain number of years; such a paper money would, no doubt, fall more or less below the value of gold and silver.

Some years ago the different banking companies of Scotland were in the practice of inserting in their bank-notes what they called an *optional clause*, by which they promised payment to the bearer, either as soon as the note should be presented, or, in the option of the directors, six months after such presentment, together with the legal interest for the said six months. But this optional clause was taken advantage of by some of the directors, and it was suppressed by act of Parliament. The exchange between London and Dumfries would sometimes be 4 per cent. against Dumfries on account of the uncertainty of their getting bank-notes exchanged for specie.

The paper currencies of North America consisted in government paper, of which the payment was not exigible till several years after it was issued, and which was subjected to a forced circulation. Its discount was sometimes 30 per cent. This law bears the marks of having originally been a scheme of fraudulent debtors to cheat their creditors.

The proportion between the value of gold and silver and that of goods of any other kind, depends in all cases, not upon the nature or quantity of any particular paper money which may be current in any particular country, but upon the richness or poverty of the mines which happen at any particular time to supply the great market of the commercial world with those metals. It depends upon the proportion between the quantity of labor which is necessary in order to bring a certain quantity of gold and silver to market and that which is necessary in order to bring thither a certain quantity of any other sort of goods.

If bankers are restrained from issuing any circulating bank-notes, or notes payable to the bearer, for less than a certain sum, and if they are subjected to the obligation of an immediate and unconditional payment of such bank-notes as soon as presented, their trade may with safety to the public be rendered in all other respects perfectly free. The late multiplication of banking companies increases the security of the public because it obliges all of them to be more circumspect in their conduct, to guard themselves against those malicious runs which rivalship is always ready to bring upon them. The failure of any one company, an accident which in the course of things must sometimes happen, becomes of less consequence to the public. This free competition, too, obliges all to be more liberal in their dealings with their customers, lest their rivals should carry them away.

Of the above quotations I only intend to review the most important. The comparison which Adam Smith draws between a guinea and that which can be obtained for it, as a revenue, makes the latter indeed the most essential. But likening the guinea to a mere bill upon all tradespeople, undervalues the signification of metal money, to the advantage of paper. A guinea is at once merchandise and a conservator of value. It never can sink to the value of worthless paper, as a bank-note can.

"*The substitution of paper in the room of gold and silver money, replaces a very expensive instrument of commerce with one much less costly.*"

To determine its relative expense the amount of circulating money in a country must be compared—

a. To the amount of things actually given in exchange for money;

b. The amount of things sold for money, but for which no money was used because they were equalized by other things;

c. The amount of things which remain fixed capital, which do not change owners, and which, from time to time, are only estimated by money or by that which stands in the place of money.

Money is not merely "that important instrument of commerce by means of which every individual has his subsistence, conveniences, and amusements regularly distributed to him in their proper proportion," but it is also the standard by which the value of all other products of the national wealth is measured.

Adam Smith, in referring to money, only considered the yearly productions which pass from hand to hand by means of money, and observed that "the difference between the 5 and 30 fold amount would average 17½ fold." Later, in the course of his investigations, he recommends the interdiction of bank-notes of less than £5 sterling. This would almost entirely exclude bank-notes from retail trade. If thereby the entire trade is filled, say one-half with metal, and the metal reserve of the banks amounts to, say, one-third of the circulating bank-notes, then the amount of metal held out of circulation would be merely the fifty-second part of the products cited under *a*. However, to that is added *b*, the sum of the amount which is not paid for with money, but which was equalized by other things, and *c*, the remaining amount of national wealth that is measured by money.

The entire national wealth of France is estimated at about 300,000,000,000 francs, and her entire currency at 5,000,000,000 francs. If of that, 2,500,000,000 francs is permitted to be paper, in place of which 833,000,000 specie is retained as protection, then there is only upon the 180th part of her products any saving of interest, for which money is designed either as an exchange medium or a scale of value.

The national wealth of Germany is estimated at about 55,000,000,000 thalers, of which the bank-notes and government paper not based upon specie only form the 275th part. Only upon this is interest saved.

However, it is not correct to call metal money a costly implement, &c., when the important functions which it performs are considered, and that the value of the things to which these functions refer is a hundred times greater than is the amount of metal money upon which interest is saved.

Concerning the nature of bank-notes, we are aware that Scotland has a number of small banks which advance to their customers with the greatest liberality.

"They invented a new contrivance called cash accounts, through which the merchants took an interest in bringing their notes into circulation, and encouraging all those with whom they have any influence to do the same."

Generosity took the place of speculation. But as reciprocal service for the assistance which they had rendered to the bank by bringing their notes into circulation, they very soon demanded unlimited advances, and as these could not be obtained directly, they used the indirect method of redrawing upon London. It continued for a long time before the banks noticed that by this indirect way they were deprived of bank-notes, which soon afterward were presented for payment in metal. The cash accounts of from £2,000 to £3,000 sterling were drawn upon the bank of Scotland, for only from £100 to £200 sterling. Probably they discovered that the frequent repayments which the author cites as a means of control may be carried on in a deceitful manner.

By this means most of the banks were rescued from the hands of the speculator, that a new bank which would be more liberal, might be established. It was done for the purpose of drawing to itself the entire business.

The author has heard it said that "the business of the city of Glasgow doubled itself in fifteen years after the establishment of the first bank," &c., and says, that "the country apparently reaped great advantage from the business."

The appearance, however, was deceptive. The author does not show the logical connection between the increase of trade and industry and the disbursement of bank-notes, and the exceeding business freedom united therewith. The increase of the commerce and industry of a country has its origin in things entirely different from unprotected bank-notes, and the excessive liberality of the banks of issue. A reliable business man can always obtain the necessary money with a pure specie currency. The small unemployed amount of money must be collected in savings-banks, banks of deposit, and banks of discount. A high discount induces the importation of specie.

Often the business impulse of a country has its origin in a spirit of enterprise arising suddenly, which at that time appears to have been the case in Scotland, and for whose growth the banks of issue are credited. It is, however, only an artificial impulse which the banks of issue produce. The end is a great business crisis, filling the country with deep distress. A few cool leaders are enriched at the expense of this misery.

The author says that "but few articles of luxury will be imported by the money forced abroad," that "the demands of idle people will not be increased in the smallest degree by these bank operations." But those specially interested in banks of issue form a class, which very soon, without any labor, through the clear gain of tribute, lead an idle life.

Banks give to the merchant, for his efforts to bring their notes into circulation, certain privileges, which the solid merchant can also obtain from a bank of deposit without the danger of being exposed to a bank of issue failure, which, according to Adam Smith, must sometimes occur in the course of events, and which, from an almost complete discontinuance during a crisis of all bank facilities, are forgotten. However, the liable merchant is constrained to assist the banks of issue in introducing their notes to the laborers, farmers, &c., because of his dependence upon the banks of issue, as they monopolize the whole business of advancing money.

Wild speculation is at the bottom of this desire for banks of issue to favor the business people, but which exposes the latter to the greatest danger, because the bank directors or stockholders are themselves speculators. The easy manner of winning money by issuing bank-notes is a universal challenge to speculation. After Parliament had legally contracted the nature of the banks of issue in Scotland, "there were still complaints over the excess of bank-note issue."

The capture of the capital of the country does not necessarily put the treasury into the hands of the enemy, but it makes the circulation of paper money precarious. The author further says:

It has been maintained that the increase of paper money, because it increases the whole money circulation, and consequently diminishes the value of the same, necessarily increases the money price of merchandise.

A similar increase occurs, as I have already mentioned in Chapter VIII, in the relation of the paper money unsupported by a metal basis to the whole money volume of the world. The £800,000 sterling referred to by Adam Smith as distributed, lowered the price of money abroad. But the science of national economy, as understood, teaches differently. If the cited example of one-fifth specie basis should prevail, the Highlander would quickly find the guinea in his hand worth but 4 instead of 20 shillings, and that, too, whether the guinea was an actual piece of gold or consisted of a bank-note at par.

The value of a guinea is determined by the number of guineas in metal or paper, and their equivalent in metal or paper money. The necessary labor for the production of metal has only an indirect influence upon its value, because the actual number present in the market is the definitive amount, including those in course of preparation.

Adam Smith cites, that from the beginning of the past century, provisions were never cheaper than in 1759, in spite of the large circulation in paper money, as evidence that paper money does not necessarily increase the money price of merchandise. But to us the manner of stating the inherent connection of these two things is incorrect.

The amount of money is much easier changed by the circulation of paper money, than by a pure specie circulation. An artificial necessity, or one called forth by the idea that it is for the best, can increase the amount of bank-notes without an immediate reaction taking place. With a pure metal basis, it is necessary to import metal from abroad. The discount increases and designates a natural limit against the artificial enlargement; and then no bank has a permanent interest to call forth an artificial necessity for money.

The history of the Bank of England shows how hazardous it is to bring a bank of issue into close relations with the government. In 1694, the bank was granted privileges for sums advanced to the government. In 1696, her bank-notes were 25 per cent.* discount. Her obligations to the government had, in the mean time, forced her to flood trade with paper money.

The author, in the course of his recital regarding the disadvantages of banks of issue, concludes with the following reflections:

The commerce and industry of the country, however, it must be acknowledged, though they may be somewhat augmented, cannot be altogether so secure when they are thus, as it were, suspended upon the Dædalian wings of paper money as when they travel about on the solid ground of gold and silver.

From this extract one would suppose that the author draws the conclusion that the disadvantages of a bank of issue far outweigh the interest accruing to the banks. But he closes Chapter II in a singular manner, with the following words:

If bankers are restrained from issuing any circulating notes, or notes payable to the bearer, for less than a certain sum; and if they are subjected to the obligation of an immediate and unconditional payment of such bank-notes as soon as presented, their trade may, with safety to the public, be rendered in all other respects perfectly free.

Only so far does Adam Smith recommend restraining the banks of issue.

The advantages which he maintains the country draws therefrom are not only undemonstrable, but it is much more certain that the country, as a whole, will only be damaged thereby, and the banks of issue alone be the gainers. If the commerce and industry of a country are augmented through a bank of issue, it is not *through* it but in *spite* of it.

It is a spirit of enterprise restrained within reasonable limits which augments commerce and industry, and not that spirit of speculation "suspended upon the Dædalian wings of paper money.

We see that through the influence of banks of issue, commerce is exposed to bankruptcy, to an increase of money distress, to the danger of depreciated values, and to many other misfortunes.

But especially are the entire interests of the state placed upon an uncertain basis through the influence of the banks of issue, and justice toward her officers, toward her army, and toward her creditors made impossible.

---

* 20 per cent. See Wealth of Nations.

XVI.

BEGGING LETTERS.

It has already been proven that bank-notes not based upon specie, because they increase the whole money circulation of the world, diminish the purchasing power of money. The interest which is gained from notes not based upon specie, in Germany, falls partly to the state, and is accepted by it. The bank-note, not based upon specie, influences the floating money capital as a tax, by which means a paper thaler and a specie thaler in the hands of the public are equally affected, because if the paper thaler is not on hand the specie thaler takes its place.

Besides this portion of specie, in conjunction with the unprotected note circulation, the banks must have for the support of their remaining notes and obligations about 120,000,000 thalers specie. This is the amount upon which the German banks of issue win tribute, because it brings into trade bank-notes not based upon specie. It is 1 per cent. of the estimated value of the entire amount of money in the world. This 1 per cent. depreciates every 10 thalers in the hands of the laborer and peasant to the amount of about 3 groschen : 100 hard-earned thalers are only worth 99 thalers. The 120,000,000 thalers of bank-notes unprotected by specie, are *begging letters*, sent by a Cresus through the country to increase his great wealth through the sweat of poverty. The proper name for the imperial bank of issue would be the *Imperial Begging Bank.*

XVII.

THE RULING OF THE MONEY MARKET THROUGH DISCOUNTS.

It is a fact long known that the banks of issue do not average as high dividends as other banks. Their stockholders, therefore, are interested in so operating as to lead them into other fields of business, and their regulations are necessarily changed. However, it has already been remarked that this would not be in the interest of the directors. The discount business is under the control of the banks of issue, with which no one can compete. If they hold a large amount of paper in reserve, *they merely gain no interest upon it* ; while the banks of deposit *lose direct interest upon their entire cash treasury*. When a bank of issue has a large reserve of notes the directors often consider it providential.

Such a note reserve, however, puts them in condition to control the special circulating districts of the money market, and this fact reveals the principal ground of their tenacious hold upon the privileges of the banks of issue. Upon the one hand the directors may give an unrighteous opinion, or approach it, and upon the other they may suddenly and unnecessarily deprive trade of its accustomed assistance. It is true, the control of the bank, from its very nature, is circumscribed to certain districts, but within these districts the directors have enough play room. Especially does the establishing of the rates of discount present such opportunity. Sometimes for weeks it is agitated by lowering or advancing. *The directors control the source of the money circulation.* They fix to a certain scale the amount and the extent of the rates of discount, which the periodical tribute power of money determines, and which also influences its purchasing power. With every advance or diminution of the discount the worth of all merchandise, exchanges, stocks, and other values rise or fall.

The Prussian bank, by its exorbitant privileges, almost absolutely governs the German money market. As I have already shown in Chapter II, it is the deputies of the central committee, and their assistants, who actually conduct the bank, and the influence which they have upon the operations of the bank is to them *a source of immeasurable gain.* They and their friends possess millions and millions of thalers' worth, whose value is influenced by these operations. Even if they were angels of virtue, this advantage would have an influence upon the mind. At all events, they have earlier knowledge of the operations of the bank than others, and are able to properly regulate their sales and purchases of stocks.

On the 16th of September the bank increased her discounts from 4 to 5 per cent., which had a great effect upon nearly all paper values. The German Trade Gazette announced at the time, the approximate gain which the bank had realized.

The sum which the privileged bankers of the Prussian bank gain in this way, through their actual management, is difficult to compute, but that which the banks of issue bring to them through their begging letters, called bank-notes, may be safely estimated as far beyond millions.

XVIII.

BANK LIBERALITY.

A pure metal basis for a money circulation is undoubtedly an object worthy of attainment. Nevertheless, nearly all present at the commercial congress at Dantzic declared in favor of banks of issue. One hopefully recommended an imperial bank, another the *wild-cat* scheme. The latter called to mind the power which the imperial bank of issue would exercise over the entire money market. But it was shown that the *wild-cat* bank exercised a similar power in its special department. The imperial-bank party pointed out, amid applause, the irregularities of the wild scheme as an anomaly no longer bearable. In opposition to this, there is no proof that an imperial bank of issue, on account of its close relation to the minister of finance, in the event of a war, would more easily threaten us with a forced circulation. The latter argument is not so clearly demonstrated as is that in reference to the wild scheme. New privileges of emission are not be granted, and the old will disappear. The Prussian bank will gradually extend her branches, and curtail more and more the operations of the other banks, not only as to that which concerns the issue of bank-notes, but also that which belongs to the fixing of the discount and the lucrative speculation in stocks which is united therewith.

The Prussian bank has established its seat in Alsace-Loraine. Since the beginning of July Bremen has possessed a branch bank. Leipzig has asked for one, and Hamburg also desires a branch bank. The extension of the Prussian bank over all Germany is only a question of time. No money power is able to compete with her so long as she maintains her right to a paper circulation without a metal basis. It would be but a matter of prudential forethought for the medium and small banks of issue to resign their privileges before they are taken from them, and gradually to change into deposit banks, but at the same time demand that the Prussian bank be compelled to do the same. The latter would certainly be richly indemnified, through the large inflow of deposits, and the bank stockholders would probably be as well off as at present. This is the opinion of high officers of the bank.

If all the existing privileges of the banks of issue were canceled, Germany's finances, in conformity with imperial justice, would in all parts of the empire rest upon a completely sound and pure metal basis.   Instead of, as at present, granting favor only to Mr. von Bleichröder, and his associates, the natural circulation of money in all parts of Germany would bring with it prosperity to the entire empire.

It is characteristic, however, of this class of men, endowed with energetic and accomplished business minds, to employ every means at their command in retaining possession of the tribute which German forbearance has for a long time paid them.

Under the shield of *liberality* they use the empire as a tool for their exchange manipulations.   *They employ a subsidized press and the power of the empire in making a pretended war against the Jesuits, in order thereby to divert public attention from the great sore which is consuming the very marrow of the empire.   They regard a prohibition against issuing notes unprotected by specie, as a violation of natural freedom, and refer for argument to Adam Smith.*

In spite of the weakness of human nature, which is reflected in the history of the Scotch banks after the Parliamentary regulations regarding an excess of bank-notes, Adam Smith, as we have seen, declares for banking privileges with restrictions.   Since that time, however, new and bitter experiences and careful observations have led to the adoption of principles altogether in opposition to the Manchester power, and which consider a complete metal basis as the only just financial policy.   Against all and every note unsupported by specie we are able to cite Adam Smith's own words, but which he himself practically applies merely to an *excess* of the same.   He says:

But those exertions of the natural liberties of a few individuals, which might endanger the security of the whole society, are, and ought to be, restrained by the laws of all governments—of the most free, as well as of the most despotic.

We would render futile these exertions, if we *"from year to year curtailed the circulation of notes unsupported by specie until a complete metal basis is secured."*

XIX.

GETTING RID OF PAPER MONEY NOT BASED UPON SPECIE BY MEANS OF A NEW UNIT OF COMPUTATION.

In my former publications I have already proven that the establishment of the coin laws, which places the new gold coin in a certain ratio to the existing silver standard, and which gives to the banks of issue the right of redeeming their notes in silver or in gold, builds a bridge, by means of which they will be able to preserve their privileges in the future gold standard.   Take, for instance, a 10-thaler note of the Prussian bank.   Formerly 10 silver thalers redeemed it.   Now it requires 30 marks in gold.   When the government finally adopts the gold in place of the silver standard, then the 10-thaler bank-note will be redeemable only in gold; then all that is necessary to preserve the valuable privileges of the Prussian bank as implements for the special use of Mr. von Bleichröder, and his associates, is merely a matter of form, viz, the permission of bank-notes in all amounts, corresponding to the mark system, from 100 marks upward, and, when that is accomplished, also from the same downward.

In order to make this bridge possible, the imperial chancellor need choose no other way than that adopted by him.   In the convention he moved that the treasury standard value be adopted for the new gold coin, and because in Prussia only the bank-notes of the Prussian bank are entitled to the rights of the treasury standard value, it would give to Mr. von Bleichröder, and his associates, a pre-eminently advantageous position in South Germany. If I am not mistaken, Mr. Camphausen, in the Diet, declared that he had read all the publications upon the coin question. With your permission, sir, I must say you have not read mine carefully, or else you are forced to adopt a measure which bestows upon Mr. von Bleichröder, and his associates, for the blood which they did *not* shed upon the battle-fields of Wörth, Gravelotte, and before Sedan, one-half the national wealth of Germany.

The plan already suggested by me leads not only to a universal coin, but also to a pure unadulterated gold standard, through no false process. As article 22 of the Vienna coin treaty prohibits the issue of bank-notes and paper money, except upon a silver basis, therefore, a new imperial law is necessary to introduce paper money into the new gold standard of the Wilhelm's thaler. A positively prohibitory law might only be necessary in the independent cities of Lübeck, Hamburg, and Bremen. If the government will only assume an independent attitude, she will not be perplexed with bank legislation united with almost insurmountable difficulties. The subject is extremely complicated. Private privileges and large moneyed interests are at stake. If positive bank legislation could be effected, which from year to year, would secure a large decrease of the paper money not based upon specie, until the full attainment of a complete metal basis, then, in the course of time, the accomplishment of these selfish purposes would be frustrated. Independent of any very extraordinary events occurring, the first great money distress would be sufficient to disarrange the whole reform, as happened to McCulloch, the *judicious* American minister of finance, who for a time retired from trade $4,000,000 paper money monthly.

The situation would be entirely different, if, in accordance with my proposition, the Wilhelm's thaler were first introduced into public and retail trade, and subsequently into wholesale trade, and if no paper were permitted in this new gold standard. According to the scale of gradual introduction, paper money would first disappear from public business, then from retail trade, and finally from wholesale trade. The bank-note privileges of the banks of issue would gradually become impracticable, and as banks of deposit they would secure higher dividends.

My proposed plan of introduction is on this wise, that instead of the new gold standard, such standard be adopted by the various distributing subtreasuries of the empire as is adjusted to the exchange in each special district. The management of the depreciating bank-notes and state paper money will be conducted with strict reference to the banks and districts under consideration, and to the industrial interests of the people. My proposed plan operates as a gradually reducing power. In the course of time, bank-notes and state paper money, will entirely disappear from public business and from retail trade, although they may be used in wholesale trade for a long time to come.

XX.

CONCLUSION.

The true and really honest portion of the entire population of Germany, are in favor of a universal coin. The cities will gain in the increase of business and traveling trade. The farmer will understand foreign prices, and our attorneys, and government officers, will more easily comprehend the value of paper. Our military, our officers, our literati, our physicians, and especially all the women of Germany, are anxious for a universal coin, which will obviate the necessity of computation, make intelligible foreign ratios of value, and dispense with exchange in traveling.

Only those special money-changers and selfish wholesale lords who, in making the necessary computations and exchanges in the various coins, have grown fat, like the oyster in his shell, do not desire a universal coin.

A universal coin will not deprive you of your capital, and it will only be necessary to use your fine brain in a manner more profitable to the whole country.

·A pure metal basis for the money circulation, as the final aim of the German bank reform, is demanded; because it is in the interest of all solid business men, and because it will firmly establish our social condition, and because it will be the means of making a forced circulation impossible.

The coin law of December 4, 1871, is altogether in the interest of the money-changers, the wholesale lords, and the banks of issue. But, as I aimed to show in my introduction, *Germany cannot abandon the idea of a universal coin, based upon a pure gold standard, unless she desires to assist the future prosperity of banking privileges instead of thwarting it.*

THE COIN QUESTION.

[From the International Exposition Gazette, Vienna, September 10, 1873.]

[The late private coin conference, whose characteristics, through our criticisms and objective reports, are already known to our readers, has permitted our esteemed co-laborer, Mr. L. Wolowski, to publish his views upon the questions there discussed, in a communication addressed to us, which, on account of absence, he was prevented from doing in the conference. Notwithstanding, we by no means agree in the following ·details upon one essential point, viz, that which relates to the double standard, having lately expressed our own views thereon, yet we cheerfully make room for the communication in the columns of this paper, because, for a long time, they have been devoted by us to the discussion and to the thorough investigation of the question. Mr. Wolowski's article is appended.—EDITOR.]

It appears to me that the standard and coin question is embarrassed by prejudice from a twofold cause; which prejudice was engendered long ago, through ideas now obsolete, and which to-day, in consequence of the progress of civilization, and the peculiarly changed ratio of the commerce of the world, should be discarded; upon the one hand preconceived opinions relating to the possibility of a common standard, and upon the other regarding the use of one single metal, viz, gold, as money material.

The fluctuations of value formerly depended upon circumstances which no longer exist, and which are still called to mind. The difficulties of communication, the want of security, the meager intelligence from distant places of the earth, prevented brisk trade in metals, and hindered the equalization of prices in the markets of the world. It is different to-day. The damage inflicted upon trade in consequence of the different kinds of coin, is considerably lessened since the exchange of every kind is daily quoted, since the numerous boundaries of the many independent states of Germany, which had gradually established the value of their own money, are obliterated. Germany *was* a complete example of these pernicious fluctuations. The money and coinage unit is now actually perfected.

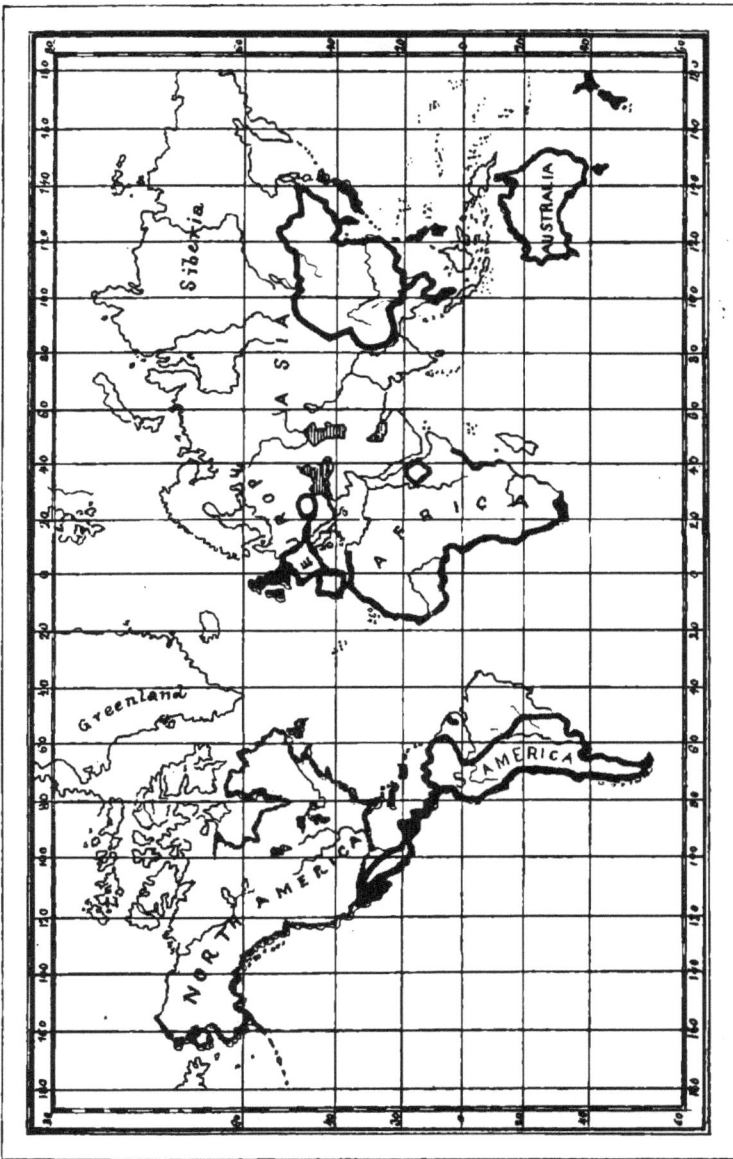

Chart I.

COIN MAP OF THE WORLD.

AUSTRALIA

Siberia

A S I A

A F R I C A

Greenland

NORTH AMERICA

S. AMERICA

H. Mis. Doc. 8.—405.

▪ Sovereigns	35,000,000 P	
▪ Francs	77,000,000	} all or part!
▪ Gold Dollars	80,000,000	
▪ Silver	521,000,000	

Egger's Money Reform.

But, although the old difficulties are lessened, there is a no less remarkable interest in a union in reference to coinage, and this unification may be effected upon a common basis, which must regard justice to all and injury to none. This was the object of the private conference lately held in Vienna.

I do not hesitate in agreeing with the members of the conference, because I believe that a fixed ratio established between the various kinds of coin, of the different countries, would be satisfactory. In this way the interests of travelers, and the much more important interests of merchants, are guaranteed, without, on the other hand, injuring the proper privileges of labor, the justice of and the respect for treaties, and the mutual social arrangements, which must all be considered in the question of the coin unit of metals, as understood in pieces of money, as is maintained by those who contend that, with reference to the depreciation in the value of silver, gold should be the only circulating medium.

Upon this question worn-out arguments are advanced without having been properly considered; an overflow, an inundation, of metal is spoken of, which would threaten the circulation at a time when the increase of trade operations demands a simplified way and manner of calculation, so that the amount of business may not still more augment the comparative insufficiency of ready money. The consequences resulting from an unusual displacement of metal coin are exaggerated, because there never has been an irregular increase of metal in the coffers of the world. Let us not deceive ourselves. It is a fact worthy of earnest consideration, that the coin reform of the German Empire would not have been possible without the French war indemnification of five milliards. The opportunity to introduce once more a circulating medium, for which until then, we had not the means, was won upon the other side of the Rhine. The question is not alone with regard to exchanging the clumsy silver pieces for the lighter and more convenient gold pieces; we must get rid of the disagreeable amount of small state and bank bills, to which, besides their inconvenience, is added the danger of an unreliable circulating value. The scarcity of gold increases the number of these small notes which, independent of many practical difficulties, operate disadvantageously to national economy.

Under the circumstances, it is therefore, not remarkable that Germany has seized the opportunity to establish a legal gold standard. But has not this object been overreached, in that the same coin standard aims to suppress the circulation of silver? This is the doubtful point to be discussed. We will examine it more closely.

First of all, we maintain that so far as a *universal coinage*, or a *universal standard*, is concerned, the new coinage and standard of Germany rather increases than diminishes the difficulties. The basis of the mark creates a new variety, which separates the German coin system from that of the other countries, resembling in this the Scandinavian system, which rests upon a gold basis, thereby adding new deficiencies to those already existing. We will not omit freely to declare that the new German coin law, which, although according to our view should not have been adopted, because it adopts the gold standard, yet in the sense of a universal standard, as we understand it, it has made an important advance, because it actually admits a new decimal fineness, which was sanctioned by the Latin Coin Union. (The coin union of states, and which really establishes the unit of the scale of purity, the principal terms of a universal standard, and, as such, constituting an actual advance.)

So far as the coinage relates only to a universal basis, I am a warm champion, but I cannot agree with those who propose one and the same concrete trade coin, formed from a fixed weight of precious metal, of a fixed purity, for the entire world. To accomplish this, every country must renounce its peculiar expressions, and accept a new coin form, everywhere based upon a unit coin standard, and which rejects every individual and national characteristic.

It is by no means necessary to go so far in order to create a simplified calculating coin for mutual exchange. The issuing of circulating money pieces of the same purity at once simplifies calculation. This is all that international relations require. An idea of agreement, with an easy reducible capacity. And the object would be attained if all pieces of money, for example, the compound of the 5-franc piece, the United States dollar, or the Austrian gulden, were so constituted. It is also by no means absolutely necessary to create a concrete money piece of the value of 25 francs, notwithstanding the good service it might furnish. The ratio between the 20-franc piece and the English pound, the Austrian 8 gulden and the German 16-mark piece, involves no arithmetical operation which could puzzle any ordinary mathematician of the smallest trading-house, especially if the trifling differences can be made up in fractional coin.

Every country calculates according to different units, which it is not easy to abandon. The variety of the usual denominations does not prevent their being understood in international trade. But the established unit of money in use in the interior of a country, is no unimportant thing. The way and manner of making payments have their peculiar characteristics; an increase in the amount called for, either in the chief or fractional coins, necessarily brings with it an increase in the price in daily payments. Certain performances which cost 20 francs in France, cost in England £1 sterling, and often, so great is the power of custom, an additional shilling is exacted in order to meet the equivalent of the old guinea. The franc suffices in France for many things which cost a shilling in England, or a gulden in Austria, so that an increase of the cost of living is often joined to normal coin pieces. As to wholesale trade, the value of things is accurately calculated according to the money in circulation. The fixing of the price underlies the universal laws of the market. And so this presents to us another question, and an important one, viz, whether the introduction of an international standard necessitates the use of but one metal for the purposes of coinage.

The fanatical advocates for gold, or for silver, must admit that the exclusive employment of one metal by one nation, and of the other metal by another nation, makes it impossible to come to an understanding in that way, while, on the contrary, the equilateral use of both facilitates a mutual contact. But this is not the only advantage arising from the use of both metals; indeed, it is the smallest, when placed in comparison with the vast national economical problems united to this fundamental question. We cannot, at this time, fully exhaust the subject, but will only express our opinion, which we hold to be correct, but which has been discarded by all those who are pledged to the universal introduction of the gold standard. The opposition of opinion is concentrated upon a point, viz, the fixing of a certain ratio between gold and silver. It has been asserted that the establishment of a fixed ratio, which, because it must necessarily be variable, is in a manner heretical. Only one metal is used, because it is intended to express only one normal value in money; otherwise, every transaction must be left to the uncertainty of a divided judgment. But one thing in this argument is forgotten, that no one can establish a fixed scale for the standard; that while the measure of weight is invariable, and also the measure of length, yet no one can, without great mistakes, equalize a coin standard to a kilogram or meter. No size can be measured by size of another nature. Money value must always be measured by another value; that is, by a variable measure. The only effort which has prospect of success, the least possible variable standard taken, would be to find a third comparison, which is not exposed to sudden fluctuations, for it is in the nature of things that their value is subject to continual variations.

The first fundamental principle of national economy teaches us, that the price expressed in money is the value of merchandise. Would the variations of ratio between merchandise and precious metal be more to be apprehended, if gold alone were used, than if gold and silver were used together? Was Turgot wrong when he said, "Gold and silver are, from the nature of things, independent of law, and, consequently, for the future, designed for coin, and, of course, for unit coin?" It is certain that herein lies the difficult points of the question.

Prejudices, which belong to the past, pretended axioms, which have been blindly conceded without drawing a careful criticism, and feigned prepossessions against the actual concord of the present, have formed a national economical article of faith from a chimera. We know that this expression will be considered bold, even presumptuous; but for years we have maintained our opinions with knowledge and good grounds. They rest upon this: that there is no fixed universal standard of value, and the least variable standard for the price of things, and consequently for the estimate of the owner as to the compass of the obligations, is effected through the mutual use of gold and silver. And this is what we hope to be able to prove.

L. WOLOWSKI.

COINAGE AND THE DOUBLE STANDARD.

VIENNA, *September* 18.

[We lately made place in our columns for the opinions of our esteemed colaborer, Mr. L. Wolowski, upon the *Coin Question*, which was so ably discussed a short time ago in Vienna; and although we differ in our comprehension of the subject, we do not hesitate to publish to-day the views of the members of the French Academy, who are warm advocates of the double standard.—EDITOR.]

The real economical question involved in the use of the metal standard has but lately arisen. It is therefore unnecessary, in relation to the great importance of this subject, to acknowledge an undue weight in favor of the opinions of old authorities, upon what was but seldom, and but briefly, discussed by them. What is, properly speaking, money? How came it in universal use? Aristotle remarks: "Mankind chose a material to serve in mutual trade, which in daily use is easy to manage, as iron, silver, or some similar substance, whose size and weight are fixed, and in order to avoid a repeated measurement, a sign of its value is made upon it by an exact coinage." And *therein* to-day lies the nature of money. The question is, concerning a product of a peculiar nature, a *tertium comparationis* for all products and all service. In order to dispense with the customary manner of exchange among savages, a direct exchange has given place to the adoption of a fixed universal product, by means of which anything may be acquired at pleasure, in this or that place, on to-day or to-morrow; this third product, this medium for all bargains estimated by the giver and receiver, is money.

Properly speaking, anything might be made into money coin, but not everything would fully meet the requirements of money, for a series of attributes are necessary, which we presume are understood. For all demands corresponding to a good coin, there is no doubt that gold, equally with silver, is well adapted; and that of equal volume, the value of the one is greater than the other, and that both have been, in a manner, by tacit agreement, universally adopted. This choice is not contradictory to the nature of things; there originates therefrom a certain ratio between the use of, and the existing quantity of precious metal, out of which grows the equalization of prices. Stability is an essential attribute of money; without doubt, it cannot be perfect, because the substance of which money is composed is a material one; but nothing must be neglected to neutralize the fluctuations, and to make them slow and gradual, dividing them among a long term of years. Money must be altogether protected from all measures which are able to change the proportion between the sum of gold and silver on the one hand, and the united trade on the other.

With reference to this purpose, grain has been proposed to be used as money, instead of the precious metals. Without mentioning the difference in quality, or the difficulty of preserving it, it suffices, at furthest, that unequal harvests would induce the abandonment of this idea. The precious metals, it is said, do not serve in ordinary use, and that is exactly why they are employed as money; they are not used as grain; the storehouses are not filled and emptied in rapid succession; on the contrary, the gold and silver products, however great, are only a fraction of the existing mass, which, through the yearly yield, is gradually increased.

The discovery of America effected, at that period, a complete revolution in prices, owing to the sudden yield of precious metal, which aggregated hundreds of millions, while in our time the billions from California and Australia exercise but a passing influence upon the price, although the mass of precious metal is reckoned according to milliards. The wear and tear to which it is subject absorbs a considerable part of the continual increase, independent of the consumption of that demanded by the arts and the industries, and for the development and expansion of luxury. The existing cash of the merchants, and, to use a vulgar expression, our pocket-money, have considerably increased. Almost everywhere the natural industries, which demand but little money circulation, are succeeded by the money industries, which, from the large amount of business, require a large capital. Even so, the gradual increase of the metal treasure corresponds to the increase of the necessities which this metal is called upon to satisfy. Although the sum increases, about which the metal treasure multiplies, yet the relative amount decreases. The production of the yellow and white metals is distributed in nearly regular yields, through a long series of years, while the relative stability of prices declines, and in consequence the accurate fulfillment of the past obligations is prevented.

If the precious metals were rapidly multiplied, the result would be a decline in their price. That experience was verified in the discovery of America. More currency would be needed to fulfill the same engagements. However, the more than usual increase of gold and silver in our century has only kept pace with the growth of the universal culture, the continual increase of population, and the rapid advance in commerce. The new billions would certainly not have satisfied these new demands, if the ingenious combinations under which the introduction of "checks," and the institution of "clearing," occupying the first rank, had not come to the assistance of fulfilling the agreements.

We have presented these views because they are very important for the proper understanding of the question, which is incorrectly called the question of the "*double standard.*" The question here is not as to a normal measure in general, but to investigate whether it is better to use the two precious metals, gold and silver, as a trade medium for all business, as a *tertium comparationis*, as has already been proven by the nature of things, or, instead, to confer this obligation upon gold alone.

One important point generally overlooked in this controversy, but which to us appears the weightiest, is the question as to the value of the quota of precious metal belonging to each individual. Commerce requires 60,000,000,000 francs in gold and silver. Now, can gold alone, which only furnishes one-half that amount, meet this requirement? What would be the consequence if a large amount of silver was suddenly withdrawn from trade? This is an important point presented to the attention of all who are employed in the study of the coin question. The question is not as to the superiority of one metal over the other, nor does it proceed from an unfounded apprehension, but it is a precautionary calculation. If money is considered a scale of value, or of labor, then is it best to discard one part of this scale, which is fitted for that purpose?

The considerable amount of metal on hand has called forth a series of reform proposals. We have had a rich surplus of gold; we demonetize it, because it is said there is danger that its value will suddenly decline; we have had a considerable surplus of silver, and it is proposed to demonetize it, to prevent a similar danger, without considering that the fear of that danger often brings a worse condition than the dreaded result itself. It is fortunate when the introduction of such propositions are prevented, as they only lead to unpleasant consequences. Concerning France especially, she may be thankful that she did not demonetize her silver before the outbreak of the late war, as had been recommended. How and under what terms could she have paid her war indemnity of 5,000,000,000, of which nearly the tenth part only was met by gold?

It is always possible to guard against a double disturbance in the same sense: If the store of metal increases, the sales, the productions, the exchange business increase in proportion. Therefore an equilibrium may be maintained. The metal product has served as a medium for the demands of the empire, which again, upon her part, as a counterpoise, offered a superabundance of metal.

What is now proposed is a reduction of the circulation of metal in opposition to the increased business movements. This would be a manifest retrograde movement, in opposition to the necessities of our time. Productions are increasing, business is enlarging, population is growing, and then, should the stores of metal be held back, introducing thereby a universal revolution, to which the discovery of America gave the signal, a revolution which would draw after it deplorable and hurtful consequences. This tendency is evincing itself at a moment when the world is recognizing the disturbances caused by the emission of bank-notes, in the disbursement of paper money, in a moment when everywhere there is a struggle to regain the stability and the accuracy of a metal currency in trade, and where this necessity is valid, especially in Germany. This, at least, is not logical.

The whole transaction may be represented under the figure of a large balance, in one scale of which is placed the amount of products, of labor, of past obligations, agreements, and bargains of all kinds, for which the price is fixed in precious metal; and in the other scale is placed the metal store of gold and silver. The balance inclines to one side or the other, according to the ratio between the store of metal and the sum of materials which it serves to balance. The inevitable result of the demonetizing of silver at such a time, would be that the scale holding the money would be lighter and rise, and if this attained to any considerable degree, then the price of all commodities, and the purport of all agreements, would be much changed, to the disadvantage of the owners, and to labor as well as to all debtors, and to the exclusive benefit of capital and creditor.

There is nothing easier than to demonstrate the unpleasant results of such a precedent. The ratio between the store of metal and of that estimated thereby, fixes the price of things; according to the change of this ratio, the price rises or falls. The more specie, the more valuable is real estate, and inversely; it is also so with labor. On the other hand, every obligation, every debt, represents a fixed expression in money. If the paying power is increased, then the sum to be returned in capital and interest is heavier. We have to day 30,000,000,000 francs in gold, and the same in silver; if that, balancing the scale which holds productions and labor, is demonetized, it will be lighter by one-half. The price of gold will be doubled, and liabilities can be met with this alone.

These considerations are sufficient to justify our opposition to the suppression of the double standard, and to the introduction of a new arrangement of normal values.

L. WOLOWSKI.

INDEX.

A.

B.

C.

V.

W.

Z.

○

www.ingramcontent.com/pod-product-compliance
Lightning Source LLC
Chambersburg PA
CBHW030848270326
41928CB00008B/1273